Chicago

REAL CITY

Chicago

www.realcity.dk.com

LONDON, NEW YORK,
MELBOURNE, MUNICH AND DELHI
www.dk.com

Produced by Departure Lounge

Contributors
J.P. Anderson, Jason Heidemann, Cara Jepsen, Heather Kenny, Margaret Littman, Patrick Sisson

Photographers
Alessandra Santarelli, Joeff Davis

Reproduced in Singapore by Colourscan
Printed and bound in Singapore by Tien Wah Press

First American Edition, 2007
07 08 09 10 9 8 7 6 5 4 3 2 1

Published in the United States by
DK Publishing, Inc.,
375 Hudson Street, New York, New York 10014

ISSN: 1933-4567
ISBN: 978-0-75662-685-3

The information in this Real City guide is checked annually.

This guide is supported by a dedicated website which provides the very latest information for visitors to Chicago; please see page 7 for the web address and password. Some information, however, is liable to change, and the publishers cannot accept responsibility for any consequences arising from the use of this book, nor for any material on third party websites, and cannot guarantee that any website address in this book will be a suitable source of travel information.
We value the views and suggestions of our readers very highly. Please write to:
Publisher, DK Eyewitness Travel Guides,
Dorling Kindersley, 80 Strand, London WC2R 0RL.

Contents

The Guide » The Website 6

Introducing Chicago 8

Top Attractions **12**

The Year **16**

Travel Information **20**

Practical Information **22**

Restaurants 24

Shopping 48

Art & Architecture 68

Performance 86

Bars & Clubs 104

Streetlife 126

Havens 138

Hotels 148

Street Finder **162**

Index by Area **176**

Index by Type **182**

General Index **188**

The Guide

Real City Chicago

Stay ahead of the crowd with **Real City Chicago**, and find the best places to eat, shop, drink, and chill out at a glance.

The guide is divided into four main sections:

Introducing Chicago – essential background information on the city, including an overview by one of the authors, the top tourist attractions, festivals and seasonal events, and useful travel and practical information.

Listings – eight themed chapters packed with incisive reviews of the best the city has to offer, in every price band and chosen by local experts.

Street Finder – map references in the listings lead you to this section, where you can plan your route and find your way around.

Indexes – the By Area and By Type indexes offer shortcuts to what you are looking for, whether it is a bar in Lincoln Park or an Italian restaurant.

The Website

www.realcity.dk.com

By purchasing this book you have been granted free access to up-to-the-minute online content about Chicago for at least 12 months. Click onto **www.realcity.dk.com** for updates, and sign up for a free weekly email with the latest information on what to see and do in Chicago.

On the website you can:

- **Find the latest news** about Chicago, including exhibitions, restaurant openings, and music events
- Check what other readers have to say and **add your own comments** and reviews
- **Plan your visit** with a customizable calendar
- See at a glance **what's in and what's not**
- Look up listings by name, by type, and by area, and check the **latest reviews**
- **Link directly** to all the websites in the book, and many more

How to register

- Click on the Chicago icon on the home page of the website to register or log in.
- Enter the city code given on this page, and follow the instructions given.
- The city code will be valid for a minimum of 12 months from the date you purchased this guide.

city code: **chicago41930**

MILES DAVIS
JOHNNY GRIFFIN
BACARDI
KNOB

introducing chicago

In many ways, Chicago is one of the most cosmopolitan of the nation's big cities. Its mix of vibrant ethnic neighborhoods, eclectic shops, lakeshore activities, and cutting-edge theater, art, and restaurants makes it a true melting pot. The blues music scene and striking architecture are hard to beat, too. This guide picks out the city's best, starting with the lowdown on America's "Second City."

INTRODUCING CHICAGO

We Chicagoans like to brag about our city, talking up the gorgeous lakefront, beautiful architecture, and cool new museums. It's partly because we can't stop defending ourselves as the "Second City," but also because we want to share why it's wonderful to live here. For me, it's the small scenes – a backyard glimpsed from the El, neighborhood architectural gems, the skyline seen from Lake Shore Drive. Even after decades of living here, I'm still awed.

Heather Kenny

North vs. South

When Chicagoans talk about the North Side and the South Side, they're often speaking about more than geography. The glamorous North Side – basically everything north of the Loop downtown – tends to get all the attention; but the vast, mainly working-class South Side, where the city's tough, brawny image was born, is a key piece of the city's portrait. Here's where you're most likely to hear the distinctive Chicago accent and find the best – albeit rundown – blues bars and soul-food restaurants, while the University of Chicago campus and the gracious homes of the historic, re-emerging Bronzeville neighborhood provide pockets of elegance. Today, the North Side/South Side division is more of a friendly rivalry than anything else – though it's a whole different story when it comes to the city's two baseball teams.

Architectural Mecca

Chicago's stunning skyline is the most obvious manifestation of its famous architectural heritage, which also includes Frank Lloyd Wright's ground-hugging Prairie School designs and Mies van der Rohe's minimalist glass-and-steel structures. The stately high-rises downtown lend a sense of old-world grandeur, while more contemporary additions continue the city's unique legacy. But Chicagoans are just as proud of humbler structures: turreted Victorian buildings, imposing greystone three-flats, and the celebrated Chicago bungalow, a squat one-story brick cottage. Every neighborhood has its surprises: a pretty carved stone lintel on an Italianate façade; a block of attached townhomes that looks as if it were lifted en masse off of a London street; ornamental details on Loop buildings viewed up close from the El (elevated train) – these all make roaming the city a real pleasure.

Summer in the City

The city's Latin motto is *Urbs in Horto*, or "city in a garden," and while it's a reference to the city's many parks, it's still a rather interesting choice for an area whose bitter winters are so notorious. But Chicagoans wring the most out of the summer months, filling them

a city primer

with countless neighborhood festivals of every stripe, open-air concerts, and outdoor markets – as well as lounging at any bar or restaurant with an alfresco area. The lakefront – with its many beaches, miles of biking and walking paths, and gleaming new Millennium Park located downtown – is the most obvious location for warm-weather enjoyment, but activity along the long-neglected riverfront has begun to pick up with riverside restaurants and cafés, and kayak and canoe rental. Meanwhile, lavishly planted and carefully tended parks all over the city are fully exploited for picnics or impromptu sunning sessions as soon as summer arrives.

Arts Incubator

The "bright lights" of Chicago may not outshine those of New York or London, but they're famous for helping to catapult local artists to the national stage. That's particularly true of the local theater scene – Steppenwolf Theatre's ensemble includes a bevy of now-famous actors, many of whom appear regularly in major movies and TV shows. Also, the seminal improvisational comedy company Second City, with its ever-changing troupe of performers and writers, is a legendary well of American comic talent. It still packs the house after more than 40 years in business. Musically, the local blues and jazz scenes may not get as much mainstream attention as has been enjoyed by local rock acts in recent years, but aficionados of both genres can find performances by world-class musicians almost any night of the week, in both intimate little bars and famous venues. Students and recent graduates of local arts schools have rejuvenated Chicago's fashion and design landscape, garnering widespread national attention for their innovative designs and resulting in increasing numbers of retail outlets devoted to local designers.

✓ The Good Value Mark

Cities can be expensive, but if you know where to go you can always discover excellent-value places. We've picked out the best of these in the Restaurants, Shopping, and Hotels chapters and indicated them with the pink Good Value mark.

INTRODUCING CHICAGO

Locals like to point visitors in the direction of lesser-known treasures, from offbeat museums to iconic buildings, and these gems are highlighted in the Art and Architecture chapter *(see pp68–85)*. But despite the long lines and (oft-undeserved) tourist-trap reputations of some places, there are certain must-see destinations for any Chicago visitor. From original skyscrapers to major museums to pleasant open spaces, these are Chicago's essential sights.

Sears Tower

5 E4

233 S. Wacker Drive, at Adams • 312 875 9696 • Ⓜ Quincy
» www.thesearstower.com Open 10–10 daily (11–8 daily Oct–Apr)

It may have lost its world title, but this 1974-built skyscraper is still the nation's tallest. Get in line on a clear day, and from the 103rd-floor Skydeck you can see across four states. The innovative and sleek design have made it one of the city's most famous icons. **Adm**

Chicago Botanic Garden

1000 Lake Cook Road, Glencoe • 847 835 5440 • Metra stop Glencoe
» www.chicago-botanic.org Open 8am–sunset daily

Based in suburban Glencoe, this vast expanse is hugely rewarding for anyone interested in Illinois' natural splendor. As well as numerous gardens, there are shoreline and prairie habitats that highlight the little-known beauty of Midwestern flora *(see p140)*.

The Magnificent Mile

5 F2

Ⓜ Grand, Chicago

This moniker applies to the stretch of Michigan Avenue north of the Chicago River and south of Oak Street. Along these busy sidewalks you'll find department stores, malls, and flagship stores. But before there was The Gap et al, The Mag Mile was famous for its architecture. Walk this strip and you'll see some of Chicago's oldest buildings: the historic Water Tower, the Tribune Tower, and the Wrigley Building.

top attractions

Lincoln Park Zoo

3 F2

2200 N. Cannon Drive • 312 742 2000 • Bus Nos. 22, 36, 73, 151, 156

>> www.lpzoo.com Open 9–6 Mon–Fri; weekend hours vary by season

One of the few free zoos in a major U.S. city, the Lincoln Park Zoo is a destination not just for those who want to see the animals. Many of the animal habitat buildings and enclosures are of interest in their own right, as is the hand-carved endangered species carousel.

Millennium Park

5 F4

312 742 1168 • Ⓜ Randolph, Madison

>> www.millenniumpark.org Open 6am–11pm daily

Chicago's No. 1 destination for locals and visitors alike, Millennium Park is not really about plants. Frank Gehry's Jay Pritzker Pavilion, Anish Kapoor's *Cloud Gate*, Jaume Plensa's Crown Fountain, and great people-watching are the real crowd-pullers *(see pp74–5)*.

The Field Museum

7 F1

1400 S. Lake Shore Drive • 312 922 9410 • Metra stop Roosevelt Road

>> www.fieldmuseum.org Open 9–5 daily

This cultural behemoth, one of the treasures of the Museum Campus *(see p132)*, houses everything from biological specimens to collections assembled for the 1893 World's Fair. Sue, the world's largest, most-complete, and best-preserved Tyrannosaurus rex, is the most famous exhibit. Blockbuster temporary shows are also held here. **Adm**

>> *The free Chinatown/Pilsen bus service (weekends, end May–end Sep) links attractions on the South Side*

Museum of Contemporary Art

5 G1

220 E. Chicago Avenue, at Mies van der Rohe • 312 280 2660 • Ⓜ Chicago
>> www.mcachicago.org Open 10–8 Tue, 11–5 Wed–Sun

This vast museum houses an impressive collection of post-1945 art. Designed by Josef Paul Kleihues, it offers inviting outdoor steps for sitting and contemplating the city, along with ample space indoors for considering works of art from every angle *(see p77)*. **Adm**

Navy Pier

5 H2

600 E. Grand Avenue • 312 595 7437 • Bus Nos. 29, 56, 65, 66, 124
>> www.navypier.com Open 10–8 Mon–Sat, 10–7 Sun; check web for full details

The waterfront location of a range of attractions, Navy Pier has been the city's top tourist destination since 1916. Highlights include the Ferris Wheel, a children's museum, the Skyline stage for concerts in summer, and an ice-rink in winter. The views are amazing year round.

Art Institute of Chicago

5 G4

111 S. Michigan Ave., at Adams • 312 443 3600 • Ⓜ Adams, Monroe
>> www.artic.edu Open 10:30–5 Mon–Fri (to 8 Thu), 10–5 Sat–Sun

It is already hard to see all that the Art Institute has to offer, but on-going expansion means it will grow by one third. Must-sees such as Grant Wood's *American Gothic*, Andy Warhol's *Mao*, and blockbuster shows draw the crowds, and the institute also has an interesting program of concerts and dance performances *(see p73)*. **Adm**

top attractions

Adler Planetarium & Astronomy Museum

7 G1

1300 S. Lake Shore Drive • 312 922 7827 • **Metra stop Roosevelt Road**

>> www.adlerplanetarium.org Open 9:30–6 daily (winter: to 4:30)

The U.S.'s first planetarium, the Adler has one of the world's largest collections of astronomical equipment. The Sky Theater hosts a re-creation of the night sky, while the StarRider Theater puts on an amazing interactive show featuring 3-D graphic projections. **Adm**

Museum of Science and Industry

9 F4

57th St. & Lake Shore Dr. • 773 684 1414 • **Metra stop 55th/56th/57th**

>> www.msichicago.org Open 9:30–4 Mon–Sat, 11–4 Sun

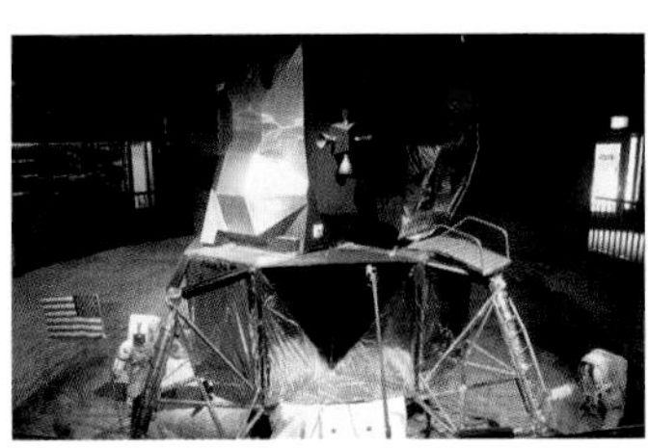

This museum opened in 1933 and was housed in the former Palace of Fine Arts, the last-remaining major structure from the 1893 World's Fair. Today, exhibits include the "working" coal mine, Apollo 8 module, vintage Silver Streak train, and German WWII submarine. **Adm**

Shedd Aquarium

7 F1

1200 S. Lake Shore Drive • 312 939 2438 • **Metra stop Roosevelt Road**

>> www.sheddaquarium.org Open 9–6 daily (winter: to 5 Mon–Fri)

Donated to the city by a former president of Marshall Field's department store in 1929, this Beaux-Arts beauty is home to hundreds of species of marine animals. The 1991-built Oceanarium has phenomenal underwater viewing galleries where you can gaze upon the likes of beluga whales and dolphins *(see p82)*. **Adm**

>> *The Adler Planetarium is open to 10pm on the first Friday of every month*

Due to the severe and protracted winters (which often extend well into spring), Chicagoans really welcome the arrival of temperate weather, and the warmer months are packed with outdoor festivals, concerts, and parades. There's almost too much to choose from: it may be tiring, but trying to cram as many outdoor activities as possible into the short summer is practically an unspoken rule.

Casimir Pulaski Day Parade

Named after a Polish general, this parade is held on a day that is an official holiday in Chicago. The city has an enormous Polish population, and this day celebrates their heritage: expect lots of Polish music and vendors selling traditional Polish foods. **First Mon in Mar**

St. Patrick's Day Parades

www.chicagostpatsparade.com; www.southsideirishparade.org

Chicago's Irish population is so big the city has two parades. The one downtown, where they also dye the Chicago River green, is most famous, but the south side Irish Parade is the local favorite. If you want a drink, stick to the west side of Western Avenue because that's the side with all the bars. **Closest Sat to 17 Mar**

57th Street Art Fair

773 493 3247, www.57thstreetartfair.org

In the Hyde Park neigborhood, at the junction with Kimbark Avenue, the big and bustling 57th Street Art Fair kicks off the city's art fair season. Reputedly the U.S.'s first judged art fair, it is guaranteed to offer high-quality paintings, sculptures, and jewelry for sale. **First weekend in Jun**

Pride Parade

www.chicagopridecalendar.org

Crowds of around 500,000 people watch Chicago's gay community march around the Boystown neighborhood *(see p128)*. The rowdy celebration of gay rights includes plenty of drag queens, fast-tempo music, and every liberal politician in the city. The Chicago Dyke March is the lesbian alternative and is generally held the day before Pride, in Andersonville to the north. **Last Sun in Jun**

Outdoor Summer Music Festivals

312 744 3315, www.chicagobluesfestival.org; 773 728 6000, www.oldtownschool.org; 847 266 5100, www.ravinia.org

On a summer weekend, it seems live music spills out of every park or pavilion in Chicago, but there are three events that should not be missed. In June, come rain or shine, the free Chicago Blues Festival, called Blues Fest

spring and summer

by locals, showcases the type of music the city considers its own, with performers such as Buddy Guy and Koko Taylor taking the stage in Grant Park. The following month, the legendary Old Town School of Folk Music *(see p102)* holds a two-day Folk and Roots Festival in Welles Park. Previous headline acts have included soul musician Oris Clay and Latin hip-hop fusion band, Ozomatli and there are also performances from students and teachers at the school. Donations are requested at the gate. Throughout the summer, the Ravinia Festival is an easy Metra train ride to suburban Highland Park to hear music by the Chicago Symphony Orchestra, pop acts such as Rufus Wainwright, and salsa stars such as La India. Skip the pricy pavilion seats and opt instead for the cheaper lawn seats where you can picnic as you watch the performance. **Jun–Sep**

Neighborhood Festivals

www.cityofchicago.org

Chicago has 77 neighborhoods and almost every one hosts at least one fun summer festival. The formula – cheap food, jewelry and T-shirt vendors, and local bands – tends to be the same whichever one you go to, but hipper neighborhoods tend to have more beer and louder music. **Jun–Aug**

Theater on the Lake

www.chicagoparkdistrict.com

Every year, the Chicago Park District asks local theater companies, including big names like Steppenwolf *(see p95)*, to remount successful shows from the preceding year at its lakeside facility. You can bring in food and drinks, making this a low-key, low-priced theater experience offering high-quality drama. **Jun–Aug**

Chicago Outdoor Film Festival

312 744 3315 or call 311, www.cityofchicago.org

Grant Park becomes a large outdoor movie theater on Tuesday nights during the summer, when the city screens free films in Butler Field. No reservations are needed, but BYO blanket, bug repellent, and popcorn. Films start when night falls. **Mid-Jul–Aug**

In the fall, Chicago's cultural calendar offers everything from trendy art openings to Lincoln Squares's Oktoberfest. Even in the midst of winter, there's more to life in Chicago than shoveling snow. Locals brave the elements to take advantage of musical performances, festive light displays, and a whole range of tempting activities that are offered as part of the Winter Delights program.

Around the Coyote

773 342 6777, www.aroundthecoyote.org

Many of the artists who used to live and work in hip Wicker Park have been pushed out by high rents. This multi-venue arts festival means, that for this weekend, the neighborhood gets some of its old vibe back. **Second weekend in Sep**

German-American Fest

847 647 9522, www.lincolnsquare.org

The Lincoln Square neighborhood was founded by German immigrants. Even though it has been gentrified, it has kept some of its European feel, and no weekend shows it off better than this annual Oktoberfest. Toast the old country with lots of German beer, bratwurst, and brass band and accordion music. **Sep or Oct**

LaSalle Bank Chicago Marathon

312 904 9800, www.chicagomarathon.com

Some 40,000 runners come to the city to race 26.2 miles (42 km) through its streets. The best places to cheer on runners are at the Cermak-Chinatown or 35th-Bronzeville-IIT El stops and in Museum Campus (Map 7 F1) near the finish line. **Second or third weekend in Oct**

Seasonal Lights

Winter is a hard fact of life in Chicago. So wrap up warm and see what locals do for the festive season with lots of electricity and a little imagination. The northwest side's Sauganash neighborhood is famous for its flashy displays of kitsch Christmas lights. Drive or walk through these wide streets to see Santa and his reindeer on what seems like almost every roof, and more mangers than you can shake a stick at. The holiday season kicks off with the Magnificent Mile Lights Festival, when this famous stretch of Michigan Avenue turns on its white lights (nearly one million on 200 trees) the Saturday after Thanksgiving. The light "procession" runs down Michigan Avenue, culminating in a firework display on the river. State Street's Macy's department store *(see p58)* offers Chicago's ever popular animatronic holiday window display. **Nov–Jan**

fall and winter

LaSalle Bank Do-It-Yourself Messiah

www.lasallebank.com/messiah

People vie for tickets to participate in the Civic Opera House's *(see p98)* annual sing-a-long to George Frideric Handel's *Messiah*. One of the city's best-loved winter events sees the predominantly amateur audience-cum-choir seated by vocal range and helped along in the performance by the Chicago Symphony Chorus. Tickets are issued from mid-November. **Dec**

Winter Delights

312 744 3315 or call 311, www.winterdelights.com

The city's two-month effort to encourage people of all ages – and with various interests – to get out of their homes includes plenty of indoor (and some outdoor) activities. Each weekend, there's a different theme, and everything from cooking demonstrations to ice skating, cabaret shows, jazz and blues performances, and even circus acts are among the (often free) events held across town. Many city hotels offer Winter Delights discount packages, too. **Jan–Feb**

Chinese New Year

www.ccamuseum.org

Dancing dragon-led parades, fortune cookies galore, and plenty of firecrackers are all part of the events that signal the start of the Chinese New Year on Cemrank Street. This free event is great fun, but not for those who are easily startled by loud noises. While in the neighborhood, check out the Chinese-American Museum of Chicago, which chronicles the local immigrant experience. **Late Jan–early Feb**

Chocolate Festival at Garfield Park Conservatory

312 746 5100, www.garfield-conservatory.org

Learn everything there is to know about everyone's favorite sweet treat at this three-day festival. Staff members explain the history of chocolate and how the fruit of the cocoa tree goes "from bean to bar." Local makers bring their wares to sample, nutritionists tell you that chocolate can be good for you, and its beauty benefits are also explained. **Weekend before Feb 14th**

Chicago's public transportation network, the Regional Transportation Authority (RTA), includes the Chicago Transit Authority (CTA) system of buses and El trains, Metra trains, and Pace suburban buses. Taxis provide a quick alternative and are recommended at night, but the RTA is generally efficient and easy to use. The following information covers the key aspects of getting around Chicago; for further sources of information, see www.echicago.co.uk.

Arrival

Chicago has two main airports: **O'Hare International Airport**, one of the world's busiest, is a major international and national hub located in the city's north-west corner. **Midway International Airport** is served by national carriers and occasional international flights. It is a 40-minute drive from downtown.

O'Hare International Airport

One of the easiest and most cost-effective ways to get to and from O'Hare is the **CTA**'s Blue Line train, which takes approximately 45 minutes to arrive downtown. Airport shuttle buses, such as **Omega Airport Shuttles,** are a good alternative. **Continental Airport Express** runs a daily route between O'Hare and downtown (6am–11:30pm). Tickets cost $25. You can also take a taxi – a typical trip from the airport to the city center costs around $35. However, if money isn't an issue, you can arrange for a limousine pickup through a service like **A1 Limousines**.

Midway International Airport

Midway is closer to downtown than O'Hare: the CTA's Orange Line is the cheapest way to get downtown and takes around 30 minutes to travel to the center. Alternatively, take a **Continental Airport Express** shuttle bus (6am–11:30pm). Tickets cost $20. Cab rides downtown cost around $25 and a limo would cost more.

By Train and Long-Distance Bus

Union Station (Map 4 D4) is served by around 40 Amtrak services each day, but is a fair walk from the nearest El stop at Clinton. **Greyhound**'s main downtown terminal is five blocks away at 630 W. Harrison St. (Map 4 D5).

Getting Around

Chicago is a sprawling city: while walking through downtown is easy and enjoyable, you'll need to use the city's public transportation system or taxis to reach neighborhoods farther out.

Chicago's Grid System

Nearly all streets in Chicago run east–west or north–south. The zero point is at the intersection of Madison Street (running east–west) and State Street (running north–south). All streets are labelled in relation to this point: for example, the section of State Street north of Madison is known as North State Street. Numbering also begins at the zero point: odd numbers are found on the east sides of north–south streets and the south sides of east–west streets. To get an idea of how far north an address is from Madison for example (or how far west from State), remember that as a rule, each block has 100 street numbers. 733 N. Halsted Street is seven blocks north of Madison and all other 700 N. addresses – for example, N. La Salle or N. Michigan – are located at the same cross street.

Public Transportation

The **RTA** operates a variety of bus and rail lines in Chicago, including the **CTA** and Metra. Though the CTA doesn't provide extensive service in many areas of the city, the busiest sections are well covered. A single ride on both buses and trains – often called simply "The El" because many of the train lines are elevated above the street – costs $2. Transfers between train lines cost an extra 25¢. Visitor Passes are available online and at a variety of downtown locations; a 1-day pass is $5, a 2-day is $9, a 3-day is $12 and a 5-day is $18. "Refillable" fare cards, can be purchased at any station or at many currency exchanges. Any extra journey started within 2 hours of boarding a train or bus only costs 25¢: a third journey within that period is free. Some bus services on main streets run 24/7 though most shut down at various times between 10pm and 2:25am. Downloadable schedules and transport maps for trains and buses are available from the CTA website *(or see inside back cover)*.

Metra trains are commuter trains connecting the city with the suburbs. The downtown terminals are either **Union Station** or the nearby Ogilvie Transportation Center.

Taxis

You can hail a cab on any busy street corner in Chicago, especially downtown and on the North Side. The meter starts at $2.25, increasing $1.80 for every mile or $2 for every six minutes of waiting. There is a $1 charge for each extra passenger over the age of 12 years. There is no extra charge for baggage or credit card use, but only a few cabs are equipped with credit card machines. You can also call for a cab: try **Yellow Cab** or **Flash Cab Chicago**.

Driving

While the grid system is a boon, driving in Chicago can be frustrating, since traffic can often become gridlocked and parking spots hard to come by and expensive. If you need to drive, there are plenty of car rental agencies, such as **Hertz** or **Enterprise**, at each airport and around the city. The speed limit on city streets is 30mph (50kph). Drivers should have a license (international if applicable) and ID on them at all times.

Bicycles and Inline Skates

Cycling is encouraged by the city and most main streets have separate bike lanes. Be careful, however, since many drivers aren't very polite and don't share the road well. Cyclists can take their bikes on Metra trains on weekends and during off-peak hours on weekdays. Bicycles are allowed on CTA trains and CTA and Pace buses equipped with bike racks outside of rush hour. **Bike Chicago** rents a variety of bikes by the hour and has several outlets and you can also try the **Millennium Park Bike Station**. Cycling and inline skating along the Lakefront Bike Path *(see p132)* is highly recommended in warmer months.

By Water

From Memorial Day to Labor Day, **Shoreline Sightseeing** offers a River Taxi between Navy Pier and Sears Tower and a Harbor Taxi between Navy Pier and the Museum Campus.

Tours

A boat on the Chicago River is an excellent vantage point from which to admire the city's world-renowned architecture: the Chicago Architecture Foundation *(see p76)* run arguably the best river tours, as well as architecture-themed walking tours. Alternatively, try a leisurely carriage ride through downtown (**www.antiquecoach-carriage.com**). Gray Line (**www.grayline.com**) offers bus tours of the city, while the Chicago Historical Society (**www.chicagohs.org**) organizes a range of walking tours through the city's varied neighborhoods. Cyclists should check out **Bike Chicago** for tours on two wheels. Other specialist tours include local ghost hunter Richard Crowe's Supernatural Tour (**www.ghosttours.com**), while Untouchables Tours (**www.gangstertour.com**) follow the trails of infamous local gansters of the 1920s and 30s. Chicago Greeters is a free service (**www.chicagogreeter.com**) where a whole range of tours for groups of 1–6 people are offered by enthusiastic and knowledgeable local residents out of sheer love of their city. For more information on Chicago tours try **www.chicago.il.org/tours.html**.

Directory

A1 Limousines
800 810 0208
www.a1ofchicago.com

Bike Chicago
312 595 9600
www.bikechicago.com

Continental Airport Express
888 284 3826
www.airportexpress.com

CTA
www.transitchicago.com

Enterprise Rent-A-Car
800 261 7331 • www.enterprise.com

Flash Cab Chicago
773 561 4444
www.flashcab.com

Greyhound
800 231 2222
www.greyhound.com

Hertz Rent-A-Car
800 654 3001 • www.hertz.com

Midway International Airport
773 838 0600
www.flychicago.com

Millennium Park Bike Station
888 245 3929
www.chicagobikestation.com

O'Hare International Airport
773 686 2200
www.ohare.com

Omega Airport Shuttles
773 483 6634
www.omegashuttle.com

RTA
312 836 7000
www.rtachicago.com

Shoreline Sightseeing
www.shorelinesightseeing.com

Union Station
312 655 2101 • www.amtrak.com

Yellow Cab Chicago
312 829 4222
www.yellowcabchicago.com

>> *Call the RTA for any enquiries regarding the CTA transport system; the website also has links to Metra and Pace*

Chicago is an incredibly friendly and accessible destination, though it offers some challenges for visitors with special needs. The Chicago Office of Tourism's website contains plenty of helpful information and useful links. The following is some essential practical advice to help you make the most of your stay; for sources of information, check www.echicago.dk.com.

Disabled Travellers

All of the CTA's 150 bus routes have lifts or ramps for disabled passengers and many CTA train stations are also accessible; a full list is available on the CTA website *(see p20)*. Guide dogs are permitted on all buses and trains. The city also maintains a website with information about city services and events for those with disabilities at **www.cityofchicago.org/disabilities**. Wheelchair-accessible taxis are available throughout the city from **Central Dispatch** (800 281 4466). All major sights, shops, and restaurants are wheelchair accessible by law.

Emergencies and Health

Drug stores (pharmacies) are open during regular business hours. Some chains such as **Walgreens** and **CVS** have 24-hour stores. Check their websites for the location nearest you. Many local grocery chains, such as **Jewel** and **Dominick's**, also have in-store pharmacies. For serious medical emergencies requiring immediate aid, call **911**, or check with your concierge or in the Yellow Pages for your nearest hospital. The **Northwestern Memorial Hospital** is convenient to downtown. Even if you have medical insurance you may have to pay for treatment yourself and then be reimbursed, but you should always check with your insurance company before receiving any treatment. If you have a dental emergency, the **Chicago Dental Society** or your concierge can advise you. If you are unlucky enough to be a victim of crime you need to fill out a police report in order for you to make use of your travel insurance.

Gay and Lesbian Chicago

The legal age for sexual consent in Illinois is 18, and most Chicagoans are tolerant of gay couples. Boystown, the country's first officially recognized gay village and the most popular gay neighborhood, is located on the north side of Chicago *(see p128)*. Most of its restaurants, bars, and stores are on Halsted Street. Andersonville, located farther north, also has a large gay and lesbian population. Sources of information include the **Lesbian & Gay Helpline**, Boystown website (**www.boystownchicago.com**) and the local gay newspaper, the weekly *Windy City Times* (**www.wctimes.com**).

Listings/What's On

A variety of local publications offer comprehensive events listings. The *Chicago Reader* (**www.chicagoreader.com**), a free paper available from streetboxes around the city, and *Time Out Chicago* (**www.timeout.com/chicago**), an inexpensive magazine available at any city newsstand, both offer extensive coverage of local entertainment options. New editions of both printed publications come out every Thursday. The Metromix website (**metromix.chicagotribune.com**), which is filled with excellent maps, is an exhaustive resource for information about restaurants, bars and clubs. Flavorpill is a free, fortnightly email offering a select crop of cultural happenings: log on to see the current edition (**chi.flavorpill.net**.)

Money

Many travel experts recommend travelers use credit cards and ATMs because they offer the best exchange rate. If you need to exchange hard currency, you can visit one of the city's many currency exchanges, which are clustered in the downtown area. However, major banks usually have more favorable exchange rates for large transactions. U.S.-dollar traveler's checks are accepted pretty much anywhere and if lost or stolen are usually easily replaced.

Opening Hours

Most **shops** are open from 9 or 10am to 6 or 7pm: if open on Sundays, hours are usually noon to 5 or 6pm. **Post offices** and **banks** usually close at 2 or 3pm on Saturdays. **Bars** in Chicago typically stay open until 2am on weekdays and 3am on Saturdays, though a few places have late-night licenses and are open until 4am on Fridays and 5am on Saturdays. **Restaurants** normally close between

10pm and 11pm on weekdays and a little later on weekends. Most **parks** are open from dawn until dusk. Post offices and banks are closed on public holidays, as are many – but not all – stores.

Phones and Communications

There are several local area codes. When dialling from one area code to another, dial 1 to precede the area code and seven-digit telephone number. The prevalence of cell phones has meant that few phone booths are still in operation: the ones that are probably require a phone card for overseas calls. Cards can be bought at convenience stores. Local calls (within the same area code) cost 35¢.

Internet cafés are becoming more commonplace, especially in Lakeview and Lincoln Park, and provide web and computer access at an hourly rate. Many cafés, books stores, and coffee shops also offer free wireless access. You can find a partial list of wi-fi spots at **www.wifi411.com.**

Stamps are sold at grocery stores as well as post offices. Blue mailboxes are found on most major street corners.

Sales Tax

Chicago's sales tax, one of the highest in Illinois, stands at 9 per cent. It is applied to all consumer goods in retail stores and is added to your purchase at the register. Cigarettes, which have an additional tax, are generally sold with the tax already included. Hotel occupancy tax is 15.4 per cent and is added to the room rate.

Security and ID

It's recommended that you carry a picture ID and a valid passport with you at all times, since all bars and clubs require you to be 21 and over and will card you (ask for proof) at the door. Most places will accept a passport for proof of age, but prefer a driver's ID. Any alcohol consumption or purchase requires ID, for example in restaurants or stores. In terms of personal security, certain areas of Chicago, especially the far west and on the south side, are best avoided.

Tipping

Restaurants do not add a gratuity to your bill, so you are expected to tip your server between 15 and 20 per cent. Unless the server is incompetent or rude, they should receive a tip. Taxi drivers and hairdressers expect between 10 and 15 per cent. Hotel porters should receive a dollar per item and hotel staff should receive a few dollars a day. Bartenders should be tipped a dollar per drink – you might find that you won't get served again if you don't.

Tourist Information

The city has two **Visitor Centers** located downtown (open daily) and a website filled with helpful travel information and advice. In addition, many hotels carry free monthly publications, such as *Where Chicago* and *Front Desk*, which provide up-to-date information on attractions and events in the city. Alternatively, you can try calling 311 for information on city-run special events.

Directory

Chicago Dental Society
312 836 7300

Chicago Office of Tourism
312 744 2400
cityofchicago.org/tourism

Chicago Visitor Centers
Chicago Cultural Center, 77 E. Randolph St.
Chicago Water Works, 163 E. Pearson St. • www.chicago.il.org

CVS
888 6074287
www.cvs.com

Dominick's
www.dominicks.com

Fire Department
911

Illinois Bureau of Tourism
800 406 6418
www.enjoyillinois.com

Jewel
www.jewelosco.com

LaSalle Currency Exchange
777 N. LaSalle St.
312 642 0220

Lesbian & Gay Helpline
773 929 4357

Mayor's Office for People with Disabilities
312 744 7050
egov.cityofchicago.org/disabilities

Northwestern Memorial Hospital
251 E. Huron St. • 312 926 2000
www.nmh.org

Police
911

United States Postal Service
www.usps.com

Walgreens
www.walgreens.com

Yahoo Yellow Pages
yp.yahoo.com

» *For information on Chicago's grid system* see p20

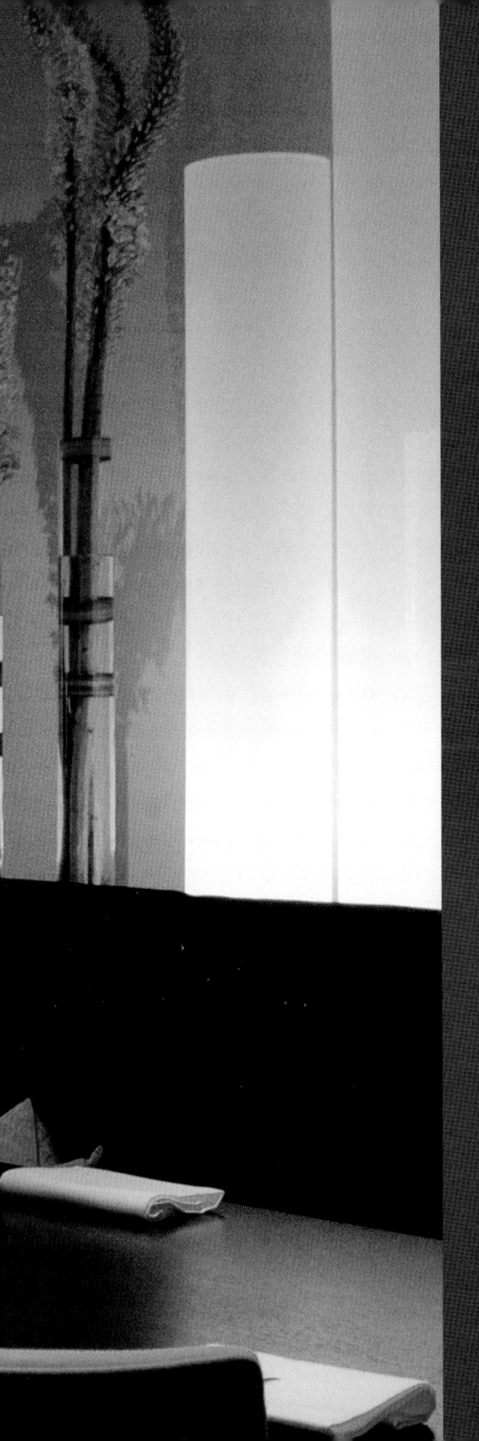

restaurants

Chicago's reputation as a haven for meat-lovers is justified. From Italian beef sandwich joints to steakhouses and hot dog stands, there may be no better place in the U.S. to satisfy carnivorous cravings. Recently, however, there's been a change. The Windy City's dining scene has become as cosmopolitan as any, offering both fine vegetarian fare and several restaurants that are leading the nation's culinary avant-garde movement.

RESTAURANTS

What I love about Chicago is that you don't need a lot of money to have a memorable meal: think hot dogs and deep-dish pizza, standout sandwiches and cheap ethnic fare. But I'm also excited at how this fast-food city's dining scene has become incredibly sophisticated, with a slew of progressive restaurants and young chefs turning out 21st-century food you won't find on either U.S. coast. Whether your tastes run high or low, you're in for some great eating.

J.P. Anderson

Trendy Scenes

Want to dine with the beautiful people? Slip into **Japonais** *(see p35)*, where local loft-dwellers sip sake cocktails and nibble on exquisite bites of upscale Japanese fare. **Nine Steakhouse** *(see p31)* is still the flashiest red-meat joint in town, while a funky/casual crowd indulges in decadent desserts at Bucktown favorite **Hot Chocolate** *(see p43)*.

Culinary Adventures

Chicago features a host of forward-thinking restaurants. Get on the right wavelength at hot destinations like **Moto** *(see p47)*, where Homaro Cantu whips up edible paper and barbecued styrofoam; **Alinea** *(see p30)*, with a slightly more accessible menu; or **Green Zebra** *(see p46)*, a fine-dining vegetarian place that makes even hardened carnivores drool.

Chicago Classics

No visit to the meat-loving Windy City would be complete without sitting down to a juicy steak at **Morton's** *(see p31)*, an overstuffed sandwich at **Manny's Coffee Shop** *(see p40)*, a Chicago-style hot dog with the works at **The Wieners Circle** *(see p32)*, or a sloppy, succulent Italian beef sandwich at River North's **Mr. Beef** *(see p34)*.

choice eats

Cultural Melting Pot

Ethnic enclaves across the city are brimming with global flavors, so you can sample samosas and curries at Devon Avenue's classy Indian destination **Tiffin** *(see p32)*, or nibble on gyros and moussaka at **Greek Islands** *(see p42)* in Greektown. On the South Side, fill up on authentic, amazingly cheap Mexican fare at **Nuevo Leon** *(see p42)*.

Rise and Dine

Chicagoans take breakfast almost as seriously as baseball. For a retro diner experience check out **Lou Mitchell's** *(see p39)*, a well-loved staple since 1923. The **Bongo Room** *(see p42)* is a favorite for flapjacks, while **Orange** *(see p29)* dishes up creative morning fare like fruit sushi and "green eggs and ham" (scrambled eggs with pancetta and basil).

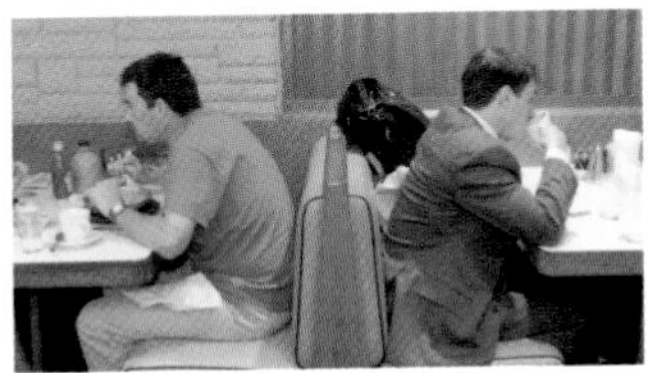

Randolph Street Hot Spots

Ten years after this industrial neighborhood became a big-time dining destination, it's still a hot ticket. Highlights include the minimalist, modern **Blackbird** *(see p45)*, which offers whip-smart New American fare, and **avec** *(see p45)* with a thrilling small plates menu. The always-crowded **Sushi Wabi** *(see p45)* is still the hippest raw-fish spot in town.

Kit Kat Lounge & Supper Club

1 B2

3700 N. Halsted St., at Waveland • 773 525 1111
>> www.kitkatchicago.com Open 5:30pm–1:30am Tue–Sun

Comfort food and drag queens may sound an incongruous combination, but it's the winning formula behind this fun, quirky Boystown restaurant and martini lounge. Couples and groups of all persuasions crowd the bar to sample Kit Kat's 98 custom cocktails (flavors such as Key Lime Pie and Big Apple are particularly popular), while several times every evening from 8pm, the resident "Kit Kat Divas" strut out to sing or lip-synch to classic and current pop songs.

The food might not be the point here, but it's no afterthought, either. The upscale, hearty menu features appealing starters like chicken and beef satay, coconut crab cakes, and pizza with *alfredo* sauce and rosemary chicken, plus main plates of Big Daddy coconut-crusted shrimp, Little Miss Saigon *ahi* tuna, and satisfying Top Hat beef tenderloin with sweet chutney and crispy shoestring fries. **Moderate**

Ann Sather *satisfying Scandinavian food*

1 B3

929 W. Belmont Ave., at Clark • 773 348 2378
>> www.annsather.com
Open 7am–3pm Mon & Tue, 7am–9pm Wed–Sun

Famous for its gooey cinnamon rolls, this old-fashioned diner is a local breakfast favorite. Swedish-style pancakes with lingonberries are a big hit in the morning; the evening menu offers classics like roast duckling, chicken croquettes, and shepherd's pie. **Cheap**

Penny's Noodles *eat on the cheap*

1 B5

950 W. Diversey Pkwy., at Sheffield • 773 281 8448
>> www.pennysnoodleshop.com
Open lunch & dinner daily

Insanely low prices and a varied menu of pan-Asian specialties have made this chain really popular with a young crowd. The food is always satisfying, from plump Vietnamese spring rolls to *tom yum* soup and generous portions of rice and noodle dishes. **Cheap**

Mia Francesca *ever-popular Italian joint*

1 B3

3311 N. Clark St., at Aldine • 773 281 3310

» **www.miafrancesca.com** Open lunch Sat & Sun, dinner daily

Families, daters, and pre-theater diners keep this cozy place buzzing nightly. This original location is so popular that 16 other Francescas have sprung up around Chicago. All offer hearty classics (calamari, thin-crust pizzas, pastas) and a modern look: dark wood, white tablecloths, and black-and-white photos. **Moderate**

The Pepper Lounge *dark, sultry date spot*

1 B2

3441 N. Sheffield Ave., at Clark • 773 665 7377

» **www.pepperlounge.com** Open dinner Tue–Sun

Tucked among Wrigleyville's sports bars is this intimate, sexy spot, where couples cuddle at close-set tables and regulars linger over martinis at the bar. The eclectic menu changes regularly, but you'll always find staples such as ruby-red tuna tartare with *tobiko* caviar, and lovely *cavatappi* pasta with herbed chicken breast. **Moderate**

Orange *funky breakfast hangout*

1 B3

3231 N. Clark St., at Belmont • 773 549 4400

Open breakfast & lunch daily

One of the city's best-loved morning haunts, this cheerful Lakeview storefront has gained a loyal following for its whimsical interpretations of breakfast classics. The menu changes often but is always full of well-presented delights; signature plates include fruit sushi (morsels of fruit such as mango and fig rolled up in sticky rice), French toast kebabs, and fancy egg dishes like "green eggs and ham" – a delicious blend of scrambled eggs, pesto and pancetta. Drinks include coffee infused with orange, plus healthy juice options. For lunch there's a selection of salads and sandwiches.

The sunny space itself is a fresh start to the day, with orange walls and pillows, stacks of oranges behind the counter, and an artificial orange tree. The crowd is young and just-out-of-bed, which makes for good people-watching while you wait (and you will wait) for a table. **Cheap**

Half Shell, Inc. *unpretentious seafood spot*

1 C5

676 W. Diversey Pkwy., at Orchard • 773 549 1773
Open lunch & dinner daily

Little-known even to locals, this subterranean bar and restaurant serves some of the best crab legs in the city (plus scallops, beef tenderloin, and more) at very reasonable prices. There's no atmosphere to speak of – just a few Christmas lights and nautical knick-knacks – but that just adds to the hidden-gem charm. **Moderate**

pingpong *stylish pan-Asian nook*

1 C3

3322 N. Broadway St., at Buckingham • 773 281 7575
» www.pingpongrestaurant.com
Open 4pm–midnight daily

In the heart of Boystown, this tiny BYOB storefront is a popular date choice for couples of all persuasions. Just about everything on the pan-Asian menu is tasty, from fresh spring rolls and tuna tartare to kicky *kung pao* chicken and sesame beef with broccoli. **Cheap**

Alinea *avant-garde food*

2 D3

1723 N. Halsted St., at Willow • 312 867 0110
» www.alinearestaurant.com Open dinner Wed–Sun

After doing time in esteemed kitchens in Evanston and the Napa Valley, chef Grant Achatz has made his solo debut with this cutting-edge venture in Lincoln Park, and it's easily the hottest restaurant in the city.

Achatz likes to play with familiar flavors: a peanut butter and jelly sandwich is transformed into grapes dipped in peanut butter, wrapped in brioche, and dusted with ground, roasted peanuts. Other intriguing combinations have included freeze-dried strawberries with foie gras, and hazelnut puree with granola.

The decor is stylish and muted, and features include sensor-tripped doors, a floating, glass-walled stairway, and an open kitchen. There is no à la carte menu; instead, diners choose a tasting menu of 6, 12, or a whopping 24 courses, which can add up to a seven-hours-plus experience. Want a table? Call now – Alinea is generally booked up months in advance. **Expensive**

North Pond *artful, modern French fare* 1 D5

2610 N. Cannon Dr., at Diversey • 773 477 5845
www.northpondrestaurant.com Open brunch Sun, dinner Tue–Sun (also lunch Tue–Sat in summer)

One of Chicago's loveliest restaurants, this picturesque special-occasion spot is located by a pond in the heart of Lincoln Park. The recently renovated Arts and Crafts-style building features rich wood and copper accents, a buzzing open kitchen, and a beautiful stone fireplace that holds a roaring fire during the winter months.

The cuisine is just as impressive. Over the years, chef Bruce Sherman has built strong relationships with local farmers, and it shows in the clean, honest flavors and seasonal emphasis of the menu. There are à la carte options, but the five-course tasting menu offers the best all-round experience. Dishes might include grilled sablefish with lemon-scented crushed potatoes, charred spring onion and green asparagus; and lemon soufflé with strawberry anise hyssop syrup. Reservations are a must. **Expensive**

Bourgeois Pig *the thinking man's café* 3 E1

738 W. Fullerton Ave., at Lincoln & Halsted
773 883 5282 • Open breakfast, lunch & dinner daily

Set in an old brownstone, this charmingly messy café draws a university crowd, who settle in with their books to sip one of the four kinds of fresh-brewed coffee. The menu offers soups, pastries, salads, and literary-sounding sandwiches like "The Sun Also Rises." Expect live music most weekend nights. **Cheap**

Meat-Lovers' Paradise

If you like steak, you're in the right place – Chicago's steakhouses offer prime cuts of Midwestern beef and high-class atmosphere. One of the nation's top chains, **Morton's** (Map 3 G5, 1050 N. State St., 312 266 4820, www.mortons.com), began right here on the Gold Coast, and is still the place to go for giant steaks with delicious sides of creamed spinach and garlic mashed potatoes. Flashy decor and a creative menu draw a glitzy crowd to **Nine Steakhouse** (Map 4 D3, 440 W. Randolph St., 312 575 9900, www.n9ne.com), while **David Burke's Primehouse** (Map 5 F2, 616 N. Rush St., 312 660 6000, www.brguestrestaurants.com), with its clean, stylish contemporary decor and forward-thinking menu, is giving the old boys a run for their money.

Karyn's Fresh Corner *health food haven*

2 D3

1901 N. Halsted St., at Armitage • 312 255 1590

>> www.karynraw.com Open lunch & dinner daily

Karyn's is a holistic health center containing two outlets that serve uncooked vegan meals. Choose from snacky bean burros and California rolls in the café to fancy dishes like basil-scented turnip "ravioli" with sundried tomato puree and macadamia whipped cream in the adjacent gourmet restaurant. **Moderate**

The Wieners Circle *hot dog heaven*

1 C5

2622 N. Clark St., at Wrightwood • 773 477 7444

Open 11am–4am daily (to 5am Sat & Sun)

You haven't truly visited the Windy City until you've tried a Chicago-style hot dog, piled high with everything from tomatoes and pickles to frighteningly neon-green relish – but never, ever catsup. This late-night walk-up in Wrigleyville is the place to do it, in spite of (or perhaps because of) the comically rude staff. **Cheap**

Café 28 *classy Cuban spot*

1800 W. Irving Park Rd., at Ravenswood • 773 528 2883

>> www.cafe28.org • Ⓜ Irving Park (Brown Line)

Open brunch Sat & Sun, lunch Tue–Fri, dinner daily

Local artists' work adds a touch of culture to this wildly popular spot where customers linger over their mojitos. Dishes include almond-crusted halibut and *ropa vieja* (Cuban beef stew), while the live-music brunch offers variations on eggs Benedict and French toast. **Moderate**

Tiffin *exceptional Indian food*

2536 W. Devon Ave., at Maplewood • 773 338 2143

Ⓜ Western (Brown Line), then bus No. 49B

>> www.tiffinrestaurant.com Open lunch & dinner daily

Tiffin is the finest restaurant in Chicago's Indian and Pakistani neighborhood. In the open kitchen, chefs prepare lip-smacking classics such as vegetable samosas, chicken tikka masala, and sag paneer. The buffet lunch is hugely popular. **Moderate**

Jin Ju *hip Andersonville Korean*

5203 N. Clark St., at Foster • 773 334 6377
Bus No. 22 Open dinner Tue–Sun

Soju (sweet potato vodka) flows like water and the spicy aromas of classic dishes such as *kimchi* (pickles) and *bibimbop* (mixed vegetables) waft through this relaxed Korean restaurant. Low lighting and sexy ambient music make Jin Ju a popular date spot; then again, it could just be the killer cucumber martinis. **Moderate**

Moody's Pub *burgers and a beer garden*

5910 N. Broadway St., at Thorndale • 773 275 2696
Ⓜ Thorndale (Red Line)
>> www.moodyspub.com Open 11:30am–12:45am Mon–Fri, 11:30am–1:45am Sat, noon–12:45am Sun

There's no finer place in the city to enjoy a hamburger. This Edgewater tavern comes into its own in summer, when you can sit in a spacious beer garden filled with silver oaks and bubbling fountains. Cash only. **Cheap**

NoMI *exquisite French dishes with a twist*

5 F1

800 N. Michigan Ave., at Chicago • 312 239 4030
>> www.nomirestaurant.com
Open breakfast, lunch & dinner daily

Located on the seventh floor of the Park Hyatt Hotel, sophisticated NoMI has full-length windows, and a world-class art collection that includes work by Dale Chihuly. But all that is secondary to the stunning modern French and sushi cuisine. **Expensive**

BIN 36 *nirvana for wine-lovers*

5 F3

339 N. Dearborn St., at Kinzie • 312 755 9463
>> www.bin36.com Open breakfast, lunch & dinner daily

The exemplary wine list and creative American food make this space (with a reservations-suggested restaurant and separate walk-in tavern) very popular. High ceilings and walls of windows give a cool, modern feel, but the food is comforting, from braised veal ravioli to mussels with curry cream. **Moderate**

>> *Devon Avenue* (see p128) *has a handful of very good, reasonably priced Indian and Pakistani restaurants*

Cafe Iberico *top-notch regional tapas*

5 E1

739 N. LaSalle St., at Chicago • 312 573 1510

>> www.cafeiberico.com Open lunch & dinner daily

This boisterous River North tapas joint is overflowing with international revelers every night of the week. Reservations are accepted only for parties of six or more, so arrive early or be prepared to wait at the bar – not such a bad option, considering that you'll have easy access to the popular red or white sangria. Large groups sit at long communal tables in several open, high-ceilinged rooms, and relaxed servers keep drinks refilled and things flowing smoothly. The menu offers regional Spanish specialties such as Andalusian-style gazpacho or grilled swordfish with white beans and spinach, plus other tapas classics like marinated olives or artichokes, baked goat cheese, grilled shrimp, and beef skewers with caramelized onions. For heartier appetites, there's seafood paella, grilled salmon steak, or beef tenderloin. But be sure to save room for dessert: the chocolate flan is unforgettable. **Moderate**

Mr. Beef *Chicago fast-food classic*

666 N. Orleans St., at Huron • 312 337 8500

Open 7am–4:45pm Mon–Fri, 10am–2pm Sat

This industrial, no-frills lunch spot in River North draws crowds of local office workers for what is arguably the best Italian beef sandwich in the city. Paper-thin slices of meat are marinated in *jus* and piled onto a chewy roll; cheese and sweet or hot peppers are optional, but a bagful of fries on the side is a must. **Cheap**

City of Pizza

Chicago-style (a.k.a. deep-dish) pizza got its start in 1943 at downtown's **Pizzeria Uno** (Map 5 F2, 29 E. Ohio St., 312 321 1000). Now part of a national chain, it still serves up satisfying pies, heavy on the crust and with chunks of savory crushed tomato. Less-touristy **Lou Malnati's** (Map 5 E2, 439 N. Wells St., 312 828 9800) favors a light, buttery crust and also does a delicious thin-crust variation. But if thin-crust is your thing, you can't beat **Pizza Metro** (Map 2 A5, 1707 W. Division St., 773 278 1753, www.pizzametro.com), a late-night spot that serves up slices with offbeat toppings. Finally, **Piece** (Map 2 A4, 1927 W. North Ave., 773 772 4422) is a brewpub and sports bar whose New Haven-style (hand-formed) pies have even won over some die-hard Chicago pizza purists.

Japonais *trendy Japanese nibbles*

4 D1

600 W. Chicago Ave., at Larrabee • 312 822 9600

www.japonaischicago.com Open lunch Mon–Fri, dinner daily

Set in a recently converted industrial building on the Chicago River, this hot spot is one of the city's most visually stunning restaurants. Inside, water flows seductively over a high-gloss red brick wall behind the host stand. Four distinctive dining and lounging spaces on two levels set very different moods, from the lavish red patent-leather chairs and gold lamé curtains of the formal Red Room to the casual rattan furniture and plush couches of the downstairs Riverwalk Café.

The food, created in separate cold and hot kitchens by executive chefs Jun Ichikawa and Gene Kato, is just as stylish, with artful, imaginative presentations. Sushi is impeccable here, with plenty of fresh *nigiri* selections plus signature *maki* including *mono*, an octopus roll topped with spicy tuna tartare and sweet *unagi* sauce. But it's the non-sushi fare that's most impressive, from the lovely, light Bin Cho salad of marinated sashimi baby tuna and shaved *daikon* radish spritzed with citrus sake vinaigrette, to treats like Seven Samurais (a dish of seven seafood tartares) and Pachinko – oysters baked with shrimp and bacon gratin and served on the half shell over aromatic sea salt.

Reservations are highly recommended to avoid waits of an hour or more, particularly on weekends. Or you can dine in the casual (no-reservations) downstairs bar and lounge, which features an abbreviated menu and a full slate of specialty cocktails, from Japanese Mai Tais and sake martinis to the Floating Orchid, a citrusy house special topped with an edible orchid. **Expensive**

ETHYL
GALLONS
2 1 0 19 18
3 17
4 16
5 15
6 14
7
8 9 10 11 12
NO
SMOKING
POTA
CHI

Osteria Via Stato *Italian hotspot*

5 F2

620 N. State St., at Ontario • 312 642 8450

>> www.leye.com Open lunch Mon–Sat, dinner daily

Italian food doesn't get much more authentic than at this delightfully rustic yet modern restaurant in River North. Everyone eats from the set-price menu, which includes a wide range of antipasti (from house-smoked salmon to light chickpea salad and Italian cured meats); simple pastas and risottos; and lighter, moderately portioned entrées such as pork shank and skate wing with capers. The smart "Just Bring Me Wine" option includes three tastings of paired wines at three different price points from the all-Italian list.

The decor is handsome yet spare, with warm wood fixtures and exposed brick. Bare lightbulbs hang from the ceiling of the low-lit dining room, and diners chat at the long, communal tables. Equally charming is the adjacent *enoteca*, a relaxed wine bar: its high tables, outdoor patio, and tempting list of casual nibbles make it a destination in itself. **Moderate**

Twin Anchors *legendary barbecue joint*

3 F3

1655 N. Sedgwick St., at Eugenie • 312 266 1616

>> www.twinanchorsribs.com Open lunch Sat & Sun, dinner daily

Located on a residential street in Old Town, this hidden gem has been serving platters of fried chicken, grilled shrimp, ribs, and steaks to its clientele since 1932. It's an old-fashioned, no-nonsense kind of place: couples, families, business diners, and retirees crowd around tables and cram into worn red-leather booths. Frank Sinatra is on the jukebox and strings of pink piggy lights decorate the wood-paneled walls. Signs around the place read "Positively No Dancing," and they mean it – a throwback to the days when excitable patrons waiting to be seated would start dancing at the bar and knock into waitresses laden with plates of meat.

Local celebrities from Frank Sinatra to David Mamet have dined at Twin Anchors, and actress Bonnie Hunt filmed part of her movie *Return to Me* here. The place still gets packed most nights with regulars looking for good, reasonably priced food. **Moderate**

Lou Mitchell's *the ultimate breakfast joint*

4 D4

565 W. Jackson Blvd., at Jefferson • 312 939 3111
Open breakfast & lunch daily

Perhaps the best breakfast place in the city, this Loop diner has been around since 1923 and fairly crackles with old Chicago charm. Bouffant-haired waitresses call customers "Hon" and work their tables with lightning-quick efficiency, doling out coffee, orange juice, and big plates of food to a mix of tourists, locals, and office workers. The interior is nothing special – tiled floor, vinyl booths, and fake plants – but that's not the point. Lou's is all about reliable, comforting morning food, from 17 kinds of fluffy omelet to banana pancakes, Belgian waffles, and piles of French toast. Lunchtime offerings include salads, burgers topped with everything from bacon to green olives, and classic sandwiches like tuna, baked meatloaf, and BLT. There are doughnut holes to nibble on while you wait for a table, plus women and kids get Milk Duds (chocolate-covered caramel candies) after they're seated. Cash only. **Cheap**

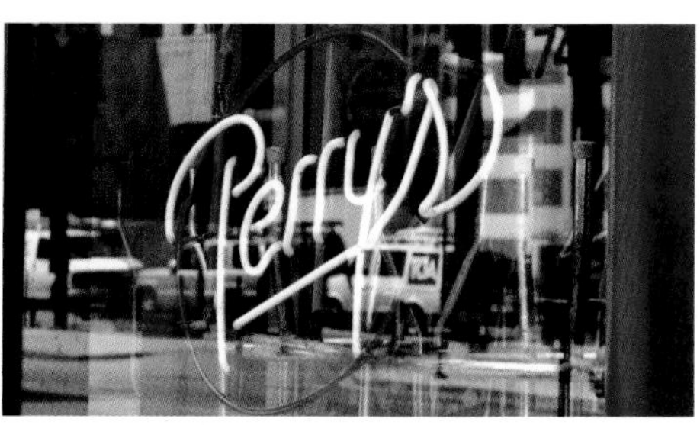

Perry's *mammoth, overstuffed sandwiches*

5 E3

180 N. Franklin St., at Randolph • 312 372 7557
>> www.perrysdeli.com Open breakfast & lunch Mon–Fri

The line usually winds out the door at this Loop lunch magnet, where giant sandwiches are piled high with meatloaf, turkey, egg, pastrami, and more. The decor is simple (fluorescent lights; walls papered with clippings and reviews) and cell phones are banned. Value-for-money daily specials also available. **Cheap**

Eleven City Diner *stylish deli delights*

7 E1

1112 S.Wabash Ave., at 11th • 312 212 1112
>> www.elevencitydiner.com
Open breakfast, lunch & dinner daily

Decked out with plush leather booths and gleaming tiled and mirrored walls, this classy diner dishes up traditional Jewish deli fare. Try matzo ball soup, latkes, sandwiches, and burgers, as well as retro soda-fountain drinks such as egg creams. **Moderate**

Gioco *exemplary contemporary Italian*

1312 S. Wabash Ave., at 13th • 312 939 3870

>> www.gioco-chicago.com Open lunch Mon–Fri, dinner daily

Set in a former speakeasy in the newly hot South Loop, this urban-chic eatery is one of the city's more stylish. The simple-yet-delicious menu includes classic Tuscan and Umbrian dishes such as beef *carpaccio* with truffle oil and gnocchi with tomato sauce and parmesan cheese. **Moderate**

Manny's Coffee Shop *classic deli*

6 C1

1141 S. Jefferson St., at Roosevelt • 312 939 2855

>> www.mannysdeli.com Open 5am–4pm Mon–Sat

A South Side institution since 1942, this café is popular with police officers, businessfolk, and retirees. They all come for the improbably thick sandwiches piled with brisket, pastrami, and especially corned beef, plus generous sides of potato pancakes and other deli staples. Free Internet access is an added perk. **Cheap**

Fine Dining Favorites

For many people, fine dining in Chicago means one place: **Charlie Trotter's** (Map 2 D2, 816 W. Armitage Ave., 773 248 6228, www.charlietrotters.com). When it comes to *haute cuisine* in this city, Trotter's conservative and cerebral-yet-ample fare is the benchmark against which everyone else is measured. Almost as accomplished and much more fun is **Tru** (Map 5 G2, 676 N. St. Clair St., 312 202 0001, www.trurestaurant.com), a gallery-like space in Streeterville where celebrity chefs Rick Tramonto and Gale Gand draw "oohs" and "ahhs" with their divine food and exquisite delivery, such as caviar that is presented on a miniature glass staircase.

Four-star cuisine comes with one of the city's finest views at **Everest** (Map 5 E5, 440 S. LaSalle St., 312 663 8920, www.everestrestaurant.com), 40 floors up in the Chicago Stock Exchange. Acclaimed chef Jean Joho takes inspiration from his Alsatian roots to turn out winning French fare, while master sommelier and local TV host Alpana Singh adds star power. The view isn't too shabby from **Spiaggia** (Map 3 H5, 980 N. Michigan Ave., 312 280 2750, www.levyrestaurants.com), either: this pricey, contemporary space at the north tip of Michigan Avenue looks onto Oak Street Beach, serves top-notch Italian food by chef Tony Mantuano, and is the setting for many a marriage proposal. A mile north in Old Town, **Kamehachi** (Map 3 F4, 1400 N. Wells St., 312 664 3663, www.kamehachi.com) was the city's first serious sushi spot and continues to be one of the best in town; it is a very popular choice for special occasions. Out in Irving Park, there's **Arun's** (4156 N. Kedzie Ave., 773 539 1909, www.arunsthai.com) – a lovely room in the city's north-west where chef Arun Sampanthavivat takes Thai cuisine to dizzying heights of presentation, flavor, and creativity.

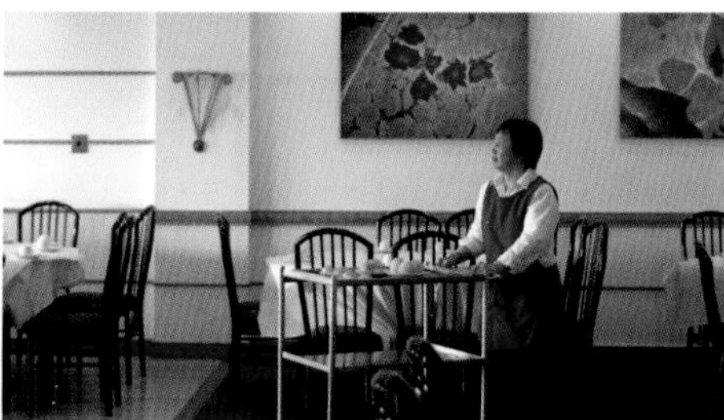

The Phoenix *Chinese behemoth*

6 D4

2131 S. Archer Ave., at Wentworth • 312 328 0848
Open breakfast, lunch & dinner daily

Some of the most authentic Chinese food in the city is served up at this 350-seat Chinatown restaurant. The two dining rooms can feel a little sterile, but the food is upbeat and always delicious, from shark-fin soup to lemon chicken and short ribs. Daily dim sum, served at breakfast and lunch, is rightly popular. **Moderate**

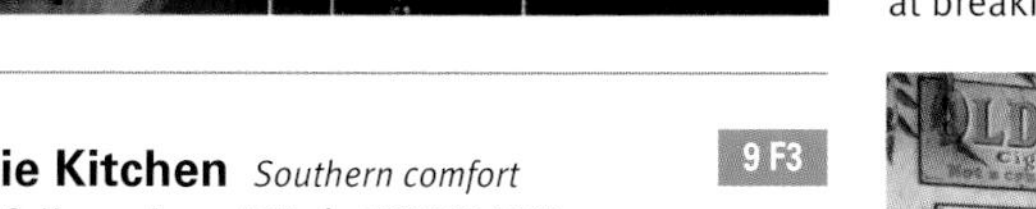

Dixie Kitchen *Southern comfort*

9 F3

5225 S. Harper Ave., at 52nd • 773 363 4943
>> **www.dixiekitchenchicago.com** Open lunch & dinner daily

Lunch draws serious crowds to this cozy Hyde Park hub, so arrive early or you'll end up waiting. The walls are covered with old American bric-a-brac, and the menu offers impressive renditions of Southern specialties: spicy gumbo, jambalaya, fried green tomatoes, oyster po'boys, and a very fine peach cobbler. **Moderate**

Opera *bold, brash Chinese*

7 E1

1301 S. Wabash Ave., at 13th • 312 461 0161
>> **www.opera-chicago.com** Open dinner daily

From the team behind Gioco, this wild, circus-like space is a riot of color and texture, with swooping wrought-iron details, walls papered with newspaper clippings, and a bold harlequin color scheme. The spacious dining room buzzes with conversation, while sizzling sounds and delicious smells waft through from the open kitchen. If you prefer more intimacy, ask for a table in one of the curtained-off "vaults."

Though the food isn't quite as over-the-top as the decor, chef Paul Wildermuth clearly has fun giving traditional Chinese dishes an upscale twist. Sweet-savory Maine lobster spring roll with tangerine mustard puts typical eggrolls to shame, while *kung pao* beef elevates a take-out favorite with NY strip steak and a spicy kiss of chili-garlic black bean sauce. To drink, try the "#1" cocktail: sake, vodka, raspberry, and sparkling wine – refreshing but lethal. **Expensive**

>> *If you haven't reserved, arrive by 12:30 for lunch or 7:30 for dinner to have more luck in getting a table*

Nuevo Leon *authentic Mexican*

1515 W. 18th St., at Ashland • 312 421 1517

Ⓜ 18th (Blue Line) Open 7am–midnight Mon–Sat (to 11pm Sun)

It's hard not to love this excellent-yet-cheap Mexican diner. The decor is simple (wood paneling in the front and orange walls in the back), but the food really hits the mark, from fresh, chunky dips to enchiladas in earthy *mole* sauce and sinfully rich *tres leches* cake. Bring your own wine and beer; cash only. **Cheap**

Tufanos *family-style Italian*

4 B5

1073 W. Vernon Park Pl., at Carpenter • 312 733 3393

Open lunch & dinner Tue–Fri, dinner Sat & Sun

Part restaurant, part neighborhood tavern, this casual Little Italy eatery dishes up some of the best pasta in town. The simple menu, written on a blackboard, offers generous portions of classics such as rigatoni with mushrooms, and draws a upbeat mix of visitors, locals, and students from the nearby university. **Moderate**

Greek Islands *authentic Greek fare*

4 C4

200 S. Halsted St., at Adams • 312 782 9855

» www.greekislands.net Open lunch & dinner daily

With an expansive, traditional menu that covers all the classics from *dolmades* to moussaka, *gyros*, and "flaming" (flambéed) cheese, this place is a standout on the Greektown strip. The four spacious dining rooms are casual and comfortable, and chefs put on a mesmerizing show in the busy open kitchen. **Moderate**

Bongo Room *brunch worth waiting for*

2 A4

1470 N. Milwaukee Ave., at Honore • 773 489 0690

» www.bongoroom.com Open 7:30am–2:30pm Mon–Fri, 9am–2:30pm Sat & Sun

Lines for weekend brunch often stretch out the door at this fashionable morning hangout. A young, hip crowd packs in for key lime cheesecake pancakes, chocolate tower French toast, and omelets with various fillings. Breakfast and lunch are also served daily. **Cheap**

Hot Chocolate *sweet and savory delights* 2 A3

1747 N. Damen Ave., at Willow • 773 489 1747
>> www.hotchocolatechicago.com
Open brunch Sat & Sun, dinner Tue–Sun

Pastry chef Mindy Segal, who wowed diners and critics at mk in River North, is now going it alone at this trendy Bucktown kitchen. And though the menu here is more casual – salads, sandwiches, milkshakes, and sweets – the results are almost as impressive.

Done up in tones of (what else?) chocolate, the space is warm and inviting. Tables fill up quickly and young professionals buzz at the long bar, sipping cocktails and nibbling on zippy green-curry mussels, warm roasted beet and goat cheese salad, and sandwiches from Kobe beef skirt steak to peanut butter and jelly.

Some folks come just for the desserts, and it's worth the trip. Old faithfuls like Banana Napoleon are offered alongside new creations such as warm brioche donuts and stout-and-caramel-flavored milkshake – all testimony to the chef's own sweet tooth. **Moderate**

Spring *excellent New American cuisine* 2 A4

2039 W. North Ave., at Damen and Milwaukee • 773 395 7100
>> springrestaurant.net Open dinner Tue–Sun

Set in a former Russian bathhouse, this soothing garden-level restaurant draws hordes of hip young couples celebrating anniversaries and birthdays. The sophisticated space is filled with warm wood and bamboo, offset by crisp white tablecloths, and a Zen garden adds to the cool, relaxed vibe.

Executive chef Shawn McClain won national acclaim for his fine vegetarian concoctions at Green Zebra *(see p46)*. Here, the menu is largely Asian-inspired with a seafood bent. Spiced prawn Thai salad is an explosion of flavor in which kicky prawns are combined with green papaya, heart of palm, mint, tamarind, and chili; milder but no less flavorful is the roasted monkfish with lentils, bacon, cipollini onions, and roast garlic sauce. The rather more casual bar menu offers tasty bites such as tempura tiger shrimp, Dungeness crab burger, and foie gras mousseline with pineapple quince. **Expensive**

Le Bouchon *intimate French bistro*

2 A2

1958 N. Damen Ave., at Armitage • 773 862 6600

>> www.lebouchonofchicago.com Open dinner Mon–Sat

Close-set tables and a cozy bistro ambiance set a romantic scene at this Bucktown nook. The simple French cuisine includes tempting plates of house-made pâté, mussels, and perfectly tender *escargots*, which precede hearty mains of garlic roast chicken, duck in red wine sauce, and *steak frites*. **Moderate**

Café Bolero *sexy Cuban beats and eats*

✓

2252 N. Western Ave., at Belden • 773 227 9000

Ⓜ Western (Blue Line)

>> www.cafebolero.com Open lunch & dinner daily

Live music, potent mojitos, and good tapas draw an upbeat international crowd to this informal Bucktown joint. Tasty Cuban dishes like *ropa vieja* (beef stew) and stuffed plantain issue from the open kitchen, while the intimate back room throbs with music. **Moderate**

Coast *creative, reasonably priced sushi*

2 A2

2045 N. Damen Ave., at Armitage • 773 235 5775

>> www.coastsushibar.com Open dinner daily

Painted concrete floors, woven leather furniture, and natural wood create a minimalist-chic look in this popular Wicker Park sushi spot. Low, low lighting and well-spaced tables make Coast popular with young couples on dates; moderate prices and a no-corkage BYOB policy only add to its appeal.

Of course, the main attraction is the innovative menu, which offers updated classics with unexpected flavor pairings and fresh, seasonal ingredients. Dishes include stuffed shiitake mushrooms with rich garlic sauce, and salmon spring roll wrapped in *shiso* leaf and served with green curry dipping sauce. Most impressive is the *maki* selection, which includes nine vegetarian rolls, more than three dozen standards (Rainbow, California, Philly), and seriously delicious signature rolls such as Ceviche – a spicy-cool mix of lime-marinated scallop, mango, shrimp, jalapeño, and cilantro. **Moderate**

avec *stylish, small plates*

4 D3

615 W. Randolph St., at Jefferson • 312 377 2002

>> www.avecrestaurant.com Open dinner daily

Right next door to chef Paul Kahan's other restaurant, Blackbird *(see below)*, this chic offering from Kahan and partner Donnie Madia has eclipsed its sibling in popularity. The recipe is simple: delectable rustic Mediterranean dishes and an excellent, well-priced wine list, served up in an appealingly modern, tight squeeze of a long, narrow room. Avec's soothing space is all inviting wood tones and gleaming metal details, with cedar-clad walls. Long communal tables face the stainless steel bar and open kitchen.

Koren Grieveson, one of the city's top young chefs, oversees a changing menu that might feature wood-roasted escargots with spicy stewed tomato and herbed breadcrumbs, spicy meatballs, or baby squid crostini. Service is whip-smart and efficient, with attractive servers who make great recommendations and know the menu inside out. **Moderate**

Blackbird *standout American fare*

4 D3

619 W. Randolph St., at Jefferson • 312 715 0708

>> www.blackbirdrestaurant.com

Open lunch & dinner Mon–Fri, dinner Sat

Local boy and award-winning chef Paul Kahan serves up top-notch modern food in this minimalist space. Expect to be wowed: from seared elk loin with fava beans and bacon to simple-but-sensational endive salad, he hits the bull's-eye just about every time. **Expensive**

Sushi Wabi *outstanding sushi*

4 C3

842 W. Randolph St., at Green • 312 563 1224

>> www.sushiwabi.com Open lunch Mon–Fri, dinner daily

The city's original trendy sushi destination, Sushi Wabi is still one of the best Japanese restaurants in town. What's the appeal? Low lighting, a stylish crowd, live DJs, an expansive menu of *nigiri* plus signature *maki* like the Godzilla roll – a mouthful of tempura shrimp, avocado, spicy mayo, and chili sauce. **Moderate**

Twisted Spoke *sassy biker bar*

4 B2

501 N. Ogden Ave., at Grand • 312 666 1500
>> www.twistedspoke.com
Open 11am–2am Mon–Fri, 9am–3am Sat, 9am–2am Sun

Harley riders and young professionals rub elbows at this great biker bar, where black-and-white glamour shots of customers on their motorcycles hang on the exposed brick walls and the servers are tattooed and pierced. Biker attitude aside, the Spoke serves up some of the city's finest comfort food: meatloaf sandwiches, pot roast, and the legendary half-pound Fatboy burger.

Brunch is the main event here, though, with standout scrambled eggs, corned beef hash, and Elvis toast (stuffed with peanut butter and bananas). Or for an offbeat "breakfast" experience, stop by the Spoke on Saturday at midnight for "Smut & Eggs," when you get to watch porn screenings (and not the soft stuff, either) while you eat. Other specials include all-you-can-eat meatloaf on Mondays, $2.50 beers on Tuesdays, and half-price whiskey on Wednesdays. **Cheap**

Green Zebra *meatless magic*

4 A1

1460 W. Chicago Ave., at Ashland • 312 243 7100
>> www.greenzebrachicago.com Open dinner Tue–Sun

Chicago's vegetarians eat exceptionally well these days, thanks in part to the creative menu at this small, harmonious space. Decorated in soothing greens and dotted with lush foliage, the room is intimate yet airy, with high ceilings and a large window at the front that frames the gritty local street scene.

The hip-but-relaxed clientele is a mix of sophisticated vegetarians and local gourmets, and chef Shawn McClain, formerly of Spring *(see p43)*, dreams up classy veggie plates that even carnivores rave about. There's heavenly sweet parsnip panna cotta with braised endive, blood orange, and pepper biscuits; and crimson lentil cake with spiced shallot and red pepper jam, and preserved lemon. The extensive wine list emphasizes European whites; servers are knowledgeable and more than happy to suggest suitable food pairings. **Moderate**

Moto *cutting-edge cuisine*

4 C3

945 W. Fulton Market, at Sangamon • 312 491 0058
>> www.motorestaurant.com Open dinner Tue–Sat

The brainchild of twentysomething chef Homaro Cantu, this avant-garde restaurant in Chicago's developing Fulton Market warehouse district is considered by many to be one of the most important dining spots in the country today. Cantu worked as a sous-chef at legendary four-star restaurant Charlie Trotter's *(see p40)* before setting up on his own here in 2004. And he has been making waves on the city's dining scene ever since, creating dishes that are edgy, futuristic, surreal – and sometimes just plain odd.

The setting is clean and sparse: a long, open room featuring unadorned ivory walls, cinnamon-leather banquettes, and chocolate-colored wooden chairs. The tweed carpet effectively muffles any sound in the hushed room. Simply put, there's nothing at all that might distract from Cantu's stunning cuisine.

And what a show this young chef puts on. One of his recent tasting menus included lobster with freshly squeezed orange soda, grilled spring vegetables with barbecued Styrofoam, Colorado lamb with Kentucky fried ice cream, and freeze-dried piña colada. Cantu has also been known to serve guests a dish, then follow it with a digital photo of the same dish printed on edible paper. And he is even an inventor of sorts: many of the utensils used in the restaurant – from the coil-handled spoons that hold sprigs of rosemary to the polymer box used to cook fish at the table – are patented creations dreamed up by Cantu himself.

With all the gadgets and odd combinations, dining at Moto can seem a little like being in a science-fiction movie, but Cantu shows a real respect for his ingredients that often results in eye-opening new flavors and textures. While not all of the craziness works, Moto does offer a unique culinary experience for adventurous eaters with money to burn. **Expensive**

dolce vita

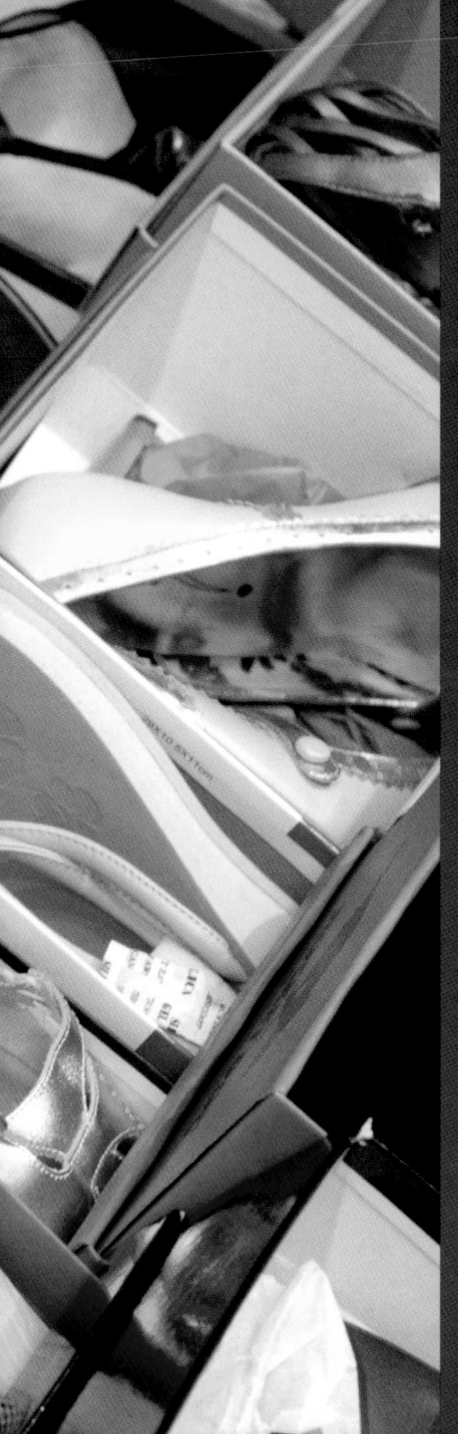

shopping

Chicago's nickname may be "the Second City," but its shopping is first class. The glamorous designer shops of the Magnificent Mile and the grand old department stores on State Street make a great starting point. But follow the locals out to the trendy boutiques in buzzing Wicker Park, Lakeview's scruffy record stores, and the charming, dusty bookshops of Hyde Park to discover what this city's retail scene is really all about.

SHOPPING

In the past ten years I've watched Chicago become a world-class shopping destination. Its big-name downtown stores have been joined by heaps of cool shops located all over the city that offer everything from clothes by independent fashion designers to futuristic furniture. I love these classy, design-conscious boutiques, but I've also got a soft spot for the scruffier places – the idiosyncratic local bookstores and musty vintage shops that have been around forever.

Heather Kenny

Something Old

At **Silver Moon** *(see p65)* the selection of vintage clothing is always top-notch, while the **Broadway Antique Market** *(see p53)* presents a history of the 20th century with kitschy salt-and-pepper shakers, old radio cabinets, and retro costume jewelry. **Jazz Record Mart** *(see p57)* has a good selection of the hot hits of yesteryear on vinyl.

Home Sweet Home

Chicago has an ever-growing array of modern interiors outlets. **CB2** *(see p55)* offers cool and contemporary home accessories to the mass market with its budget-priced options; the wares at **Stitch** *(see p67)* are similarly sleek but more upscale; while shoppers with a more artistic aesthetic check out what's on offer at **Material Possessions** *(see p59)*.

Local Favorites

Bookworms rub shoulders at the labyrinthine second-hand bookstore **Myopic Books** *(see p65)*, which functions as an ersatz neighborhood clubhouse, while the cognoscenti pick up graphic novels, zines, and anarchist newspapers at **Quimby's** *(see p64)*. For some Chicago-made clothing, seek out **Eskell's** *(see p56)* unique designs for women.

choice shops

Tasty Treats

You can spend hours in the aisles of **Fox & Obel** *(see p59)* discovering gastronomic goodies – or check out **The Chopping Block** *(see p52)*, where the small selection of artisanal olive oils and vinegars is the best of the best. To satisfy the urge for an exotic treat, **Vosges Haut Chocolat**'s *(see p57)* rich truffles, candy, and ice cream hit the spot.

Racks of Style

As far as designer fashion goes, Chicago can hold its own. The industrial space of **p45** *(see p66)* is brimming with of-the-moment styles by smaller designers (including local artists). Seek out **Robin Richman** *(see p67)* for avant-garde men's and women's clothing and opulent jewelry, and **Hejfina** *(see p63)* for clothes with a sophisticated edge.

Sole Passion

Shoe addicts love **Lori's Shoes** *(see p54)*, where all of the sizes and styles – from sandals to stilettoes – are already out on the floor. The men's and women's shoes at **City Soles** *(see p64)* have a funky, offbeat vibe; but for really fierce footwear, head to the Gold Coast's **G'bani** *(see p58)* for high-altitude, big-attitude heels.

His Stuff *men's staples with flair*

5314 N. Clark St., at Berwyn • 773 989 9111 • Bus No. 22
>> www.hisstuffchicago.com
Open 11–9 Tue–Fri, 11–7 Sat, noon–6 Sun

The owners of this boutique favor basic styles that have great tailoring and details. Sandals from J Shoes will appeal to guys with more daring tastes, while jeans-and-T-shirt types will like the Italian denim from Energie and button-down shirts by Z Brand.

The Chopping Block *cooking with style*

4747 N. Lincoln Ave., at Lawrence • 773 472 6700
>> www.thechoppingblock.net • Ⓜ Western (Brown Line)
Open 10–7 Mon–Fri, 10–6 Sat, 10–4 Sun

Even kitchen no-hopers will love the slim bottles of olive oil, jars of spices and sea salts, and glossy cookbooks here. For serious chefs, there are All-Clad pots and pans and OXO Good Grips utensils. Be sure to check the event schedule for cooking classes and wine tastings.

Merz Apothecary *old-world toiletries*

4716 N. Lincoln Ave., at Leland • 773 989 0900
Ⓜ Western (Brown Line)
>> www.merzapothecary.com Open 9–6 Mon–Sat

The original Merz Apothecary opened in 1875, and while this appealingly old-fashioned looking shop was only built in 1982, you won't care about that once you start testing all the wonderful lotions and potions. Merz carries a range of international and domestic bath and body products and natural health preparations, and has a loyal clientele among the many Europeans in the area as well as those simply looking for a change from the usual drugstore fare. You could spend hours sniffing Luxo Banho soaps from Portugal, heavenly Farmacia di Santa Maria Novella colognes from Italy, and Archipelago Botanicals candles from Los Angeles. The staff are as in-tune with your insides as with your outside and will happily offer advice to those interested in trying out natural and homeopathic remedies.

Broadway Antique Market (BAM)

6130 N. Broadway, at Glenlake • 773 743 5444
Ⓜ Granville (Red Line)
>> www.bamchicago.com Open 11–7 Mon–Sat, 11–6 Sun

This antiques mall has been a must-see for enthusiasts of 20th-century furniture, housewares, art, and knick-knacks for the past 15 years. Seventy-five dealers fill both huge floors of BAM's Art Deco building with everything from beautiful Arts-and-Crafts-inspired dining tables to Bakelite jewelry – plus a good dose of kitsch.

Upstairs, case after case of salt and pepper shakers and postcards can be a bit overwhelming for the casual browser, but the working jukebox, old typewriters, and beaded evening purses help to hold the attention. Follow the leopard-print carpeting to the furniture area, where soft jazz helps to create the feel of a 1950s cocktail party. Wrought-iron patio sets and leather-and-chrome sofas abound, but you might also find a Victorian fainting couch or a 1920s baby carriage hidden in a corner. Go on the weekend for the best buzz.

Endo-Exo Apothecary *chic grooming* 2 D2

2034 N. Halsted St., at Armitage • 773 525 0500
>> www.endoexo.com Open 11–7 Mon–Fri, 10–6 Sat, 11–5 Sun

A mix of vintage apothecary cabinets and modern cases hold an assortment of exclusive makeup, bath and body ranges, and fragrances. Product junkies can indulge in Tarte cosmetics and skin concoctions from Sundari and Bliss, while those after celestial scents will love the Tocca candles and Red Flower perfumes.

Mint *local threads* 1 B3

2150 N. Seminary Ave., at Belmont • 773 528 1983
>> www.mintboutique.com
Open 11–6 Tue–Fri, 10–5 Sat, 11–5 Sun

"Made in Chicago" is the theme at this tiny shop stocking the work of local designers. Pick up a unique necklace of beads and semiprecious stones or a clutch bag made of zebra-stripe fabric. There are clothes too, like singular shirts with collars made out of silk ties.

Lori's Shoes *shoe nirvana*

2 D2

824 W. Armitage Ave., at Halstead • 773 281 5655
>> www.lorisshoes.com
Open 11–7 Mon–Thu, 11–6 Fri, 10–6 Sat, noon–5 Sun

Apart from some cute tiles painted with shoes at the entrance, this store's decor definitely comes second to the merchandise. The focus is on the maze of boxes in the main room, where barefoot women search for their size and compete for mirror-space. Brands are mainly mid-range, such as Steve Madden and Franco Sarto, but there's a wide selection of styles in everything from boots to sandals. Good deals can be found on the permanent sale racks lining the walls. And even if you don't find the perfect slipper, you'll probably be seduced by one of the many luxuriously beaded evening bags, trendy purses, or leather totes on display. Be warned: some Saturday afternoons it can seem like every shoe-crazy woman in Chicago (and her bored boyfriend) is packed into this shop and blocking access to those Mary Janes you've got your eye on.

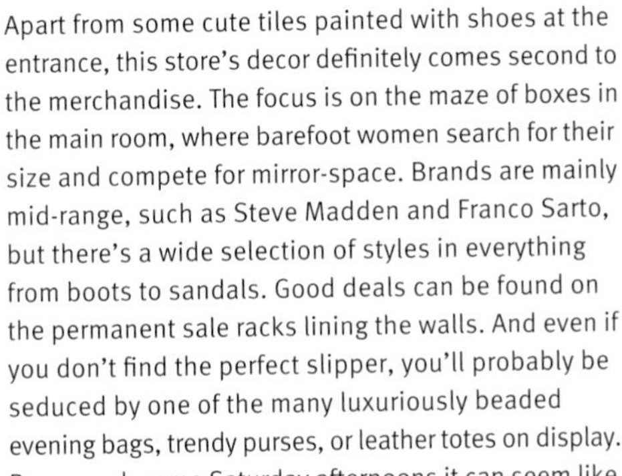

Calvin Tran *modern versatility*

2 D2

2154 N. Halsted St., at Webster • 773 529 4070
>> www.calvintran.com Open 11–7 Mon–Sat, noon–6 Sun

New Yorker Calvin Tran studied fashion in Chicago, and once a month or so he can be found in his spacious, airy boutique helping his customers decide which of his flowing pieces suits them best. Asymmetrical, poncho-like tops in soft fabrics are a trademark, as are cowl necklines and unfinished hems. Classic dressers will go for the 1940s-inspired tweed jackets, pants, and skirts with fresh details like flirty, kicky hems, plus sumptuous silk dresses and blouses in black-and-white patterns influenced by Tran's Vietnamese heritage.

Tran likes to create multifunctional pieces, such as skirts that can be pulled up to become strapless dresses, or halter tops with extra-long sides that can be tied in several ways. Luckily his hands-on approach is mirrored by the friendly staff, who are happy to show how such transformations can be achieved.

CB2 *21st-century design*

2 D4

800 W. North Ave., at Halsted • 312 787 8329
>> www.cb2.com
Open 10–8 Mon–Fri, 10–7 Sat, 11–6 Sun

The gleaming white-on-white look of this homewares and furniture store indicates the contemporary leanings of the merchandise within. An offshoot of the more traditional Crate & Barrel (on the next block), this is the place for the design-conscious customer to stock up on everything from orange- and green-tinted martini glasses to molded wooden dining chairs.

Creative displays often suggest quirky solutions such as using votive candleholders as shot glasses or glass block picture frames as centerpieces, while the mini-rooms displayed around the store offer fresh ideas for your home. Inexpensive Asian-inspired porcelain dinnerware and wooden vases that look like they jumped out of a Cubist painting are hard to resist, as are bins full of fun, small items like iPod holders and soaps with a map of Chicago embedded inside.

Art Effect *everything but the kitchen sink*

2 D2

1935 W. Armitage Ave., at Bissell
>> www.arteffectchicago.com
Open 11–7 Mon–Fri, 10–6 Sat, noon–5 Sun

In the 20 years that this much-loved boutique has been in business, it's become an integral part of the Chicago shopping scene. The three bright, airy rooms are full of women's clothing and accessories, housewares, gifts, items for bath and body, and any number of quirky doodads, making it the ultimate gift-buying destination. The store's shabby French-chic decor reflects the Continental leanings of some of the offerings, such as French soaps and books on Provençal design. Items for the home include delicate sake sets and plastic trays in bright colors.

Clothing tends to be feminine or sporty – lacy dresses and silk blouses, casual blazers, and a whole set of shelves devoted to T-shirts – while the jewelry section includes both distinctive contemporary designs and cute inexpensive earrings and necklaces.

1 A2

Jake *on a denim theme*

3740 N. Southport Ave., at Grace • 773 929 5253
>> www.shopjake.com
Open 11–7 Mon–Fri, 10–6 Sat, noon–5 Sun

This smallish, somewhat pricey boutique focuses on denim and up-to-the-minute ideas of what to wear with it. Expect labels such as Habitual and Earnest Sewn, plus items such as spangled tops and camisoles for women and casual shirts for the guys.

1 A2

Trousseau *tasteful lingerie*

3543 N. Southport Ave., at Addison • 773 472 2727
Open 11–7 Mon–Fri, 10–6 Sat, noon–5 Sun

The frothy, flirty undergarments here are especially popular with brides-to-be, but Trousseau's ladylike yet sexy lingerie – beaded nighties and wispy g-strings – will appeal to any girl. Even sportier types who prefer subdued flannel to daring lacy French bras will leave happy. Staff will ensure your bra fits perfectly, too.

1 B3

Chicago Comics *comic collection*

✓

3244 N. Clark St., at Belmont • 773 528 1983
>> www.chicagocomics.com
Open noon–8 Mon–Fri (to 10 Fri), 11–10 Sat, noon–6 Sun

Horn-rimmed glasses are favored by both clientele and staff at this store, where cool nerds browse the racks of Japanese manga, European titles, alternative comics, and more mainstream superhero fare. There are also back issues, underground zines, and graphic novels.

2 D2

Eskell

953 W. Webster., at Sheffield • 773 477 9390
>> www.eskell.com Open 11–7 Tue–Sat, noon–6 Sun

Old friends Kelly Whitesell and Elizabeth Del Castillo run this women's clothing store, which features their own bohemian-yet-sophisticated creations, lines from other up-and-coming designers, and some vintage items. Expect interesting details and retro-hipster pieces like a blousy minidress printed with tree limbs.

Boulevard of Dreams

Since the 1920s, the Mag Mile (*see p12*, www.themagnificentmile.com) has been known for its chic department stores and high-end boutiques. Today, it is the city's prime shopping district and many stores are found in "vertical malls," such as Water Tower Place (No. 835). Expect crowds, especially on weekends and holidays.

Vosges Haut Chocolat *exotic truffles* 5 F2

Nordstrom, 520 N. Michigan Ave., at Ohio • 312 644 9450

>> www.vosgeschocolate.com Open 10–8 Mon–Sat, 11–6 Sun

Located on the upper floor of a mall, the original Vosges boutique is a temple to those who worship high-quality chocolate. The truffles are dense yet feather-light, and come in flavors that are far from run-of-the-mill. Owner and chocolatier Katrina Markoff, who studied *patisserie* at Le Cordon Bleu in Paris and has plied her trade in Asia, Europe, and Australia, prefers to use less-familiar ingredients such as wasabi, tarragon, and pandan leaf.

The original Exotic collection offers combinations like milk chocolate with coconut and sweet curry, or the Parisian-inspired dark chocolate with star anise, fennel, and pastis liqueur. Other collections include the Aztec, featuring cinnamon, chilies, and Mexican vanilla, and the Green, with eastern flavors such as green tea and cardamom. If you can't wait to try the stuff, there's a small seating area, and you can also order ice cream or hot chocolate in flavors based on the truffles.

Jazz Record Mart *bebop to blues* 5 F2

27 E. Illinois St., at Wabash • 312 222 1467

>> www.jazzrecordmart.com Open 10–8 Mon–Sat, noon–7 Sun

Tens of thousands of new and used jazz and blues LPs, 78s, 45s, and CDs from the mainstream to the obscure fill this local institution. There's even a section devoted to essential listening for beginners. If you can't find the album you're looking for here, chances are the staff can tell you where to get it.

Independent Record Stores

Living in the home of the blues and a major rock 'n' roll center, Chicagoans take their music very seriously. **Dusty Groove** (Map 2 B5, 1120 N. Ashland Ave., 773 342 2179, www.dustygroove.com) grew up out of a mail-order outfit for funk, soul, jazz, and hip-hop. **Rock Records** (Map 5 E3, 175 W. Washington Blvd., 312 346 3489) is a good source of imports, rareties, and novelties or, if you are nostalgic for vinyl, head over to **Dave's Records** (Map 1 C5, 2604 N. Clark St., 773 929 6325), which sells new and used LPs of all genres. **Reckless Records** (Map 1 C3, 3161 N. Broadway, 773 404 5080, www.reckless.com) is a quintessential rock record store, complete with scruffy bins and too-cool-for-you staffers.

Ikram *haute fashion*

5 F1

873 N. Rush St., at Chestnut • 312 587 1000

>> www.ikramonline.com Open 10–6 Mon–Sat

Not for the faint of heart or the light of wallet, Ikram is like an art gallery devoted to designer fashion. This is where you'll find pieces straight from the runways of Paris and New York, chosen by owner Ikram Goldman's discriminating and experienced eye. Beautiful baubles, shoes, and a few vintage items are added temptations.

G'bani *shopping Italian style*

5 F1

949 N. State St., at Oak • 312 440 1718

>> www.gbani.com Open 10–7 Mon–Sat, noon–5 Sun

This boutique gets as much attention for its politically provocative window displays as for its gorgeous range of men's and women's footwear and chic Italian clothing. But the flowing chiffon dresses, crisp linen shirts, and bejeweled evening sandals transcend such issues – the only party line here is "looking fabulous, dahling."

Downtown Department Stores

Until recently, Marshall Field's was the undisputed granddaddy of Chicago's department stores. Now owned by **Macy's**, the former flagship store (Map 5 F3, 111 N. State St., www.fields.com) still contains a grand atrium and boutiques by established names like Donna Karan and Calvin Klein, plus more youth-led labels such as Theory and Kenneth Cole. The mood at **Carson Pirie Scott** (Map 5 F4, 1 S. State St., www.carsons.com) is more downscale, but there are fresh, affordable styles from mainstream labels like Nine West and a good range of handbags and jewelry.

Just a hop away, North Michigan Avenue hosts a run of other big retailers, including many relatively new arrivals. **Lord & Taylor** at No. 835 (Map 5 F1, www.lordandtaylor.com) has suffered an identity crisis of late: it now offers hip lines by the likes of Vivienne Tam alongside the more conservative styles favored by its older clientele. **Bloomingdale's**, at No. 900 (Map 5 F1, www.bloomingdales.com), and **Nordstrom**, just off Michigan (Map 5 F2, 55 E. Grand Ave., www.nordstrom.com), focus on the trendier pieces – from Diane von Furstenberg's stretchy silk blouses to James Perse's perfectly cut T-shirts. Bloomingdale's also has must-have handbags by Kate Spade and Dooney & Burke, while Nordstrom is known for its large shoe section. At No. 700, **Saks** (Map 5 F1, www.saks.com) pitches a little higher, offering designer names and exclusive cosmetics; its men's store across the street has similar merchandise in a more intimate setting. Nearby at No. 737, **Neiman Marcus** (Map 5 F1, www.neimanmarcus.com) is not a budget shopping stop either, as its nickname, "needless markup," implies. It's valued by fashion-savvy locals for stocking lines by newer designers, such as Zac Posen and Derek Lam, that are difficult to find in the U.S. outside of New York.

Sara Jane *girly clothes*

3 F4

1343 N. Wells St., at Evergreen • 312 335 1962
Open 11–6 Mon & Sat, 11–7 Tue–Fri, noon–5 Sun

With its rainbow-hued racks of clothing, this is a store for women who like color – and lots of it. Unabashedly feminine designs are the rule: patchwork strapless dresses and soft, breezy blue-and-green beaded tops are a few of the casual offerings on hand. Even standard white shirts are embroidered with tiny details.

Material Possessions *form & function*

5 F1

704 N. Wabash St., at Huron • 312 280 4885
>> www.materialpossessions.com
Open 10–6 Mon–Sat, noon–5 Sun

As the name implies, here you'll find expensive must-haves for the home: satin bedsheets, resin bowls, and horn salad servers. Yet style never trumps function – this is luxury meant for living. Tableware is a specialty, and you can even design your own custom dinnerware.

Paper Source *stationery and cards*

5 E1

232 W. Chicago Ave., at Franklin • 312 337 0798
>> www.paper-source.com
Open 10–7 Mon–Fri, 10–5 Sat, noon–5 Sun

This is *the* spot to pick up beautiful paper in both delicate and bold prints, plus handmade cards, bound journals, cool storage boxes, rubber stamps, art and design books, and craft kits. Paper Source also hosts classes on everything from card-making to calligraphy.

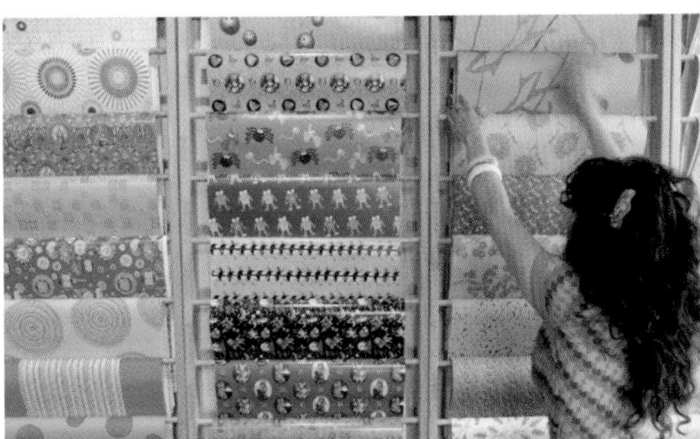

Fox & Obel *gourmet food emporium*

5 G2

401 E. Illinois St., at McClurg • 312 410 7301
>> www.fox-obel.com Open 7am–9pm daily

This high-end market offers up the finest European olive oils, cheeses from around the world, and condiments for cuisines ranging from North African to Danish. The deli and bakery counters provide mouth-watering to-go options, while the café is a pleasant place to dine in or relax after a day seeing downtown's sights.

>> Many downtown department stores offer free personal shopping services

Oak Street *upscale shopping hub*

3 G5

E. Oak St., between State and Michigan
>> www.oakstreetchicago.com

Oak Street is Chicago's answer to Rodeo Drive. It's a top shopping destination, though the pretty, old buildings, tree-lined street, and people-watching make this block-long stretch a pleasant stroll whatever your intention. Keep in mind, though, that many stores don't open until noon and are closed on Sundays.

There's designer fashion galore for those with the means to buy it, starting in the white minimalist building that houses Italian fashion powerhouse **Prada** (No. 30). **Jil Sander** (No. 48) also has a store selling the company's spare designs, as does **Yves St. Laurent** (No. 51). **Hermes** (No. 110) offers iconic bags and scarves, while across the street (No. 101) **Kate Spade**'s pop-preppy accessories and homewares attract a more youthful crowd. **Ultimo** (No. 114) is popular with those at the fashion forefront for carrying provocative designers like John Galliano and Yohji Yamamoto; tiny **Chasalla** (No. 70) tends to focus on sexier designers such as Dolce & Gabbana and Roberto Cavalli. **Barney's New York** (No. 25) is locally infamous for the haughtiness of the staff, but that doesn't bother the shoppers eager for its singular brand of Manhattan cool.

More down-to-earth options include **Sugar Magnolia** (No. 34), where the offerings could be described as "haute hippie" – swirly, floaty dresses and skirts. For shoes and accessories, **Tod's** (No. 121) and **Camper** (No. 61) have outposts, and there's a **MAC** store (No. 40) for those looking for anything from a new lipstick to a total makeover. Don't pass up **Bravco** (No. 43), which carries every type of haircare product you can imagine. For fragrance, seek out **La Maison du Parfum** (No. 104), the first U.S. location for this French retailer, which prides itself on its natural ingredients. If none of the scents seem quite right, you can have one custom-blended for you, the ultimate luxury.

Penelope's *cool clothes for cool people*

2 A5

1913 W. Division St., at Wolcott • 773 395 2351
>> www.penelopeschicago.com
Open 11–7 Mon–Sat, noon–6 Sun

Named after the owner's pug, this airy shop is popular for its funky styles – which range from terry-cloth dresses to 1970s-inspired track-suit jackets and pink corduroy blazers. What else would you expect from a store with a working vintage Ms. Pac-Man machine?

Silver Room *jewelry and more*

2 A4

1442 N. Milwaukee Ave., at Evergreen • 773 278 7130
>> www.thesilverroom.com Open 11–8 Mon–Sat, 11–6 Sun

The medium may be limited to silver, but the rings, bracelets, and necklaces here range from ethnic to flashy – and many are made by local talent. Try on a choker festooned with delicate filaments, or a necklace of African-style beads. There's also a selection of body jewelry, chunky watches, and sunglasses.

Hejfina *design-conscious fashion*

2 A4

1529 N. Milwaukee Ave., at Honore • 773 772 0002
>> www.hejfina.com Open 11–7 Tue–Sat, noon–6 Sun & Mon

Owner Heiji Choy-Black fills her lifestyle boutique with clothes, shoes, and accessories that show a passion for design. Clothing rails offer chic separates for men and women by the likes of APC, Isabel Marant, and Line 6 by Martin Margiela, while 1950s shelves hold titles on such modernist giants as Antoni Gaudí.

Budget Shopping

H&M (Map 5 F1, 840 N. Michigan Ave., www.hm.com) is always hopping with customers snapping up basics and knockoffs of runway fashions. The wait for the dressing rooms can be interminable, but that's a small price to pay for the small price you'll pay.

For big name brands, try **TJ Maxx** (Map 5 F4, 11 N. State St., www.tjmaxx.com) or **Filene's Basement** (Map 5 F1, 830 N. Michigan Ave., www.filenes basement.com); they are also good places for trendy items on the downswing – and more user-friendly than **Marshall's** (Map 5 F2, 600 N. Michigan Ave., www.marshallsonline.com), where clothes are sorted by style and size rather than designer (so it takes time to find a good buy) and the ambience is comparable to that of a cheap drugstore.

City Soles and Niche *funky footwear*

2 A4

2001 W. North Ave., at Damen & Milwaukee • 773 489 2001

>> www.citysoles.com Open 11–8 Mon–Sat (to 9 Thu), 11–6 Sun

These twin stores fill a huge space in the center of artsy Wicker Park with cutting-edge shoes. While City Soles' mood is urban funky – think candy-colored wedges from Camper and futuristic sneakers courtesy of Tsubo – Niche is more high end, with sleek Costume National heels and handmade shoes by Cydwoq.

Jolie Joli *eye-catching looks*

2 A3

1623 N. Damen Ave., at North • 773 342 7272

>> www.joliejoli.com Open 11–7 Mon–Fri, 11–6 Sat, noon–5 Sun

Located in a former fire station, this shop specializes in trendy, classy clothes with eye-catching details. For girls, there are pretty draped tops in silk and satin or short jackets covered in silver sequins. Guys can choose from the selection of 4 You casual shirts, Ted Baker shirts in Japanese-inspired prints, and corduroy jackets.

Quimby's *weird, wild books*

2 A4

1854 W. North Ave., at Honore • 773 342 0910

>> www.quimbys.com

Open noon–10 Mon–Fri, 11–10 Sat, noon–6 Sun

This store proudly adheres to its mission of stocking all things "surreal and bizarre" in the printed format, and attracts serious collectors and ironic hipsters alike. It has become a respected neighborhood institution, filling a niche where more traditional booksellers dare not tread, and feels like a comfortable local bookstore, complete with kooky characters and handwritten signs.

Like sister store Chicago Comics *(see p56)*, Quimby's carries comic books, but they are generally either darker graphic novels or quirky takes on modern life. There's also an assortment of self-assembled publications by enterprising artists. The zines range from the slick to the stapled and cover subjects from music to feminism. There are books on just about every off-the-wall subject too, from conspiracy theories to guerilla filmmaking – plus regular events such as book signings.

Silver Moon *vintage must-see*

2 A4

1755 W. North Ave., at Wood • 773 235 5797
>> www.silvermoonvintage.com
Open noon–8 Tue–Sat, noon–5 Sun

Don't let the contemporary facade fool you: this place is all about premium vintage threads for true lovers of bygone fashion, with prices to match. The sales area is painted Art Deco-style in red, white, and black, with oddities like a mechanical peep show lending an authentic air. For men who yearn for a more formal era, smoking jackets and fedoras hang alongside silver-topped walking sticks and accessories such as vintage cufflinks and pocket watches. And, if kitsch pieces are more your style, there are plenty of silk Hawaiian shirts and 1950s cocktail dresses to choose from.

The store has its own label with vintage-inspired pieces and interesting reworked items. Co-owner Liz Meyer, who styles and designs for Steven Tyler, the flamboyant lead singer of Aerosmith, occasionally stocks pieces from his private collection.

Independent Bookstores

While independents all over the country are facing threats from chains and online outfits, a core group of bookstores in Chicago have loyal followings. Uptown's **Women and Children First** (5233 N. Clark St., 773 769 9299, www.womenandchildrenfirst.com) has been selling books with a feminist bent since 1979. These days it has fiction by women writers, gay publications, magazines, and kids' books. Further south, the **Unabridged Bookstore** (Map 1 C3, 3251 N. Broadway St., 773 883 9119) has large gay and lesbian, and childrens sections; staff recommendations are posted all over the store.

Over in Wicker Park, **Myopic Books** (Map 2 A4, 1564 N. Milwaukee Ave., 773 862 4882, www.myopicbookstore.com) is a classic used bookstore: a warren of yellowing titles stacked up on towering shelves where customers hang out and read for hours. Downtown, **The Savvy Traveller** (Map 5 F4, 310 S. Michigan Ave., 312 913 9800, www.thesavvytraveller.com) has tons of guidebooks, plus travel narratives, photography books, and gadgets like pocket flashlights. Homesick Europeans should stop by **Europa Books** (Map 5 F1, 832 N. State St., 312 335 9677), which offers foreign newspapers and magazines as well as European literature.

The home of the University of Chicago *(see p83)*, you'd expect Hyde Park to be good for books. The **Seminary Co-op** (Map 9 D4, 5757 S. University Ave., 773 752 4381, www.semcoop.com), is the place for academic books, while its sister shop, the **57th Street Bookstore** (Map 9 E4, 1301 E. 57th St., 773 684 1300) carries general-interest titles. **O'Gara & Wilson** (Map 9 E4, 1448 E. 57th St., 773 363 0993), reputedly the oldest bookstore in Chicago, is an antiquarian's dream, with thousands of used books on literature, art, and history, many of them rare or out-of-print editions.

>> Wicker Park is studded with cool shops – take a walk down Damen and Chicago avenues and Division Street

p45 *forward-looking fashion*

2 A3

1645 N. Damen Ave., at North • 773 862 4523
>> www.p45.com Open 11–7 Mon–Sat, noon–5 Sun

When p45 opened its doors in 1997, it was a pioneer in up-and-coming Wicker Park, whose gritty feel and high concentration of artsy inhabitants made it an ideal spot for a shop that would launch and showcase the work of local fashion design talent. Since then, p45 has kept pace with both the upwardly mobile population and the increasing competition, expanding its mission to include lines by emerging designers from New York and Los Angeles. Truly the only shop of its kind in Chicago, it remains a beacon for forward-thinking fashion addicts, who flock to the industrial loft-like space, with its Plexiglass dressing rooms and exposed pipes, for the cutting-edge looks.

Rather than following obvious trends, owners Tricia Tunstall and Judy Yin favor the sophisticated, urban styles they like to wear themselves, which means that items look fresh for years – definitely a plus given the amount of money you'll spend. Their hands-on approach extends to conducting "closet consultations" at home for customers interested in jump-starting their personal look. Perennial favorites include Ulla Johnson's draped jersey dresses and tops, which flatter most figures, and Susana Monaco's stretchy tank tops and dresses. More avant-garde are the funky pieces by local designers: Shane Gabier's witty creations (think a half-skirt – to go over pants – and a sweater with an attached scarf), and Lara Miller's convertible knits, which go from sweater to shrug or dress to cape in seconds.

Accessories are available here too, and include fanciful vintage-inspired hats and shoes by red-hot designer Eugenia Kim, plus jewelry that's mostly on the sleek side – such as silver bangles, drop earrings, and necklaces of tiny wooden beads.

Apartment No. 9 *masculine basics*

2 A3

1804 N. Damen Ave., at Churchill • 773 395 2999
>> www.apartmentnumber9.com
Open 11–7 Mon–Fri, 11–6 Sat, noon–5 Sun

Sisters Sarah and Amy Blessing designed their small menswear boutique to appeal to that most difficult of customers: the average guy who hates to shop. With its white walls and minimum of fussy details, the space resembles a bachelor's apartment. Jeans are piled casually on a leather ottoman and cargo shorts dangle from hooks, inviting customers to touch the merchandise, of which there is a lot. The styles are as relaxed as the surroundings: well-cut basics such as button-down shirts in stripes and subtle prints from Etro and Seize sur Vingt, army jackets by Dsquared, and distressed khakis from Generra. Dressier options include wool houndstooth trousers by Michael Kors and Paul Smith jackets. There are also little luxuries like silk ties and cashmere socks, and a whimsical touch is added by items such as cufflinks made from typewriter keys.

Stitch *luxury for the home*

2 A3

1723 N. Damen Ave., at Wabansia • 773 782 1570
>> www.stitchchicago.com Open 11–7 Mon–Sat, noon–6 Sun

Bucktown's first "lifestyle boutique," Stitch leans toward the modernist sensibility. Each carefully selected item reflects the movement's tenets of organic materials and clean lines: low-slung sofas share the space with leather clutches, wooden jewelry, and silver candleholders shaped like antlers.

Robin Richman *unique clothing*

2 A2

2108 N. Damen Ave., at Charleston • 773 278 6150
Open 11–6 Mon–Sat, noon–5 Sun

The distinctive shabby-chic look of this boutique hints at the mix of modern and vintage-inspired style within. Robin set up shop to highlight her handknit sweaters, but she also carries edgy yet feminine dresses and suits by New York designer Gary Graham, plus endearingly old-fashioned-looking shoes and sweet jewelry.

art & architecture

Following the Great Chicago Fire in 1871, a flurry of rebuilding led to the construction of the first sky-scrapers and the emergence of the ground-breaking Chicago School of Architecture. The city's "virtual museum" of architecture is only rivaled by its real museums, which range from quirky niche collections to world-acclaimed art exhibits.

ART AND ARCHITECTURE

My first-day-of-spring tradition is to drive south on Lake Shore Drive toward the Loop. In front of me is the elegant Drake Hotel, the towering John Hancock Building, and countless museums, big and small, to explore. After months of winter asking, "Why would anyone live here?", I wonder "Why would anyone live anywhere else?" Few cities have art and architecture that are so essential to their diversity, their recreation, and their personality as Chicago.

Margaret Littman

Frank Lloyd Wright's Legacy

Chicago is ground zero when it comes to the architect of Prairie Style. Start at **The Rookery** *(see p76)* where Wright's atrium is at the heart of this former city hall. Move on to the **Frederic C. Robie House** *(see p83)*, arguably his best-known work. Then head to **Oak Park** *(see p80)*, a suburb dotted with many buildings designed by the great man.

The Great Outdoors

"Short but sweet" is an apt description of Chicago's milder months, but when the sun's out, so are the locals. They flock to the many attractions of **Millennium Park** *(see p74–5)* or view modern architectural icons from the **West Wacker Drive Riverwalk** *(see p72)*. The large sculpture garden at **Douglas Dawson Gallery** *(see p77)* permits more solitary strolls.

World-Class Art

There is a well-founded civic pride in the city's major art museums. From the **Museum of Contemporary Art**'s *(see p77)* ground-breaking works to the U.S.'s leading collection of Latino art at the **Mexican Fine Arts Center & Museum** *(see p81)*, and the diverse collections of the **Art Institute of Chicago** *(see p73)*, serious art-lovers are spoiled for choice.

choice sights

Modern Architecture

Forty years after it was built, few buildings still engender as much debate in Chicago as the corncob-like towers of **Marina City** *(see p80)*. Another love-it-or-hate-it building is Helmut Jahn's **James R. Thompson Center** *(see p77)*, while further south, the **IIT** *(see p85)* is a mecca for aficionados of Mies van der Rohe's "skin-and-bone" style of design.

The Chicago School

This late-19th-century architectural style, characterized by the use of steel-frame construction, terra-cotta cladding, and the "Chicago window," is illustrated by several of the city's architectural icons. Check out Daniel Burnham's **Monadnock Building** *(see p80),* or his early skyscraper, the **Reliance Building** *(see p80)*, now the Hotel Burnham.

Specialized Museums

Chicago's niche museums scrutinize many aspects of humanity. The **International Museum of Surgical Sciences** *(see p72)* houses surgical artifacts spanning 4,000 years, while the **Leather Archives & Museum** *(see p72)* focuses on this gay subculture. The **Museum of Broadcast Communications** *(see p77)* has lots of TV- and radio-related exhibits.

International Museum of Surgical Sciences *surgical history*

3 G3

1524 N. Lake Shore Dr., at North • 312 642 6502

>> www.imss.org Open 10–4 Tue–Sat (May–Sep: Tue–Sun)

This museum is filled with items that span 4,000 years of surgery. From depictions of Stone-Age circumcision and early C-sections to devices once used to correct bowlegs, the often-bizarre exhibits elicit a sense of relief that we live in more modern times. **Adm**

Leather Archives & Museum *leather galore*

6418 N. Greenview Ave., at Devon • 773 761 9200

>> www.leatherarchives.org • Ⓜ Loyola (Red Line)

Open noon–8 Thu & Fri, noon–5 Sat & Sun

Curious about the world of leather? Then this place is for you. Tamer exhibits include murals from Chicago's now-closed Gold Coast (one of the world's first leather bars) and a look at the history of the black motorcycle jacket; racier items include S&M "knick-knacks." **Adm**

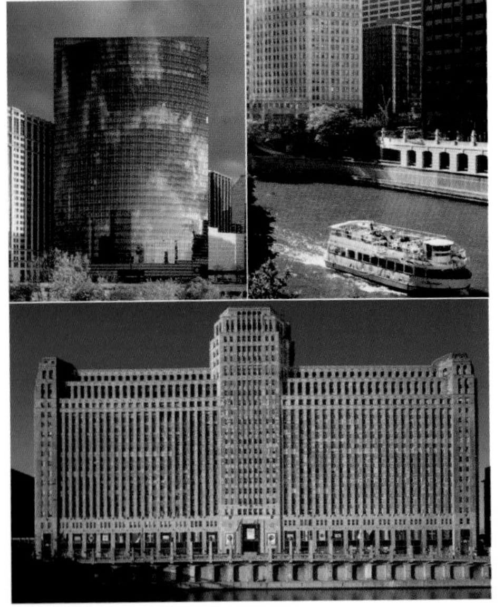

West Wacker Drive Riverwalk

5 E3

When the two-tiered Wacker Drive isn't under re-construction (an ongoing project), the stretch of its lower-level Riverwalk between Michigan Avenue and Lake Street is home to a few waterfront cafés and picnic spots. But architecture aficionados come here to look up as the shores of the Chicago River are one of the best places to see the city's icons of modern architecture. These include the mammoth 1930 Merchandise Mart *(bottom)*, which, when built, was the largest office building in existence, warranting its own zip code. Other skyscrapers that can be seen from the river banks include Skidmore, Owings, and Merrill's monolithic Quaker Tower (1987); Mies van der Rohe's spartan IBM Building (1971); and the graceful curve of Kohn Pederson Fox Associate's 333 W. Wacker Drive (1983, *top left)*. Farther east at Lake Shore Drive, Ellen Lanyon's River- walk Gateway murals (28 ceramic panels depicting the city's history) are the city's largest piece of public art.

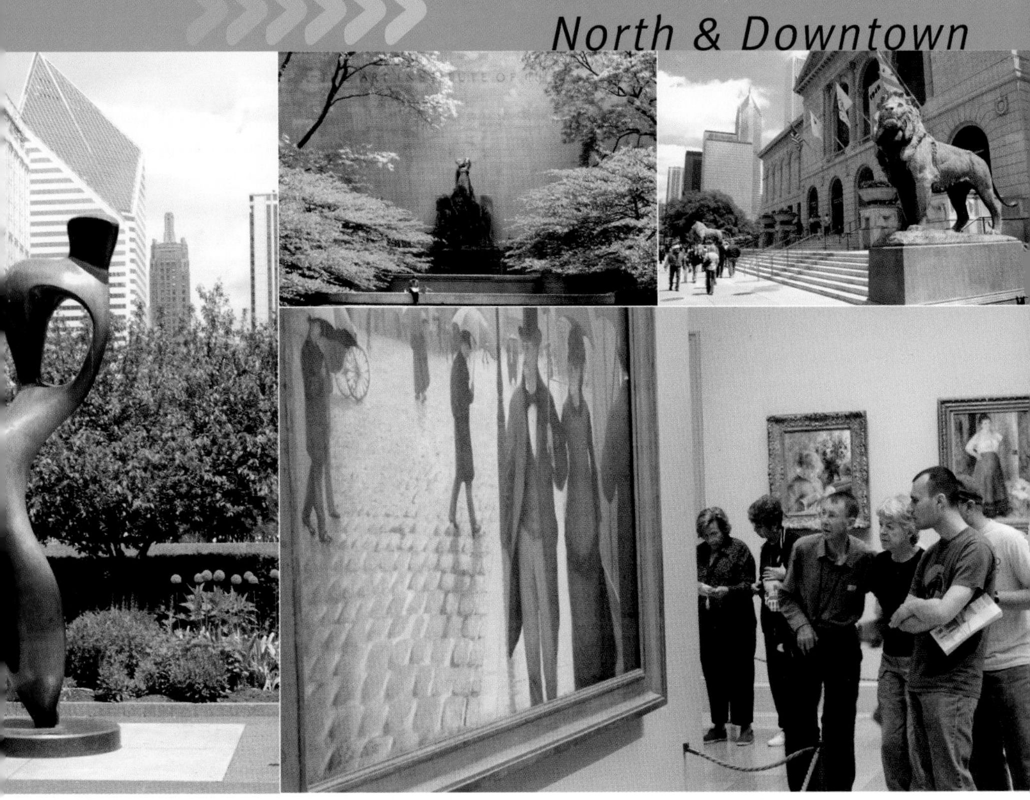

Art Institute of Chicago *world-class art* 5 G4

111 S. Michigan Ave., at Adams • 312 443 3600
» www.artic.edu Open 10:30–5 Mon–Fri (to 8 Thu), 10–5 Sat & Sun (summer: to 9 Thu & Fri)

Built after the Great Chicago Fire of 1871, the Art Institute of Chicago, with its grand entrance flanked by stone lions, is probably the city's best-known and best-loved cultural institution.

It is hard to know where to start when entering this museum, and locals as well as students at the presti-gious School of the Art Institute of Chicago all have their own recommendations. The permanent collection includes significant Asian, American, and European painting and sculpture, as well as world-famous modern art, textile, and photography collections. Visitors who have only a few hours to race through the museum should be sure to seek out the renowned works: George Seurat's *A Sunday on La Grande Jatte*, Grant Wood's *American Gothic*, and Edward Hopper's *Nighthawks*. However, it would be a shame to miss out on more unusual highlights, such as the Arthur Rubloff Paperweight Collection and the Thorne Miniature Rooms. The latter might sound like dollhouses that would only interest 10-year-old girls, but the collection of detailed reproductions of interiors – conceived by Chicago socialite Narcissa Ward Thorne in the 1930s – is one of the institute's most popular attractions.

In addition to the permanant exhibits, the institute keeps things fresh by hosting blockbusting shows and special events such as concerts or dance performances, often linked to the shows. **Adm**

» *Some river boat tours depart from the lower-level corner of Michigan Avenue and Wacker Drive*

Millennium Park *public space perfected* 5 F4

Entrances on Michigan Ave., Randolph St. & Monroe St.
Welcome Center: 201 E. Randolph St. • 312 742 1168
>> www.millenniumpark.org Open 6am–11pm daily

Millennium Park finally opened four years after this millennium began, but as soon as it was completed any cynicism on the part of local taxpayers disappeared. In its first six months, more than 2 million people visited the park, and the following year the City of Chicago added blue-shirt-wearing hospitality workers to help guide visitors through its 24.5 acres (10 ha). The park has become a top city attraction: a collection of captivating public art, water sculptures, and architecture. Its also one of the best places in town for people-watching.

At its center is the **Jay Pritzker Pavilion**, a Frank Gehry-designed outdoor amphitheater, as acoustically perfect as it is aesthetically pleasing. The stage is topped with curlicues of steel, winding 120 ft (36.5 m) above the ground. Steel pipes create a trellis-like structure that functions as a visual device as well as a means – through the speakers attached to it – for sound to be distributed over both the amphitheater and the Great Lawn seating area. That lawn was designed so that it drains immediately and the grass dry enough for concert-goers to sit on within an hour of a downpour.

From the Pavilion, visitors can now walk east toward Lake Michigan over the **BP Bridge**, Gehry's first bridge design, which spans the multi-lane Columbus Avenue. The bridge is also architecturally impressive, though in winter its steel panels are tricky to navigate when covered with ice.

Millennium Park is stamped with Gehry's signature, but it is Anish Kapoor's *Cloud Gate* sculpture that has become the park's highest-profile attraction. Called "the bean" by locals, the sculpture creates a 12-ft (3.6-m) arch that allows visitors to walk under it and see their reflections – and that of the skyline – in the smooth stainless steel surface.

The **Crown Fountain**, close to Michigan Avenue, is another main attraction. The fountain comprises two towers that play digital loops on LED screens: the faces of more than 1,000 Chicago residents are depicted in this mesmerizing installation that was created by the Spanish artist Jaume Plensa, who was inspired by the diversity of Chicago's population. From time to time, water spews from the towers onto the ground below: in warmer months, children (and grown-ups with a childish streak) head here to take off their shoes and paddle and frolic.

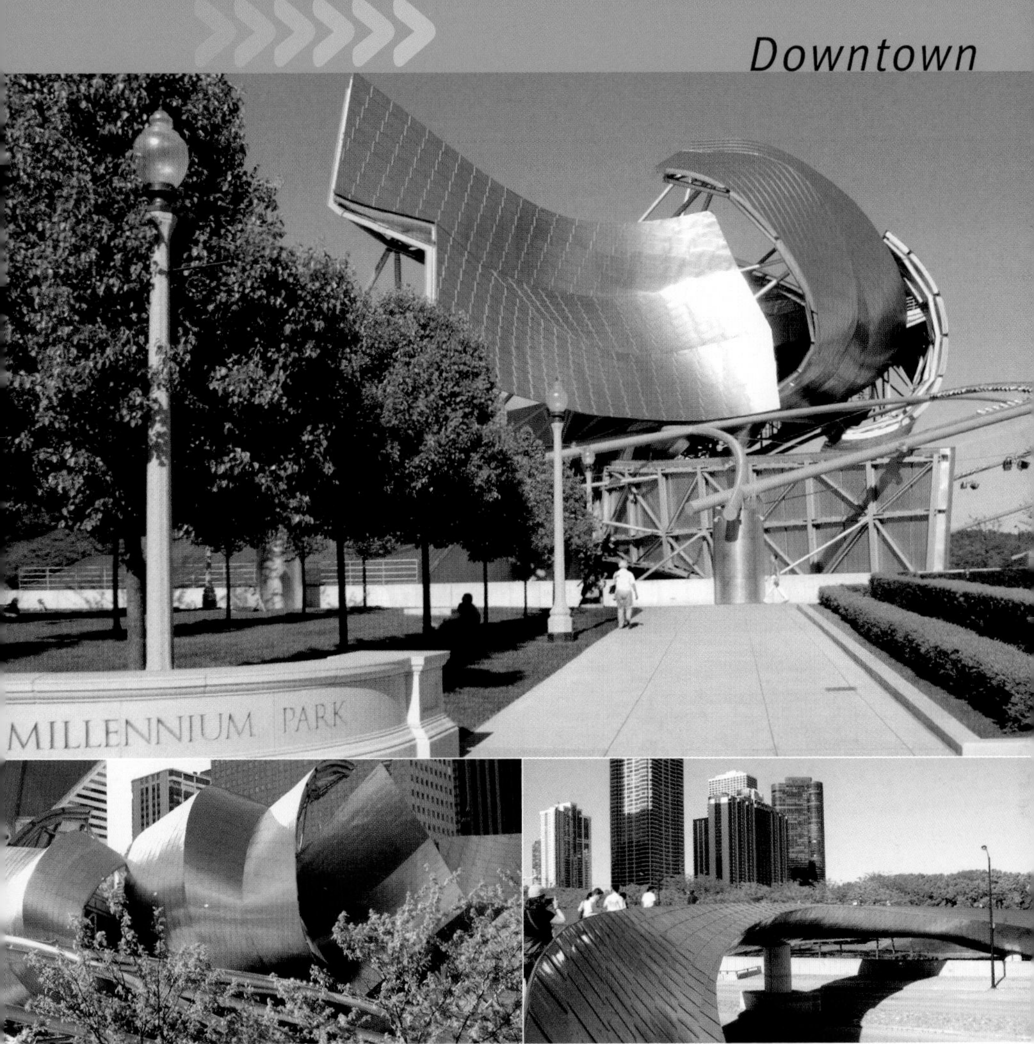

Beyond the bustle of *Cloud Gate* and the Crown Fountain lies one of the park's more serene attractions, the **Lurie Garden**. Its landscaping is easily on a par with that of the much larger, much visited Chicago Botanic Garden *(see p140)*. Native plantings cover the garden's terrain, and include the "shoulder" hedge, a tangible representation of poet Carl Sandburg's reference to Chicago as the "City of Big Shoulders."

Millennium Park also hosts seasonal attractions like the McCormick Tribune Plaza ice rink that offers free skating in winter. Farther north, the Millennium Monument is a semi-ciruclar colonnade that forms a striking backdrop for temporary art exhibitions. For more details on what the park has to offer, stop by the Welcome Center or take its free tour by downloading an mp3 file from www.antennaaudio.com.

>> Admission is charged for some Millennium Park concerts and other activities, as well as for showers and lockers

Chicago Cultural Center *free culture* 5 F3

78 E. Washington St., at Michigan • 312 744 6630
>> www.cityofchicago.org Open 10–7 Mon–Thu, 10–6 Fri, 10–5 Sat, 11–5 Sun; tours Wed, Fri & Sat at 1:15

This grand former city library building (nicknamed the "people's palace") is worth a visit for its architecture alone. The books were moved to the Harold Washington Library *(see p145)*, and an extensive free cultural program means it now really lives up to its moniker.

Chicago Architecture Foundation 5 F4

224 S. Michigan Ave., at Jackson • 312 922 3432
>> www.architecture.org Open 9–6:30 Mon–Sat, 9–6 Sun

Housed in the historic Santa Fe Building, this center is ground zero for everything relating to the city's built environment. Temporary exhibits and lectures attract serious architecture fans. More accessible are tours led by enthusiastic guides, including the city's best river tour. The gift shop is also excellent. **Adm**

Gallery 37 Center for the Arts 5 F3

66 E. Randolph St., at Wabash • 312 744 8925
>> www.gallery37.org Open 10–6 Mon–Sat

Unusually, this center's fifth-floor CenterSpace Gallery often features exhibitions of works by both professional and student artists hung side-by-side. Proceeds from sales help fund Gallery 37's educational programs for all of the community. Free dance, jazz, and drama performances are also open to the public.

The Rookery *office building with a history* 5 E4

209 S. LaSalle St., at Adams • 312 553 6150
Lobby open 8–6 daily

It may not be Frank Lloyd Wright's best-known work, but his glorious, sky-lit atrium is at the heart of this 1888 former city hall. The Rookery – named for the birds that once roosted on the roof – is noted as being the first building where both masonry load-bearing and skeletal frame construction techniques were employed.

Museum of Broadcast Communications *for TV and radio addicts*

5 F2

400 N. State St., at Kinzie • 312 245 8200

>> www.museum.tv Call for more details

Formerly located in the Chicago Cultural Center, this museum is due to re-open in its own impressive space in 2007. Interactive studios, TV and radio history exhibits, and more than 85,000 hours of archived TV and radio shows are among the draws.

James R. Thompson Center

5 E3

100 W. Randolph St., at Lasalle

Public spaces open to public 8:30–6 Mon–Fri

This once-controversial building was designed by Helmut Jahn in 1985 to be a democratic fusion of government offices and public spaces such as stores and restaurants. Glass elevators shuttle passengers up and down the atrium, from the top of which there's a great view of the concourse below.

Museum of Contemporary Art

5 G1

220 E. Chicago Ave., at Mies van der Rohe • 312 280 2660

>> www.mcachicago.org Open 10–8 Tue, 10–5 Wed–Sun

German architect Josef Paul Kleihues' first U.S. building has had a dramatic impact on the Windy City. Since opening in 1996 – with seven times the space it had before – the minimalist museum has become a must-see. The excellent collection of groundbreaking post-1945 art also spills into the pristine gardens. **Adm**

Douglas Dawson Gallery *exotic art*

4 C2

400 N. Morgan St., at Kinzie • 312 226 7975

>> www.douglasdawson.com Open 10–5:30 Mon–Fri, 10–5 Sat

When Douglas Dawson moved his gallery here from River North, it signaled the arrival of the West Loop Gallery District. The focus is on non-Western artworks. But the real attraction is the vast garden where impressive stone monoliths and larger sculptures that are too big to be displayed indoors can be found.

Museum of Holography *optical illusions*

4 B3

1134 W. Washington Blvd., at May • 312 226 1007

>> www.holographiccenter.com Open 12:30–4:30 Wed–Sun

More a shrine to technology than a museum *per se*, this small collection is concerned with everything you could wish to know about holographic images. The focus is on holograms as art, but the museum explains how they are created as well. It also has a research center for those who want to learn even more. **Adm**

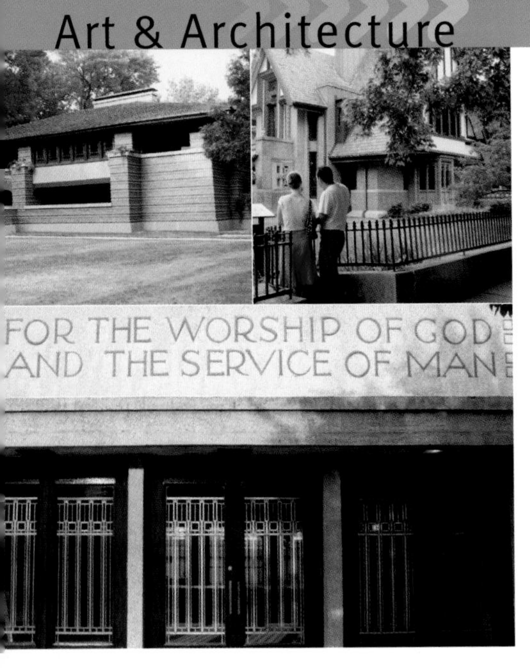

Oak Park *Frank Lloyd Wright's home base*

Visitors' Center: 158 N. Forest Ave., at Lake
Ⓜ Oak Park (Green Line) • 708 529 7800
>> www.visitoakpark.com Open 10–4:30 daily

For American architecture buffs, Oak Park means just one thing: Frank Lloyd Wright. This western suburb has 36 houses designed by Wright between 1889 and 1913. A pupil of Louis Sullivan, Wright's use and development of open-plan design in residential architecture put him among history's best regarded architects.

The neighborhood's buildings illustrate Wright's formative years, and include his own home and studio, where he developed his Prairie Style of colors and use of natural materials. Other local highlights include the poured-concrete **Unity Temple**, still a working church, which Wright considered his first contribution to modern architecture. Most of the other houses he designed are closed to the public, but there are numerous tours of the exteriors; for maps and information, stop by the Oak Park Visitors' Center.

Architectural Icons

What do Daniel Burnham and Donald Trump have in common? They're both associated with the design of iconic buildings that have made a strong impact on the Chicago skyline. While Trump's new riverside behemoth isn't yet erected (due for completion in 2008), there's plenty to keep your neck craning up.

North of the Chicago River, on Michigan Avenue, are two of the best-loved 1920s-era landmarks: the **Wrigley Building** (Map 5 F2, at No. 400) with its distinctive towers and two-story tall clock, and the **Tribune Tower** (Map 5 F2, at No. 435) diagonally opposite. The latter, built in a Gothic style, was designed to be the "world's most beautiful office building" and incorporates archaeological artifacts from around the globe in its base. North of the 1920s duo is the **John Hancock Center** *(see p144)*, a 1964 skyscraper that tapers the higher it climbs, making it seem even taller than its 1,127 ft (343 m). From the Hancock you can see **Marina City** (Map 5 F3, 300 N. State St., www.marina-city.com), a "city within a city" crowned by two round towers affectionately called "the corncobs."

South of the river are two examples of more classic Chicago architecture. Built in 1890, the **Reliance Building** *(see p155)* is considered the predecessor of the modern skyscraper. Designed by Burnham's office, it is an excellent example of Chicago School of Architecture construction. Burnham also designed the north half of the **Monadnock Building** (Map 5 E4, 53 W. Jackson Blvd., www.monadnockbuilding.com). Supporting 16 floors, its load-bearing masonry walls were considered an astonishing engineering feat. Farther west, the **Sears Tower** (Map 5 E4, 233 S. Wacker Dr., www.thesearstower.com), whose 103rd-floor Skydeck is a prime city attraction, is a staggering 1,450 ft (440 m) high.

Mexican Fine Arts Center & Museum

1852 W. 19th St., at Wolcott • 312 738 1503 • Ⓜ 18th (Blue Line)
>> www.mfacmchicago.org Open 10–5 Tue–Sun

Pilsen *(see p137)* is home to one of the largest Mexican-American communities in the U.S., and occupying pride of place in the neighborhood is the Mexican Fine Arts Center. With its open-air plaza, wide range of cultural festivals, and workshops, the space is much more than a museum. A notable highlight is the annual Day of the Dead celebration (November 1), but rotating exhibits include visual arts that are worthy of the center's status as the nation's largest Latino cultural institution.

The permanent collection includes etchings by Francisco Toledo, religious art devoted to the Virgin of Guadalupe, and murals by the revolutionary painter and Mexico's best-known male artist, Diego Rivera. Handmade goods that reflect the aesthetic of the works in the museum are sold in the gift shop and at a popular holiday bazaar each December.

Intuit *outside looking in*

4 B1

756 N. Milwaukee Ave., at Ogden • 312 243 9088
>> www.art.org Open noon–5 Wed–Sat

When Intuit was founded in 1991, outsider artists such as Henry Darger and Sister Gertrude Morgan didn't get much wall space in traditional galleries. This gallery is devoted to exhibiting autodidacts and, along with its sister space, the Carl Hammer Gallery *(see p84)*, has made Chicago a major hub for folk and outsider art.

Museum of Contemporary Photography *digital revelations*

5 F5

600 S. Michigan Ave., at Harrison • 312 663 5554
>> www.mocp.org Open 10–5 Mon–Fri (to 8 Thu), noon–5 Sat

This campus museum actually promotes all digital art forms, especially works that reflect cultural and political images. There are over 7,000 photos in the permanent, U.S.-focused collection and rotating exhibits are drawn from the work of Midwestern artists.

>> *Oak Park is home to Ernest Hemingway's birthplace (339 N. Oak Park Ave., 708 848 2222; open to visitors)*

Spertus Museum *the Jewish experience* 5 F5

618 S. Michigan Ave., at Balbo • 312 322 1700

>> www.spertus.edu

Open 10–5 Sun–Wed, 10–7 Thu, 10–3 Fri

Spertus has a large permanant collection as well as temporary exhibits relating to the experience of the Jewish diaspora, but offers plenty of cultural events too. Music, film shows, lectures, and theater are all part of the stimulating mix. **Adm**

Museum Mania

Valid for nine days after its first use, CityPass offers unlimited admission to six city museums, including the Art Institute of Chicago and the Field Museum, for half the regular admission price (if you visit them all) – plus the chance to skip long lines. The pass can be purchased online (www.citypass.com) or at any participating museum.

Shedd Aquarium *not just fish* 7 F1

1200 S. Lake Shore Dr., at Museum Campus • 312 939 2438

>> www.sheddaquarium.org Open 9–6 daily (winter to 5 Mon–Fri)

For many visitors, the main attraction here is the Oceanarium, an extension featuring different marine habitats and an amazing infinity pool for marine mammals. Architecture fans are often just as mesmerized by the ornate 1929 building and the underwater viewing area of the Oceanarium. **Adm**

Prairie Avenue Historic District 7 E3

Prairie Ave., between 18th & Cullerton

>> www.glessnerhouse.org For info on tours call 312 326 1480

In the late 1800s, Prairie Avenue was where Marshall Field (of department store fame) and his well-heeled friends lived. As the city grew, their opulent residences were eventually surrounded by factories and the area declined, but 11 of these remarkable homes remain. Two have been restored to their former glory: the Arts and Crafts **Glessner House Museum** (1800 Prairie Ave.), designed by architect H. H. Richardson, and, one block east, the **Clarke House Museum** (1827 S. Indiana Ave.). Both offer visits by guided tour only. Built in the Greek Revival style and containing pioneer-era furnishings, Clarke House is the city's oldest. It is nestled within the Women's Park and Gardens, a tranquil space with a fountain and a commemorative path, which is also worth a visit. More opportunities for personal reflection exist at the moving **National Vietnam Veterans Art Museum** (1801 S. Indiana Ave., 312 326 0270).

University of Chicago Campus

8 D4

>> **www.uchicago.edu** For opening times of individual campus sights, call 773 702 1234

A well-respected center of learning, this campus holds treasures even for those who are not academically minded. Two on-site museums house collections that are worlds apart: the **Oriental Institute** specializes in ancient artifacts from Egypt, Sudan, Palestine, and Asia – its new Edgar and Deborah Jannotta Mesopotamian Gallery alone has more than 1,300 objects – while the compact **Smart Museum** contains a surprising amount of notable modern art. The Smart's highlight is work by the Chicagoan pop-culture painter Ed Paschke.

In fine weather, stroll through the university grounds, including the Smart's Elden Sculpture Garden, before heading to the building that makes the campus a kind of pilgrimage site – the 1909 **Frederick C. Robie House**. Arguably Frank Lloyd Wright's best-known work, it is open for tours, but even viewing the exterior offers great insight into Wright's own Prairie Style of architecture.

DuSable Museum of African-American History *historical insight*

8 C4

740 E. 56th Pl., at Cottage Grove • 773 947 0600

>> **www.dusablemuseum.org** Open 10–5 Tue–Sat, noon–5 Sun

Named for the trader who was Chicago's first settler, this museum's temporary shows have included a look at black music pre-Motown, and African-American inventors. Don't miss the permanent exhibit on former (and beloved) Mayor Harold Washington. **Adm**

Downtown Public Art

Chicagoans are proud of their architecture, but it's the public works of art that are more often used as landmarks. Among the best known are Picasso's untitled sculpture, *"the Picasso,"* in Daley Plaza (Map 5 E3), and Alexander Calder's bright-red *Flamingo* that contrasts with the black backdrop of Mies van der Rohe's Federal Center in the Federal Plaza (Map 5 E4). Jean DuBuffet's monochrome fiberglass *Monument with Standing Beast* keeps guard at the James R. Thompson Center (Map 5 E3, *see p77*), while Marc Chagall's more colorful mosaic sculpture *Four Seasons* brightens up the Chase Plaza (Map 5 E4). Claus Oldenburg's baseball-inspired *Batcolumn* (Map 4 D4, 600 W. Madison St.) reflects the city's love of sports.

>> *For more of Frank Lloyd Wrights' work, visit the west side suburb of Oak Park* (see p80)

Historic Pullman District *company town*

Bet. 111th & 155th streets, Ellis & Cottage Grove aves.
Metra Central Electric stop Pullman
>> **www.pullmanil.org** Visitor Center: 11,141 S. Cottage Grove Ave., 773 785 8901; open 11–3 Tue–Sun

George M. Pullman, founder of the Pullman Palace Car Company, is credited with causing the U.S.A.'s first labor strike in 1894 when he lowered workers' wages without lowering their rents. But his legacy to urban planning was more positive. His "most perfect town" on the far South Side – now a landmark – comprises block after block of brick rowhouses, a shopping arcade, and other public buildings including the Hotel Florence (currently closed for repair).

A fire ravaged the original Pullman Factory in the 1990s, but passionate enthusiasts have worked to preserve other parts of the community. The area is now worth spending some time in: walk the manicured streets, and admire Arcade Park and the exteriors of privately owned historic homes.

Major Art Hubs

Interesting art galleries can be found in almost every Chicago neighborhood and suburb, but there are three main drags where there is a concentration of galleries with complementary, if not similar, collections. River North's Wells Street (Map 5 E1) is the best known – and the most upscale. The pieces here range from American and European contemporary photography to Latin American art, and the dealers' eye for quality makes for a worthwhile stroll regardless of your purchasing power. Not to be missed is the **Carl Hammer Gallery** (No. 740, 312 266 8512, www.hammergallery.com) one of the country's leading sellers of outsider art.

An increasing number of art dealers are taking their cue from the artists who were drawn to the big lofts and lower rents of the West Loop. While River North still boasts more galleries, West Loop is where the buzz is, particularly along Fulton Market (Map 4 C3), with its contemporary art, creative furniture, and homewares stores. In addition to the **Douglas Dawson Gallery** *(see p77)*, must-sees include the **Linda Warren Gallery** (No. 1052, 312 432 9500, www.lindawarrengallery.com), where emerging artists rarely shown in Chicago are exhibited. The West Loop's increase in popularity is also thanks to the Friday night gallery openings that lure an influx of attractive singles.

To the southwest, Pilsen has long housed artists of Mexican descent as well as the Mexican Fine Art Center and Museum *(see p81)*, but now the area is home to artists of all persuasions. Halstead Street's **Dubhe Carreño Gallery** (No. 1841, 312 666 3150, www.dubhecarrenogallery.com), with its exhibits of modern ceramic art, is one of the neighborhood's leaders. Because the area is still establishing itself as an art hub, works here tend to be more affordable and gallery hours less predictable.

Illinois Institute of Technology (IIT)

3300 S. Federal St., at 33rd • 312 567 3000
Ⓜ 35th-Bronzeville-IIT (Green Line)
>> www.iit.edu Tours available, call for details

The University of Chicago may top the IIT in some academic rankings, but when it comes to modern architecture, the Hyde Park campus doesn't hold a candle to this Bridgeport academic institution.

Influential German architect Ludwig Mies van der Rohe, who became the head of the institute's architecture program in 1938, designed the south side campus. Its 12 acres (5 ha) have long been a mecca for those who admire the architect's steel-and-concrete frames and curtain walls of brick and glass, which were, at the time, such a dramatic departure from traditional university design. The Crown Hall, which now houses the architecture school, was Mies' favorite example of his universal design.

Things got even more interesting in 2003 when Dutch architect (and Pritzker Prize Laureate) Rem Koolhaas designed a new campus center, the McCormick Tribune Campus Center (MTCC). His design connects the academic and residential parts of the campus with pathways that are reminiscent of interior streets. Also, rather than hiding the El train and its tracks, which divide the campus, Koolhaas made them a feature, creating a visually striking concrete-and-stainless-steel tunnel that encircles the elevated tracks where they enter at the top of the glass building. Not only is this structure a work of art, it also helps muffle the sound of screeching trains. Visitors enter the MTCC – which also contains a store stocking architecture-related books, T-shirts, and other souvenirs for design enthusiasts – by passing through a 20-ft (6-m) high mural of Mies van der Rohe.

Just south of the campus center is State Street Village, a collection of three student dorm buildings designed in 2002 by Helmut Jahn, a former student of Mies and one of Chicago's most-loved (or loathed, depending on your perspective) architects.

>> *1: Crown Hall; 2: McCormack Tribune Campus Center; 3: State Street Village*

Roland
SABIAN

performance

New York may get all the glory, but the Windy City has one of the nation's most highly regarded and diverse performance communities. From classic opera to cutting-edge drama, Chicago has it all. The home of the blues is also the birthplace of improv comedy, which thrives at a whole host of clubs, while music venues – including, in summer, the lakefront and parks – feature every conceivable genre.

PERFORMANCE

This gritty city has long been an incubator for local talent, spawning everything from the amplified Chicago blues sound to improv and poetry slams. Over 200 theater companies and countless dancers and musicians ensure plenty of choice on any given night, ranging from young talent blowing minds in storefront venues to slick productions in custom-built complexes. For nonsmokers, the citywide smoking ban now makes every venue a pleasure to visit.

Cara Jepsen

Roots Music

Blues and jazz have flourished in Chicago since the early 20th century. Friendly **Rosa's Lounge** *(see p99)* offers local blues acts in a neighborhood setting, while the historic **Green Mill** *(see pp92–3)* puts on nightly jazz. Jam sessions at the **Velvet Lounge** *(see p101)* on Sundays and **New Apartment Lounge** *(see p102)* on Tuesdays should not be missed.

Art-House Cinema

A popular film location itself, Chicago offers all kinds of movie experience; but for foreign and indie films and retrospectives, try the **Gene Siskel Film Center** *(see p98)*, or enjoy the **Music Box Theatre**'s *(see p90)* historic setting. The not-for-profit **Facets Cinémathèque** *(see p90)* often has the most adventurous programming of them all.

Cutting-Edge Performance

Young local talent tests the boundaries of drama and music at **Viaduct Theater** *(see p99)* and dance and home-grown theater at **Links Hall** *(see p91)*. **HotHouse** *(see p103)* showcases the latest in international music and local performance art, while **The Second City** *(see p90)* – the birthplace of improv – provides topical comedy seven nights a week.

choice acts

High Culture

Many a mayor has boasted that Chicago is a world-class city, and it's hard to argue otherwise when it comes to high culture. Just see what's on offer at the **Symphony Center** *(see p98)*, **Civic Opera House** *(see p98)* or **Joan W. and Irving B. Harris Theatre for Music & Dance** *(see p99)*, home to several younger, but still well-respected, organizations.

Windy City Drama

American dramatic talent converges on Chicago, ensuring that the scene is always fresh. The **Goodman Theatre** *(see p98)* presents consistently high-quality work, and the **Steppenwolf** *(see p95)* is known as much for its elaborate sets as the intense acting style. **eta Creative Arts Foundation** *(see p102)* is the city's best African-American drama company.

Indie Rock Scene

Chicago's indie music scene is always evolving: **Metro** *(see p94)* presents up-and-coming bands, while **The Empty Bottle**'s *(see p102)* dive-bar atmosphere suits its edgier indie rock acts. The same holds true for the **Abbey Pub** *(see p102)* – a neighborhood Irish bar with live music – or try unpretentious **Hideout** *(see p102)* for alt-country and rock.

Facets Cinémathèque *independent film* 2 B1

1517 W. Fullerton Ave., at Ashland • 773 281 9075

>> www.facets.org Store open 10–10 Mon–Sat, noon–10 Sun

Independent films are the forte of this not-for-profit venue, where film-makers sometimes field questions after their work is screened. The unpretentious, 125-seat theater also hosts several offbeat festivals, including the Chicago Latin Film Festival. The video store here carries a dizzying 60,000 titles for sale and rental.

The Second City *improv comedy mecca* 3 F3

1616 N. Wells St., at North • 312 664 4032

>> www.secondcity.com Box office open 10–10 or after last show

Tomorrow's stars perform sketches and improv comedy at this renowned institution, which has produced names such as actor Bill Murray since 1959. Mainstage is the most comfortable of the three theaters, with cabaret-style seating and a full bar. The cast performs pure improv after the show every night except Friday.

Music Box Theatre *movie palace* 1 A1

3733 N. Southport Ave., at Grace • 773 871 6604

>> www.musicboxtheatre.com

Taking in a movie at this beautifully preserved 1929 theater is like stepping back in time. The 750-seat gem is designed to resemble an old Italian courtyard, and, in addition to ornate columns and faux-marble loggia, there are twinkling stars and projected clouds, which float across the dark blue ceiling.

Independent American and foreign films are the main draw here, and the programming includes classic cinema matinées and cult midnight screenings on weekends, when the theater's pipe organ rises from the floor to provide entertainment between performances. A similarly charming, 100-seat adjoining theater (constructed in 1991) screens specialty films and documentaries attracting smaller audiences. The main theater allegedly has a ghost – a former longtime employee named Whitey who still likes to keep a watchful eye on the place.

Links Hall *cutting-edge shows*

3435 N. Sheffield Ave., at Clark • 773 281 0824

» www.linkshall.org Weekend performances only; box office open 9–5 daily for reservations

Since 1978, this non-profit, bare-bones, 75-seat theater has served as a launch pad for experimental dancers and other performers. A highlight is the winter solstice percussion concerts, when local musicians Hamid Drake and Michael Zerang perform as the sun rises.

Live Bait Theater *local performance art*

1 A1

3914 N. Clark St., at Irving Park • 773 871 1212

» www.livebaittheater.org Box office opens 30 min before show

Live Bait has premiered over 100 works by emerging Chicago playwrights and performers since 1987. The two intimate theaters boast great sight lines and productions range from plays by local playwright and artistic director Sharon Evans to the summer Fillet of Solo festival featuring the city's best solo performers.

Athenaeum Theatre *theater complex*

1 A4

2936 N. Southport Ave., at Lincoln • 773 935 6860

» www.athenaeumtheatre.com Box office open 3–8 Mon–Fri, 2 hrs before showtime Sat & Sun

Built in 1911, this is one of Chicago's few Broadway-style theaters. Offerings range from edgy physical theater to straight drama and the popular DanceChicago Festival (in the fall), which often makes for an interesting mix of theater-goers in the lobby.

Comedy Clubs

The American improvisational (improv) comedy scene began in Chicago in the late 1950s with The Compass Players (who later morphed into the more mainstream **The Second City**). **I.O.** (Map 1 B2, 3541 N. Clark St., 773 880 0199, www.iochicago.net) created a team-driven, long-form improv style in the early 1980s, while in the 1990s the iconoclastic **Annoyance Theater** (4840 N. Broadway St., 773 929 6200, www.annoyanceproductions.com) broke all the rules with its popular *Real Live Brady Bunch* show. Crowd-pulling national stand-up acts hit the stage at the cramped **Zanies** (Map 3 F4, 1548 N. Wells St., 312 337 4027, www.zanies.com), and in late spring, performers swarm to various venues for the city's annual **Improv Festival** (www.cif.com).

Green Mill Jazz Club *jazz and poetry*
4802 N. Broadway St., at Lawrence • 773 878 5552
Ⓜ Lawrence (Red Line)
>> www.greenmilljazz.com (Uptown Poetry Slam: www.slampapi.com) Open noon–4am daily (to 5am Sat); music 8pm–1:30am

The country's oldest continuously running jazz club was built in 1907 and originally named Pop Morris' Garden. Once a large, elegant complex with a beer garden and dancing, it is now a smoky live music venue with limited seating, fantastic music, and a very rich history.

In 1910 a new owner was inspired by Paris' Moulin Rouge cabaret, but re-named the club Green Mill Garden (to avoid implying any connection with the city's red-light district as the surrounding Uptown area was then a fancy suburb). A few years later, comedian Charlie Chaplin would drink at the bar after making movies at the nearby Essanay Studios. During 1930s prohibition, the club became an upscale gangster haunt and speakeasy. Performers at that time included jazz greats such as Billie Holiday, Al Jolson, Tommy Dorsey, and Benny Goodman. Much of the Art Deco interior still looks the way it did when notorious gangster Al "Scarface" Capone sat at one of the tall, crescent-shaped booths near the bar, while keeping a watchful eye on the door. His picture still hangs behind the bar, next to a portrait of mob hitman Jack "Machine Gun" McGurn, who was part-owner of the club and is thought to have been the prime trigger-man behind the 1929 St. Valentine's Day Massacre. A trap door beneath the back bar still leads to a tunnel where bootleg liquor was once brought in.

In later years, singer and actor Frank Sinatra was a regular visitor, but the place fell on hard times when the neighborhood declined in the 1970s and 80s. Today the area is rapidly gentrifying, but the club – minus the beer garden – remains largely unchanged: there's still a baby grand piano and a small stage by the bar, and the original paintings decorate the walls.

There are three sets of live music every night, ranging from crooners such as Kurt Elling to swing orchestras on Thursday night, when dancing is encouraged. For some performances there's a strict no-talking policy. It is best to arrive very early or very late to get a seat as the capacity is just 178. Food is not served, but you can bring food in to your booth from the Mexican restaurant next door. Beware: the bathrooms are located next to the stage, so a trip during a performance means you could inadvertently become part of the show.

One of the club's biggest draws is the Sunday night Uptown Poetry Slam, a spoken word contest started in 1984 by construction worker and poet Marc Smith that inspired similar events all over the U.S. Smith still hosts the slams, which start at 7pm with an open mic. A featured poet performs at 8pm, and the slam starts at 9pm. Seasoned poets and local amateurs perform in the hope of winning lottery tickets or a $10 prize. Judges are chosen from the audience, and the poetry is usually pretty good, though the crowd is encouraged to hiss and boo mediocre performers off the stage. If you visit the bar during quieter, daylight hours, ask the bartender to show you the club's massive and fascinating scrapbook.

Aragon Ballroom *historic concert hall*

1106 W. Lawrence Ave., at Broadway • 773 561 9500

Ⓜ Lawrence (Red Line)

>> www.aragon.com Box office open 9–6 Mon–Fri

This once-upscale hall, with its opulent Moorish design, is sometimes referred to as the Aragon "brawl room." Since the 1970s, patrons have guzzled beer and rocked to bands ranging from Foghat to U2. The schedule also includes salsa, blues, and boxing.

Metro *rock in style*

1 A1

3730 N. Clark St., at Grace • 773 549 0203

>> www.metrochicago.com

Box office open noon–8 Mon–Sat, noon–6 Sun

This former theater debuted as an alternative rock club in 1982 with a $5-per-ticket REM concert. The Smashing Pumpkins honed their skills here, and acts from Prince to Beck have also graced the stage. The downstairs Smartbar club *(see p113)* books hot DJs.

Best Blues Clubs

The Windy City has been a center for blues since the Great Migration (1910–60), when African-Americans flooded northern cities in search of jobs, and solo bluesmen started jamming with each other at the old Maxwell Street Market. By the late 1940s they had added horns and a backbeat and amplified their instruments to create the Chicago Blues sound popularized by "Big" Willie Dixon, Howlin' Wolf, and Muddy Waters. Today you can gape at memorabilia and hear blues every night of the week at **Buddy Guy's Legends** (Map 5 F5, 754 S. Wabash Ave., 312 427 0333, www.buddyguys.com). The north side's **B.L.U.E.S.** (Map 1 C5, 2519 N. Halsted St., 773 528 1012, www.chicagobluesbar.com) and **Kingston Mines** (Map 1 C5, 2548 N. Halsted St., 773 477 4646, www.kingstonmines.com) are more gritty but not necessarily more authentic, while Downtown's **Blue Chicago** (Map 5 E2 & 5 E1, 536 & 736 N. Clark St., 312 642 6261, www.bluechicago.com) books many female performers. The swanky **Cotton Club** (Map 7 E3, 1710 S. Michigan Ave., 312 341 9787) features jazz and R&B as well as blues, while the strictly blues **Rosa's Lounge** *(see p99)* is an altogether more homey affair.

For open-air concerts, the **Chicago Blues Festival** takes place each June *(see p16)*, and there are jam sessions on sunny Sunday mornings at the new, less characterful, **Maxwell Street Market** *(see p136)*. Here, Piano C. Red with his Flat Foot Boogie Band often set up near 16th Street and Canal Street, at the south end of the market. Many of his backup players are from Elmore James Junior's blues band (Elmore Junior also sits in, as do various legends from around the city). Additionally, you can hear live Mexican and other Central American music at this market.

Steppenwolf Theatre Company

2 D3

1650 N. Halsted St., at North • 312 335 1650

>> www.steppenwolf.org Box office 11–5 Mon, 11–7 Tue–Sun

Co-founded by film actor Gary Sinise in a suburban church in 1976, this actor-focused theater company is known for its realistic performances of American dramas. Today's complex was built in 1991, and the amenities include a swanky upstairs lounge and three stages. The 515-seat Mainstage is known for stunning sets, which have incorporated suspended catwalks, thunderstorms, and moving automobiles. The big draw, however, is the high-caliber, 35-member ensemble, which now includes John Mahoney (from *Frasier*), Laurie Metcalf (from *Roseanne*), and film actor John Malkovich. Its occasional Traffic series promotes unique collaborations between artists from different disciplines. The two other theaters stage smaller productions by emerging playwrights and young theater companies. Reduced-price day-of-show tickets are available on a first-come basis from 11am daily.

Lookingglass Theatre Company

5 F1

821 N. Michigan Ave,. at Chicago • 312 337 0665

>> www.lookingglasstheatre.org

Box office open noon–showtime Tue–Sun

Co-founded by *Friends* star David Schwimmer, this highly original company occupies a modern theater housed in one of the few buildings to survive the Great Chicago Fire of 1871. It specializes in adapting classic works of literature for the stage.

Chicago Theatre *downtown jewel*

5 F3

175 N. State St., at Washington • 312 462 6363

>> www.thechicagotheatre.com Box office noon–6 Mon–Fri

This grandiose landmark, which features a seven-story auditorium, opened as a movie palace in 1921. Restored to its former glory, it is now one of the city's top venues, with a program ranging from bands like Nick Cave and the Bad Seeds to comedian Steve Harvey and touring Broadway shows.

>> *In summer months, the Chicago Theatre offers tours of its premises*

Mill

Symphony Center *world-class orchestra* 5 F4

220 S. Michigan Ave., at Adams • 312 294 3000

>> www.cso.org Box office open 10–6 Mon–Sat, 11–4 Sun

The 1904 Symphony Center is home to the Chicago Symphony Orchestra (CSO) which, under the direction of Sir George Solti, won 31 Grammy Awards. In 1997, Daniel Barenboim succeeded Solti and modernized the repertoire. Premium acoustics complement a dazzling program featuring guest musicians like Ravi Shankar.

Goodman Theatre *theater district anchor* 5 F3

170 N. Dearborn St., at Randolph • 312 443 3800

>> www.goodmantheatre.org Box office open 10–5 Mon–Fri

High-quality productions by U.S. and international playwrights are the hallmark of this award-winning, 80-year-old company. The modern complex houses an 830-seat main stage plus a smaller theater, which regularly hosts premieres of new plays. Their annual production of *A Christmas Carol* is a local favorite.

Civic Opera House *opera on the river* 4 D4

20 N. Wacker Dr., at State • 312 332 2244

>> www.lyricopera.org Box office open noon–6 Mon–Sat

With performers such as Pavarotti and Carreras gracing its stage, it's not surprising that most performances at this world-famous venue – the home of the Lyric Opera company – sell out. But even non-ticket holders can stop by to admire the its splendor, including the grand foyer. Call for details of day-of-performance tickets.

Ticket Agencies

Many concerts, sporting, and theatrical events can be reserved through **Ticketmaster** (312 559 1212; www.ticketmaster.com). Half-price tickets to same-day shows can be bought in person at **Hot Tix** booths (www.hottix.org). Branches of both outlets can be found at Tower Records (214 S. Wabash Ave. and 2301 N.Clark St.); cash only.

Gene Siskel Film Center *indie films* 5 F3

164 N. State St., at Randolph • 312 846 2800

>> www.siskelfilmcenter.com

Named for the late *Chicago Tribune* film critic, this Art Institute-affiliated institution is a cherished part of Chicago's entertainment scene. It has a café/gallery and two theaters that screen locally produced work, retrospectives, an ongoing "music in movies" series, and festivals of films from around the globe.

Jazz Showcase *non-smoking jazz* 5 E2

59 W. Grand Ave., at Clark • 312 670 2473
>> www.jazzshowcase.com
Maggiano's Little Italy: 312 644 7700; call for show times

Owner Joe Siegel has been bringing leading jazz musicians to his club for over 50 years. The venue has cabaret-style seating for 150 on a first-come basis and Maggiano's Little Italy restaurant across the street offers dinner packages, which include a reserved seat.

Joan W. & Irving B. Harris Theatre for Music & Dance *theater in Millennium Park* 5 G3

205 E. Randolph Dr., at Stetson • 312 334 7777
>> www.harristheaterchicago.org Box office noon–6 Mon–Fri

This state-of-the-art, 1,525-seat theater is located entirely underground except for the stunning glass lobby. A dozen medium-size arts organizations share the space, including the exciting Hubbard Street Dance Chicago and the adventurous Chicago Opera Theater.

Rosa's Lounge *down-home blues*

3420 W. Armitage Ave., at Kimball • 773 342 0452
Bus No. 73 & No. 82
>> www.rosaslounge.com Open Tue–Sat

The city's most welcoming blues bar is a family affair, run by drummer Tony Mangiullo and his mother, Rosa, since 1984. Chicago's best blues artists along with some out-of-towners draw a mostly local crowd. Rosa is usually behind the bar, and there's a pool table in back.

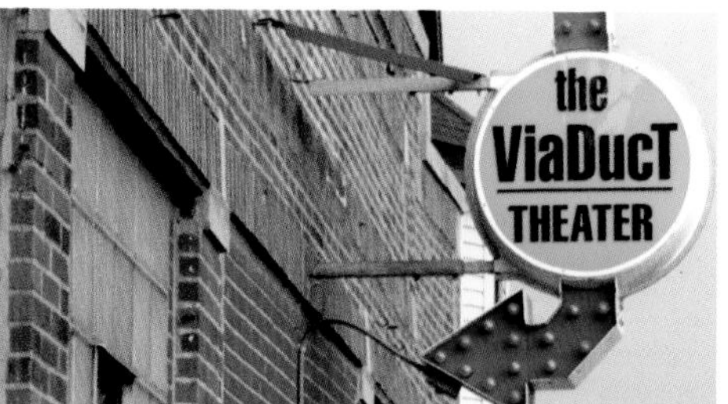

Viaduct Theater *cutting-edge performance*

3111 N. Western Ave., at Barry • 773 296 6024
Bus No. 49 & No. 77
>> www.viaducttheater.com Box office open 9–5 Mon–Fri

This former warehouse was transformed into a bustling three-theater space in 1997. The specialty here is edgy drama, live music, performance art, and film. It's a relaxed venue, attracting a young, hip crowd who appreciate the more off-beat offerings.

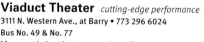

>> *The CSO plays many dates each summer at the prestigious Ravinia Festival* (see p17)

Chopin Theatre *radical performance* 2 B5

1543 W. Division St., at Ashland • 773 278 1500
>> www.chopintheatre.com Box office opens 1 hr before performance, call for reservations

This unusual theater complex started out as a Polish Community Center in 1918, and was saved from demolition by current owners Zygmunt Dyrkacz (a Polish immigrant) and Lela Headd. These days the Chopin is best known for its astonishingly eclectic programming, which runs from cutting-edge theater, film, and poetry open mics to Middle Eastern dance and live jazz. Touring Polish theater companies also make occasional appearances – Chicago has one of the largest Polish populations outside of Warsaw.

Some 500 productions a year wind up at the 226-seat main stage and 175-seat studio theater. Theatrical offerings can range from experimental drama to new plays by local African-American playwrights to cult favorites such as *Cannibal Cheerleaders on Crack*. The theater is also home base for the Guild Complex, a local cultural organization that fosters cross-cultural exchange and sponsors readings, open mics, contests, workshops, and conferences. In September, the theater is one of the venues that host Wicker Park's massive Around the Coyote arts festival *(see p18)*.

The building's white glazed terra-cotta exterior belies the opulent interior, which is dominated by a colorful and impressive grand foyer. A cushy lounge decorated with antique furniture and oriental rugs provides a appealing rest area during intermission, while photos and artwork by local painters adorn the walls.

The charming Algren café (the famous Chicago writer Nelson Algren lived locally) also forms part of the complex, and serves coffee and soft drinks which can be consumed there or brought into the theater: a BYOB policy operates in the auditorium.

Velvet Lounge *experimental jazz*

7 E4

67 E. Cermak Rd., at Michigan • 312 791 9050
» www.velvetlounge.net Shows at 9:30 Wed–Sat, 8 Sun

Named for septuagenarian owner Fred Anderson's velvety tenor sax playing, this club moved to its posh digs with the financial help of fans in 2005. Sunday jam session regulars include Anderson and members of the Association for the Advancement of Creative Musicians, which he co-founded in the late 1960s.

Spoken Word Café *music and poetry*

8 B1

4655 S. Martin Luther King Dr., at 47th • 773 373 2233
Open 8–6 Mon–Thu, 8–4 Fri, noon–4 & 7–late Sat

This intimate café in historic Bronzeville seats just 50 and features anything from blues to poetry open mics and comedy on Saturday nights. The "Love Jones" house drink (hazelnut, honey, espresso) pays tribute to the 1997 film showcasing Chicago's African-American poetry scene, which still thrives here.

Spectator Sports

With two football teams, two hockey teams, and two baseball teams, Chicago is a sports-loving town. One of the most historic places in the world to see a baseball game is the ivy-covered **Wrigley Field** (Map 1 B2, 773 404 2827, chicago.cubs.mlb.com), where the city's beloved Cubs still play. Although they tend to lose, it can still be difficult to score a ticket, but it is always possible to gain entrance by taking a tour. The South Side's White Sox have a better record and a newer stadium at **U.S. Cellular Field** (312 674 1000, chicago.whitesox.mlb.com), a.k.a "Sox Park." It has more comfortable seating and an expanded menu, and it is also a lot easier to get a seat. The Chicago Blackhawks hockey team puts on an exciting show at the west side's **United Center** (312 455 4000, www.unitedcenter.com). That's also where the famous Chicago Bulls still play basketball, only with a little less finesse than when Michael Jordan was on the team (when they won five NBA championships). American Hockey League 2002 champions the Chicago Wolves win more titles than the 'Hawks, and play at the **Allstate Arena** (847 724 4625, www.chicagowolves.com) in Rosemont. It's still easy to get a ticket for the Chicago Fire soccer team, based in their new **Bridgeview Stadium** (312 705 7200, www.mlsnet.com/mls/chf/) in the southern suburbs. The Chicago Bears football team tends to lose more often than not since winning the 1985 Superbowl: they play at the revitalized **Soldier Field** (Map 7 F2, 847 295 6600, www.chicagobears.com), which locals liken to a flying saucer caught on the old building's Neoclassical stone columns. A fun alternative is the Chicago Force, a professional women's tackle football team. They play in the spring at **Doyle Stadium** (7740 S. Western Ave., www.chicagoforcefootball.com) and often win.

» In April, the baseball season kicks off with each team's eagerly awaited Opening Day

Court Theatre *classic theater*

8 D3

5535 S. Ellis Ave., at 55th • 773 753 4472
>> www.courttheatre.org Box office open noon–5 daily

This University of Chicago-affiliated, not-for-profit theater company has been presenting classic plays ever since the success of three out-of-doors Molière productions in 1955. The comfortable 251-seat Abelson Auditorium is home to consistently high-quality work, making the journey south worthwhile.

New Apartment Lounge *jazz club*

504 E. 75th St., at Eberhart • 773 483 7728 • Ⓜ 79th St (Red Line) Jam sessions 10:30 Tue; shows 7 & 10 Fri–Sun

Best known for its Tuesday night jam sessions with eightysomething sax legend Von Freeman, this beloved dive bar expanded in 2005. There are now soft-jazz vocalists or DJs on weekends, but Tuesdays are still the real draw. After 1am, amateurs can take the stage and back up Freeman's brilliant improvisation.

eta Creative Arts Foundation

7558 S. South Chicago Ave., at 76th • 773 752 3955
>> www.etacreativearts.org • Metra stop 75th
Box office opens 1 hr before shows

Nearly all of the 100-plus original dramas presented by the eta since 1971 have been world premieres, and all were written by African-Americans. The dynamic center hosts a 200-seat theater and weekend family matinees feature young eta drama students.

Indie Music Venues

An ever-changing array of clubs nurtures Chicago's flourishing indie scene. **The Empty Bottle** (1035 N. Western Ave., 773 276 3600) books consistently high-quality acts and serves cheap beer. The non-smoking, acoustically excellent **Old Town School of Folk Music** (4544 N. Lincoln Ave., 773 728 6000) features everything from dancehall reggae to local teen rockers, and folk music. The smoky **Hideout** (Map 2 C3, 1354 W. Wabansia Ave., 773 227 4433) is off the beaten track but its roster of rock and alt-country groups draws an unpretentious crowd, making it worth the trip. The **Abbey Pub** (3420 W. Grace St., 773 478 4408) can hold 500, and books slightly bigger indie rock acts plus the occasional Irish band.

HotHouse *progressive culture*

5 F5

31 E. Balbo Ave., at Wabash • 312 362 9707

>> www.hothouse.net

Box office open noon–5 Mon–Fri & 1 hr before the show

One of the city's most luxurious venues, HotHouse offers the best in provocative musical and cultural programming, and attracts a truly diverse audience.

The club began in 1987 as an eclectic Wicker Park venue specializing in international and Afro-Caribbean music. It flourished there until 1995, when it gave up its Wicker Park base to become a not-for-profit organization linked to the Center for International Performance and Exhibition (CIPEX). Thanks to a combination of fundraising, loans, and grants, HotHouse was able to move to its current location further downtown in 1998 – and it has been gaining steadily in popularity ever since.

HotHouse works with local arts organizations to curate a varied schedule that includes world music, performance art, variety shows, and hip-hop poetry. Latin dance and folk music, avant-garde improvisers, films and open mics are also on the roster – which basically includes anything outside of the mainstream. Try to catch local jazz singer and pianist Yoko Noge, whose band fuses African and Japanese-tinged music with jazz and blues every Monday night.

The large, modern center houses an art gallery and initiated several festivals, including the Chicago World Music Festival, which is held each fall. In the main performance space, which seats 300, floor-to-ceiling windows frame the Chicago skyline, while a giant mural of a jazz band adorns the wall behind the stage. The two remaining walls are lined with large, cozy red booths, and cabaret-style tables and chairs fill the rest of the space. Seating works on a first-come, first-served basis, and while there's a two-drink minimum per person, it's not strictly enforced. There's no kitchen, but it's fine to bring in food from nearby restaurants such as the legendary Harold's Chicken Shack, at 636 S. Wabash Avenue.

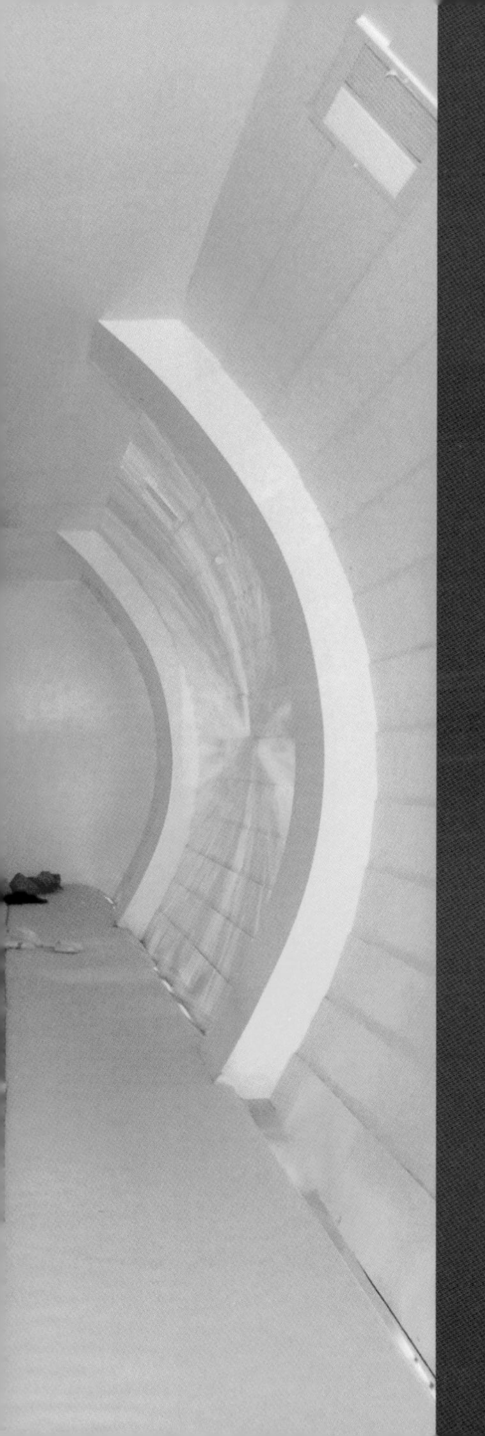

bars & clubs

The "Second City" is often associated with the gangster Al Capone and bootlegging, but the days of Prohibition are long gone and now nothing can stop Chicagoans from having a good time. Today, Chicago has an abundance of excellent nightlife venues: from exclusive cocktail lounges to friendly neighborhood hangouts and rambunctious sports bars, it's all there for the taking.

BARS & CLUBS

Chicago offers a range of bars as diverse and sophisticated as that in any major metropolis; but despite its cosmopolitan character, the city will always have a humble, Midwestern mentality. No matter how upscale its nightlife becomes, Chicagoans aren't stuck-up or jaded, respecting both opulent clubs and no-frills neighborhood bars equally. It's a revelation to party in a city with almost unlimited opportunities for nocturnal adventures and so little pretension.

Patrick Sisson

Dance Tracks and Speaker Stacks

In the early '80s, Chicago was the birthplace of house. That energy and propulsive sound still course through clubs like **Zentra** *(see p108)* and **Smartbar** *(see p113)*, but nightlife has diversified. With everything from experimental DJs at **Sonotheque** *(see p123)* to rock-oriented parties at the **Cobra Lounge** *(see p125)*, there are plenty of reasons to party.

One-of-a-Kind Treasures

Offbeat bars are a perfect antidote to the city's crowded clubs and carbon-copy Irish pubs. Add some unique destinations to your list, like bohemian **Danny's Tavern** *(see p125)*, punk-rock pub **Delilah's** *(see p111)*, reggae hotspot **Wild Hare** *(see p112)*, aviation-inspired **Jet Vodka Lounge** *(see p115)*, or quirky **Cans Bar and Canteen** *(see p125)*.

Superlative Sips

The bartending world has been shaken (and stirred) by recent trends that have made premium drinks more popular than ever, and Chicago has plenty of places to indulge. Try peerless foreign beer at **Hopleaf** *(see p114)*, drink delicious vintages at **Webster's Wine Bar** *(see p108)*, and down top-shelf tequila in various guises at **Salud** *(see p124)*.

choice nightlife

Places to Play

Nothing complements drinking like a good game, whether it's on a big-screen TV at **John Barleycorn's** *(see p110)*, or played by two attracted adults at hip lounges like **Fulton Lounge** *(see p123)* or **Spoon** *(see p108)*. A big sports town that also lays claim to having the U.S.'s first singles' bars, Chicago has plenty for both spectators and participants.

Top-Shelf Spots

For nights when you want to party like a rock star (or spend money like you are one), try some of Chicago's more upscale spots. Thanks to the stunning view at **Whiskey Sky** *(see p120)*, amazing cocktails at **Elm Street Liquors** *(see p115)*, and elite clientele at **reserve** *(see p122)*, you'll feel like a VIP just walking through the doors of these places.

Neighborhood Joints

Chicago, because of its size and diversity, is often called a city of neighborhoods. And nothing makes an area coalesce like reliable neighborhood pubs, including laid-back after-work joints like **Wabash Tap** *(see p121)* in the South Loop, **Union Park** *(see p121)* in the West Loop, or Wicker Park's **Pontiac Café** *(see p125)*, a summertime mecca.

Zentra *clubbing casbah*

2 D4

923 W. Weed St., at Fremont • 312 787 0400

>> www.zentranightclub.com Open 10pm–4am Wed–Sun

A Hindu-themed club complete with wall hangings and lush outdoor garden, Zentra is a Chicago institution offering the best in dance music. House and hip-hop rule most evenings, and local legends such as Derrick Carter, Diz, and Hiroki spin at the popular Jack Friday parties every weekend. **Adm**

Spoon *swanky singles spot*

3 F5

1240 N. Wells St., at Scott • 312 642 5522

>> www.spoonchicago.com

Open 6pm–2am Wed–Sat (to 3am Sat), 9pm–2am Sun

It's easy to strike up a conversation at this cozy cocktail bar. With its plush seats, private booths, and a loft-like second level, the interior is comfortable and inviting. It's the hippest thing on the block and draws a young, attractive, and mostly singles crowd.

Webster's Wine Bar *intimate wine bar*

2 B2

1480 W. Webster Ave., at Clyborn • 773 868 0608

>> www.websterwinebar.com Open to 2am daily (to 3am Sat)

Long couches, candlelight, savory bites, and an extensive list of wines from around the world combine to make this one of Chicago's most romantic spots. A Latin inscription near the door reads "in wine there is truth." After a night sipping the fine wine here, everything does seem to fall nicely into place.

Wrightwood Tap *neighborhood tavern*

1 B5

1059 W. Wrightwood Ave., at Seminary • 773 549 4949

>> www.bar1events.com

Open 4pm–2am Mon–Fri, 11am–3am Sat, 11am–2am Sun

It's not surprising that this charming pub exudes a welcoming atmosphere – it was once someone's house. The retro bar attracts a laid-back crowd, and occasional acoustic sets and cheap beer make this the type of friendly bar that should be on every corner.

Lilly's *offbeat music club*

2 D2

2513 N. Lincoln Ave., at Altgeld • 773 525 2422

Open 9pm–2am daily

A former blues club, Lilly's has been resurrected as a rock venue and smoky, underground dive bar. Bands (usually student groups from nearby DePaul University) rock out as patrons watch from the tiny balcony or a series of booths. Cheap booze, especially the loaded Long Island Iced Tea, is an added attraction. **Adm**

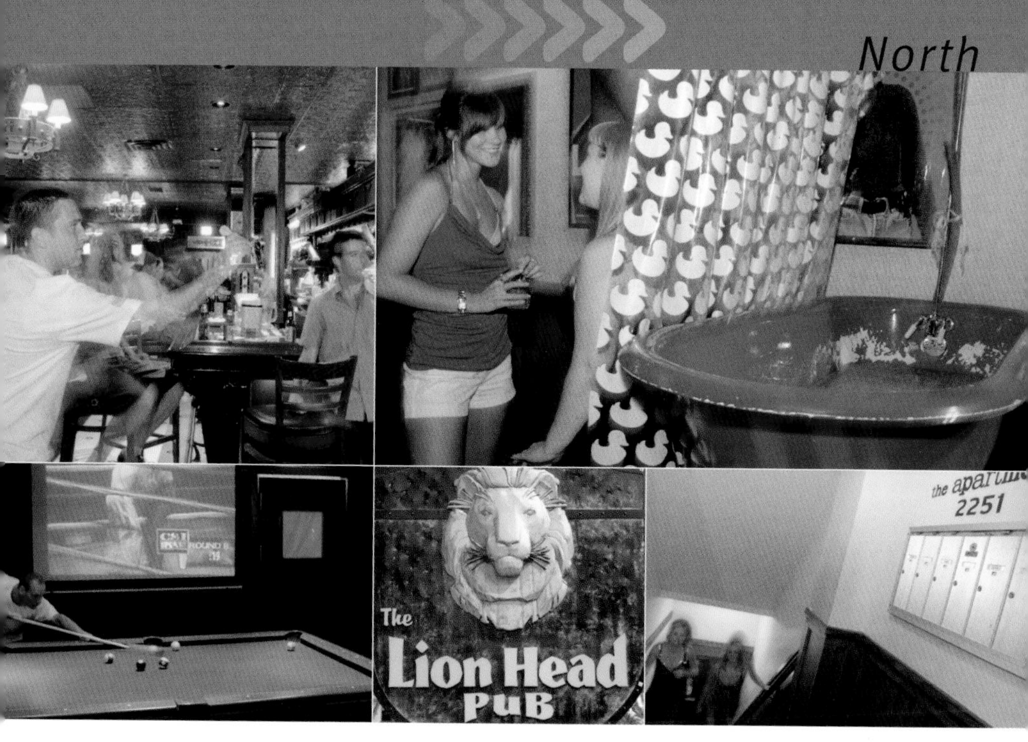

Apartment/Lion Head Pub

3 E1

2251 N. Lincoln Ave., at Webster • 773 348 5100
>> www.lionheadpub.net
Apartment open 9pm–2am Wed–Sat (to 3am Sat); Lion Head open 3pm–2am Mon–Fri, 11am–3am Sat; 11am–2am Sun

This two-in-one bar combination is a nightspot with a split personality and is ideal for those who want variety with minimum effort. Couples or groups of friends may find this place is able to keep everyone happy.

The upstairs Apartment lounge looks like the pad of a twentysomething party animal. Music posters of artists from Snoop Dogg to Nirvana cover the walls, a big TV sits in the middle of the living room, and the kitchen lies in disarray. This setup is cleverly transformed into a bar: the kitchen table becomes the main bar, the "apartment's" bathtub is filled with ice and beer and used as a side bar, beds serve as intimate seating while, in the "living room," couches provide plenty of space to relax. A few finishing touches, such as tapestries on the ceiling, colored lights, and a fireplace capped with a huge moose head, lend the interior additional character. The bumping R&B and rap tunes and the crowd – mostly college grads from nearby Lincoln Park – give this bar the feel of a real house party (minus the free beer).

Downstairs, the Lion Head pub is all testosterone. Though it bills itself as an English pub, it's actually more like a loud-and-proud American sports bar: a maze of tables surrounds the two main bars, and most of the chairs are pointed towards the bank of televisions broadcasting non-stop sports. A 3,000-song digital jukebox pumps out classic rock and metal tunes, and most of the guys order Table Topper beer pitchers, huge glass cylinders of beer that provide dedicated drinkers with a way of avoiding the long wait for the next pint. Various perennial bar favorites – such as pool, foosball, and the popular Golden Tee golf video game – are located throughout the pub.

Aliveone *long live live music*

1 C5

2683 N. Halsted St., at Schubert • 773 348 9800

>> www.aliveone.com Open to 2am Sun–Fri, 2pm–3am Sat

No other bar in the city is more devoted to music than this dark, smoky Lincoln Park spot, whose jukebox is crammed with "in concert" recordings of classic rock and jam bands. Everything from Led Zeppelin and Jimi Hendrix to the Grateful Dead gets spun inside Aliveone, which, with its massive display of framed rock star photos and vintage concert posters, is a temple of sorts to the gods of rock 'n' roll. A young, music-savvy clientele comes here most evenings to line the bar and sip the impressive selection of on-tap micro-brewed American beers. There's a pool table area near the back of the bar, but it's usually converted into seating early in the evening to accommodate the crowd. As an added musical draw, the back room – a space filled with wild, colorful paintings and posters, and lounge seating – has a separate bar and often hosts DJs on weekends.

John Barleycorn *classic Chicago tavern*

3 E1

658 W. Belden Ave., at Lincoln • 773 348 8899

>> www.johnbarleycorn.com

Open 3pm–2am Mon–Fri, 11am–3am Sat, 9am–2am Sun

Opened in the 1890s and run as a speakeasy during Prohibition, this bar shows its age, but in a good way. The cavernous interior is all dark wood and model ships, creating a classy setting for the boisterous party atmosphere. There's also an outside patio.

Spin *decadent dance club*

1 B3

800 W. Belmont Ave., at Halsted • 773 327 7711

>> www.spin-nightclub.com

Open to 2am Mon–Fri, 2pm–3am Sat, 2pm–2am Sun

Energetic, eclectic, and a bit risqué, Spin attracts a mix of straight and gay clubbers to some of the city's wildest parties. VJs "spin" the latest music videos, but it's events like the Friday Shower Contest that give this club its free-spirited reputation. **Adm**

Delilah's *punk-rock paradise*

1 A5

2771 N. Lincoln Ave., at Diversey • 773 472 2771
>> www.delilahschicago.com
Open to 2am Sat–Mon (to 3am Sat)

An iconoclast adrift in a sea of conservative bars, Delilah's stands out as one of the most unique spots in the city. Its well-deserved reputation as a punk bar is aided by its wild interior (huge, bug-eyed murals and a hallway littered with the remains of a broken computer), cheap drinks, and excellent music selection, which includes punk, ska, rockabilly, and country spun by local guest DJs. But Delilah's is so much more than a standard punk bar: it stocks one of the largest selections of premium imported beers in Chicago, regularly holds beer-tasting events, has a well-chosen range of wines, and offers well over 100 different varieties of whiskey. The owner even distills his own house brand. In addition, there are often movie screenings on the bar's small televisions. A place this original deserves to be experienced.

Sidetrack *gay and lesbian video bar*

1 C3

3349 N. Halsted St., at Buckingham • 773 477 9189
>> www.sidetrackchicago.com Open 3pm–2am daily (to 3 Sat)

This flashy, multi-level gay bar is an anchor of the Boystown neighborhood. Each of the four large rooms features slick modern furniture and TVs blasting out music videos and musicals. In summer, the enormous wooden rooftop deck provides a perfect setting to enjoy one of the bar's signature frozen drinks.

Hydrate *upscale gay lounge and club*

1 B3

3458 N. Halsted St., at Newport • 773 975 9244
>> www.hydratechicago.com
Open 8pm–4am Sun–Fri, 6pm–5am Sat

This sleek venue has a fancy cocktail lounge at the front and a large dance floor out back that is regularly presided over by famous DJs like Frankie Knuckles. The club has an inventive, constantly changing decor and a "mister" to keep dancers cool and hydrated. **Adm**

>> *For late-night eats on the North Side, grab a memorable hot dog at The Wieners Circle* (see p32)

Wild Hare *the nation's reggae heart*

1 B2

3530 N. Clark St., at Eddy • 773 327 4273
>> www.wildharereggae.com
Open 8pm–2am daily (to 3am Sat)

It's only natural to assume that any bar that considers itself the reggae capital of America must have an owner who's smoked a little too much weed. But that's not the case with Wild Hare, a truly uplifting music club that easily lives up to its lofty claim – and its well-deserved reputation. Inside, a huge blacklight mural depicting the evolution of the Rastaman spells things out for those that still don't believe in the club's devotion to the musical genre. Originally known by the cumbersome title Wild Hare & Singing Armadillo Frog Sanctuary, this club books the best reggae bands on the planet, regularly bringing Jamaican artists such as Yellowman and Burning Spear to Chicago and offering stage time to local acts like Aswah Greggorri. The more modern dancehall sounds are downplayed in favor of classic roots reggae and there are live performances seven nights a week on the well-lit, elevated stage. There aren't many seats, so be ready to dance along with the booming bass sounds emanating from the speakers for most of the evening.

Since Jamaican bands play here so often, the club has also become a home-away-from-home of sorts for many of Chicago's Jamaican immigrants, and island culture is evident everywhere. The bar features a potent home-made rum punch, along with signature Jamaican brew Red Stripe. The bar also reaches out to the neighborhood as a whole. Special events, such as post-game parties after Cubs' baseball games (Wrigley Field is just nearby) and free admission for ladies on Wednesday nights, are attempts to spread the club's positive vibrations. **Adm**

Smartbar *for true clubbers*

1 A2

3730 N. Clark St, at Waveland • 773 549 4140
>> www.smartbarchicago.com
Open 10pm–4am Wed–Sat (to 5am Sat)

With a sleek interior and an eye-popping mural, this late-night legend is dance floor-focused: just feel the booming musical crossfire created by the state-of-the-art speakers. On the decks, expect international DJs and sets from members of bands like New Order. **Adm**

Hungry Brain *atmospheric watering hole*

2319 W. Belmont Ave., at Oakley • 773 935 2118 • Ⓜ Belmont (Brown Line), then bus No. 77 Open 8pm–late Tue–Sun

Filled with thrift store couches, strings of Christmas lights and a small stage that presents occasional jazz jams, this bar has more character than most. Serving up cheap beer with a no-nonsense attitude, it attracts hipsters and barflies seeking somewhere far removed from the singles scene.

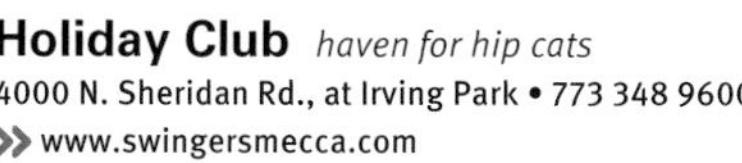

Holiday Club *haven for hip cats*

1 C1

4000 N. Sheridan Rd., at Irving Park • 773 348 9600
>> www.swingersmecca.com
Open 6pm–2am daily (to 3am Sat, from 10am Sun)

Resembling a swinging 1950s bachelor pad, this place has more sparkle than a Vegas show. Check out the photo booth and the cozy seating, try some old-school cocktails and, if you've overindulged on Saturday night, stop by Sunday morning for the reviving retro brunch.

Crew *upscale gay sports bar*

4804 N. Broadway, at Racine • 773 784 2739 • Ⓜ Lawrence (Red Line) Open 11:30am–2am Mon–Fri, 11am–2am Sat & Sun
>> www.worldsgreatestbar.com

This sports-themed gay bar makes many regular sports bars seem like second-stringers. The gourmet bar and food selection, neighborhood feel, and vast TV screen score points, while the clean, modern design and humorous touches avoid the usual frat boy frumpiness.

>> *Crew is next door to Chicago's famous Green Mill Jazz Club* (see p92)

Carol's *classic Uptown country hangout*

4659 N. Clark St., at Leland • 773 334 2402 • Ⓜ Lawrence (Red Line) Open 9–2am Mon & Tue, 11am–4am Wed–Sun (to 5am Sat)

Chicago's Uptown used to be a haven for country-and-western music, and this spectacular dive bar is one of the last remaining venues. A dingy room filled with cafeteria tables and affable bartenders, Carol's attracts a late-night crowd on weekends. Strap on that ten-gallon hat and sing along to the excellent house band.

Big Chicks *sister act*

5024 N. Sheridan Rd., at Carmen • 773 728 5511 • Ⓜ Argyle (Red Line) Open to 2am Mon–Fri, 3pm–3am Sat, 11am–2am Sun **>> www.bigchicks.com**

A gay- and lesbian-friendly bar that also welcomes straight drinkers, Big Chicks is the epitome of openness and hospitality. The small, cozy space has a comfortable bar, plenty of woman-themed art on the walls, and an outdoor patio. The drinks are cheap.

Hopleaf *beer lovers' paradise*

5148 N. Clark St., at Foster • 773 334 9851 • Ⓜ Berwyn (Red Line) >> www.hopleaf.com Open 3pm–2am daily (to 3am Sat)

Boasting an exhaustive beer list and a subdued interior, Hopleaf is a perfect spot to sit and savor a strong pint. Beer isn't just a drink, it's an art form at this popular Andersonville bar. Literally hundreds of brews are available in bottles and on draft, including dozens of micro-brewed American ales and one of the city's largest selections of Belgian beer such as Chimay and Delirium Tremens. (Note: many have an above-average alcohol content and pack a potent punch.) Several brands are even served, with reverence, in specialized, unusually shaped glasses.

A front bar and upper mezzanine are set aside for serious drinking, while the back room serves dinner, with a menu focusing on Belgian cuisine such as *moules frites* and braised rabbit. A soundtrack featuring cool jazz, and brick walls displaying colorful, retro beer posters add to the mellow mood.

Elm Street Liquors *fashionable hang-out* 3 G5

12 W. Elm St., at State • 312 337 3200

>> www.elmstreetliquors.com

Open to 2am Mon–Fri, noon–3am Sat, 3pm–9pm Sun

This hip slice of New York-style nightlife lies hidden behind an unmarked door on a side street and boasts just the kind of creative cocktail menu and minimalist design that attract bar-hopping socialites. Grab a seat, sample a signature champagne cocktail, and chill.

Howl at the Moon *the original karaoke* 5 E2

26 W. Hubbard St., at Dearborn • 312 863 7427

>> www.howlatthemoon.com Open to 2am daily (from 7pm Sun)

A rowdy but not rough piano bar devoid of pretension, Howl at the Moon is all about fun music, cheap drinks, and losing your inhibitions. Charismatic dueling piano players belt out audience requests and always keep the energy level elevated. Potent drinks help fuel the audience sing-along. **Adm**

Jet Vodka Lounge *swanky spirits* 2 D4

1551 Sheffield Ave., at North • 312 440 9140

>> www.gojetgo.com Open 8pm–late Wed–Sun

A playful cross between a private jet and a cocktail bar, Jet Vodka Lounge is aerodynamic, petite, and posh. If you look runway ready and want to party, this is the place to take off. Designed to look like the inside of a Boeing 777, the cozy nightclub runs with the aviation theme, boasting servers dressed as flight attendants, an airport terminal-style entrance, and curved walls bathed in colored lights and video screens. But it's clear there's no coach class on this flight. The staff serves an upscale and chic clientele who request private tables in the VIP cabin area and personal bottles of booze stylishly presented in ice buckets. Most guests at least sample the high-end vodka selection, which contains some 130 types from around the globe. If you have trouble sorting though the list, a selection of flights and flavored varieties are available. **Adm**

Sound-bar *highly evolved clubbing* 5 E2

226 W. Ontario St., at Franklin • 312 787 4480

>> www.sound-bar.com Open 9pm–4am Thu–Sat (to 5am Sat)

Though Chicago is recognized around the world as a capital of house music, it lacks the kind of behemoth dance clubs common to many major cities. Or at least it did until this multi-hued, multi-sensory monster arrived. Attracting the world's best DJs with its state-of-the-art dance floor, this fashionable nightspot gives club kids and big spenders plenty of reasons to dance, drink, and get debauched. Sound-bar's interior is as colorful and showy as a peacock. The two-level space is divided into several rooms that feature sleek, minimalist furniture and cutting-edge modern design. The tangerine-colored lobby bar greets guests as they enter the club, but dominating the ground floor is the large rectangular dance floor, with its maze of smoke machines and video projectors. It boasts one of the best sound systems in the city, giving the high-profile headlining DJs a perfect platform to get the crowd dancing.

The lower level is a little more sedate: the colored, glass-encased rooms – each with its own bar – are made for lounging and are where many of the club's top-notch resident DJs like John Curley, PNS, and Johnny Chaos spin laid-back sets all night. The dress code is strictly fashionable, ranging from the casually cool to the outlandishly exhibitionist, and guests are expected to check their coat at the door. They should also count on spending lots of cash, since cocktails come at a premium. Mixed drinks and martinis are the norm, as is bottle service (reserving a table and ordering an expensive bottle of hard liquor, which comes with complimentary mixers). Sound-bar is a big-money move, but that's perhaps to be expected at a venue where people want to be seen and go wild. **Adm**

Rockit Bar and Grill *upscale sports bar* 5 F2

22 W. Hubbard St., at State • 312 645 6000
>> www.rockitbarandgrill.com
Open 11:30am–2am daily (to 3am Sat, from 11am Sun)

This River North hangout occupying a lavishly appointed two-level warehouse is a step up from the frat-boy formula found in most sports bars. The ground floor is a cross between restaurant and lounge space, filled with high-backed leather chairs and secluded booths, while the open and airy upper level is a more traditional bar area, where fixtures include plasma-screens and a pair of custom-made pool tables.

Rockit's flashy design is courtesy of Nate Berkus, personal designer to Oprah Winfrey, but the cool-and-classy look isn't all it has to offer. Just as important is the delectable menu. This is bar food as imagined by a master chef; comfort food transformed into *cuisine*. Menu items such as the delectable sweet potato fries sprinkled with brown sugar, white bean hummus, or curry onion rings are perfect for satisfying a late-night craving, while those searching for dinner can choose from an inventive and well-executed menu based around pizzas and sandwiches. Or try the signature dish, the indulgent Rockit Burger made with exquisitely prepared Kobe beef. The cocktail menu is equally eclectic, featuring drinks such as caramel apple martini and fruity Rockit punch to satisfy a sweet tooth, along with a beer list that offers a good selection of American and European brews.

The music is an updated mix of classic and 90s rock, and the venue draws a crowd of beautiful young bar-hoppers – which is no surprise considering that the two owners, Billy Dec and Brad Young, are veteran promoters on the city's club scene. Unlike a regular sports bar, the real game isn't the one that's being broadcast on the screens in the bar – it's the one being played out between the attractive singles in the lower-level lounge all trying to meet someone special.

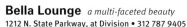

Bella Lounge *a multi-faceted beauty*

1212 N. State Parkway, at Division • 312 787 9405

>> www.bellalounge.com Open to 2am daily (to 3am Sat)

This gorgeous cocktail lounge and restaurant attracts the cream of the Gold Coast neighborhood. Bella comprises several different sections (including a gleaming bar and leather-clad front lounge), which keeps the well-dressed crowd circulating and sipping cocktails, such as the bar's signature lemon-flavored Bella Drop.

Cactus *Chicago's "beach" party*

3 G5

1112 N. State St., at Cedar • 312 642 5999

>> www.cactusgoldcoast.com Open 11am–2am daily (to 3 Sat)

After spending time at this Gold Coast bar, it's not hard to see why its motto is "Man Vs. Margarita." Cactus is an ideal spot to sip frozen drinks like the fruity Rum Runner and soak up the summer sun. With reggae and laid-back grooves playing, the beach is the only thing missing from this year-round Spring Break party.

Le Passage *upscale, underground lounge*

5 F1

937 N. Rush St., at Walton • 312 255 0022

>> www.lepassage.tv Open 9pm–4am Thu–Sat (to 5am Sat)

An exclusive and chic late-night club, this is one of the city's most popular nightspots. Customers enter via an alley and descend a narrow staircase. Inside, Le Passage exudes class, with its plush furniture and astrological frescos. It's appropriate decor, since many a star has been spotted within. **Adm**

Drinks With a View

The best view in Chicago belongs to the elegant **Signature Lounge** (www.signatureroom.com), a bar located on the 96th floor of the Hancock Building *(see p144)*. Guests can snack on appetizers and sip cocktails as they gaze out on views that go for miles. A close contender is the intimate **Whiskey Sky**, located just a few blocks away on the top of the posh W Chicago Lakeshore *(see p157)*. The sleek, minimalist bar, filled with plush black couches, offers a stunning panorama of Lake Michigan – along with a glimpse of part of the city's skyline. The comparatively low-lying **Rock Bottom Brewery** (Map 5 F2, 1 W. Grand Ave., www.rockbottom.com) doesn't offer a such a pretty view, but drinking their craft-brewed beer on the rooftop patio is still a treat.

Chicago Legends *an older clubbing set*

7 E3

2109 S. Wabash Ave., at 21st • 312 326 0300
Open 3pm–2am Wed–Fri & Sun, 7pm–3am Sat

If you're looking for a more mature crowd, head over to Chicago Legends, where 25 is the minimum age you need to be to get in the door. This massive club spices things up with everything from rap to live blues and jazz acts. The dress code here is also grown up; don't come sporting athletic attire or gym shoes. **Adm**

Junior's Sports Lounge *game on*

6 B2

724 S. Halsted St., at Maxwell • 312 421 2277
» www.juniorschicago.com
Open 11am–2am Mon–Fri, 10am–3am Sat, 10am–2am Sun

Despite the dozens of flat-screen TVs that cover every surface of this sports bar's modern interior (including one in each booth), Junior's doesn't give you a sports overload. In fact, it's a very relaxed place to spectate and savor gourmet appetizers and beer.

Wabash Tap *music saloon*

7 E1

1233 S. Wabash Ave., at Roosevelt • 312 360 9488
Open 11am–2 am daily (to 3am Sat)

This South Side bar was built for ditching your cares, clinking plenty of glasses and stretching the happy hour into a whole evening. The beer is cheap, the menu of stick-to-your-guts bar food is satisfying, and the patrons are friendly and outgoing. A cover is charged when bands play on the small stage.

Tantrum *martinis for the in-crowd*

6 D1

1023 S. State St., at 11th • 312 939 9160
Open to 2am Mon–Sat (to 3am Sat)

The plush chairs, tapered light fixtures, and a color palette of yellow, green and purple help make Tantrum's cozy interior feel like a warm embrace. Or maybe that's the feeling you get from sampling one too many items from the bar's excellent flavored (and moderately priced) martini list.

Union Park *massive watering hole*

228 S. Racine Ave., at Jackson • 312 243 9002
» www.unionparkchicago.com
Open 11am–2am daily (to 3am Sat)

A relaxed neighborhood pub where the loyal patrons can stake a claim at the bar, order dinner and watch the game on one of the bar's TVs. And of course, nothing attracts the crowds like the inexpensive beer, sangria, and dangerously affordable martinis.

reserve *high-class hangout*

4 C3

858 W. Lake St., at Peoria • 312 455 1111

>> www.reserve-chicago.com

Open 9pm–2am Tue–Fri, 9pm–3am Sat

The beautiful people flock to this break-the-bank club, turning its Asian-themed interior into a veritable runway. Located in West Loop's Warehouse District, reserve's shoddy neighborhood belies its upscale ambitions. The lower level is a lounge with a beautiful bar accented with a golden, tree-shaped sculpture and brimming with low-slung couches – perfect for sitting and sipping pricey cocktails and champagne. Bottle service – the relatively expensive practise of purchasing a bottle of top-shelf liquor, which is served with a selection of mixers – is very popular among the club's moneyed clientele. Upstairs, the long dance floor is lined by a slim bar on one side and an elevated DJ booth on the other that pumps out high-energy music. It's an ideal setting for enjoyment and indulgence. Expect a cover charge on weekends.

Funky Buddha Lounge *multicultural mix*

4 C2

728 W. Grand Ave., at Halstead • 312 666 1695

>> www.funkybuddha.com Open 9pm–2am daily (to 3am Sat)

A fusion of Moroccan lounge, Eastern art museum, and nightclub, Funky Buddha's U-shaped space is cozy but never crowded. The eclectic attitude carries over to the stage and DJ booth that feature everything from hip-hop stars to local open-mic nights. There's also a strictly enforced non-smoking room. **Adm**

Sports Bars

With Chicago's many diehard fans, the sports bar is a major civic institution. One of the most famous is **Cubby Bear Lounge** (Map 1 B2, 1059 W. Addison St., 773 327 1662), a post-game destination located across the street from the legendary Wrigley Field *(see p101)*. Down the street is **Slugger's** (Map 1 B2, 3540 N. Clark St., 773 248 0055), a cavernous pub with its own batting cages that swells with ranks of eager Cubs fans on game day. **Kincaide's** (Map 2 D2, 950 W. Armitage Ave., 773 348 0010) is another massive, beer-filled temple to all things sports. Finally, the multi-level **Hunt Club** (Map 3 G5, 1100 N. State St., 312 988 7887) offers a more refined place to watch the game, and with its multiple TVs you can watch up to seven games at once.

Fulton Lounge *libidinous lounge* 4 C3

955 W. Fulton Market, at Morgan • 312 942 9500

>> www.fultonlounge.com Open to 2am Mon–Sat (to 3am Sat)

This refined bar offers a crowded, charged atmosphere that's not so boisterous that it prevents you from having a conversation with friends. Slightly hidden in an unassuming section of the West Loop, Fulton Lounge is also very inviting, with wide French doors opening onto a large, breezy front patio.

Inside, a glass-topped bar cuts through one part of the long, exposed brick building. The rest of the space is dotted with stylish couches and chairs – coveted real estate when this place gets packed. Sharply dressed singles, many coming from nearby Randolph Street's restaurant row for after-dinner drinks, turn up to mingle and flirt. Fulton Lounge offers a standard array of chic cocktails and has a rotating, seasonal drink menu that leans toward sweet, fruity libations. But the real draw at this off-the-beaten path bar is its upbeat mood.

Sonotheque *sophisticated lounge of sound* 4 A1

1444 W. Chicago Ave., bet. Ashland & Noble • 312 226 7600

>> www.sonotheque.net

Open 9pm–2am Mon–Thu, 7pm–2am Fri & Sun, 7pm–3am Sat

From the understated modern design to the quality DJs, every aspect of this hip bar is dedicated to delivering a high-end sensory experience to a very urban, music-savvy crowd. A cascade of solid steel tiles tumbles down the exterior of the venue and draws clubbers into a small lobby area. The darkened main room, filled with sleek couches and textured wall decorations, surrounds a cocoon-like glass DJ booth, across from which is a long, dimly lit bar that is capped with a pair of TVs playing esoteric videos.

The layout resembles a slick aircraft hanger, yet the club's most important component is the excellent sound system. Everything from house and hip-hop to reggae and Indian beats is in the mix, and the club's (and the city's best) promoters routinely book top national and international talent. **Adm**

darkroom *photo-themed boho bar*

2210 W. Chicago Ave., at Leavitt • 773 276 1411 • Bus No. 66
>> www.darkroombar.com Open 8pm–2am daily (to 3am Sat)

An enclave for local hipsters, darkroom exudes cool. The interior is decorated with portraits by local photographers, the wrap-around bar is inlaid with photos, and cheap drinks and a dance floor attract a large crowd. Make a move for one of the black booths, tune into the beats, and wait for something to develop.

Vintage Wine Bar *eclectic wine tasting* 2 A5

1942 W. Division St., at Winchester • 773 772 3400
>> www.vintage-chicago.com
Open 5pm–2am Mon–Fri, 5pm–3am Sat, 5pm–1am Sun

A snub to pretentious wine snobs, Vintage subscribes to a more egalitarian philosophy of wine drinking and appreciation. The bar's wine list focuses on less popular vintages and regions but doesn't sacrifice quality. The funky interior encourages the loungey, laid-back vibe.

Salud Tequila Lounge *tequila hotspot* 2 A4

1471 N. Milwaukee Ave., at Honore • 773 235 5577
>> www.saludlounge.com Open to 2am daily (to 2:30am Sat)

This sophisticated bar proves there's more to tequila than a bitter taste and bad hangovers. Salud serves over 80 types of the infamous Mexican spirit, including special reserve selections. Some, like the *anejo* varieties, are so rich and smooth you can sip and savor rather than slam. For a different angle, Salud's cocktails exhibit a similar level of taste and refinement. Fruity concoctions like the Tequila Mockingbird have no hint of the main ingredient, and even the potent Margaritas lack the typical bite. Alternatively, the tequila flights are perfect for sampling three different types of this drink.

Inside, the bar has a riotous look, with stucco walls, a tree-shaped feature bearing bottles of tequila, and murals that depict the distillation process. A small patio offers extra space in summer. You can always order a beer at Salud, but that kind of defeats the purpose of coming here.

Pontiac Café *a perfect people-watching patio* 2 A4

1531 N. Damen Ave., at North • 773 252 7767
Open 11am–2am Sun–Fri, 11am–3am Sat

It may occupy a former garage near a busy intersection, but Pontiac Café is a charming place to kick back, especially on the patio, which provides ample space to sit, drink and watch the crowds pass by. Things get wilder on Friday nights with the Rock 'n' Roll Karaoke, when would-be singers get a live backing band.

Cans Bar and Canteen *kitsch flashback* 2 A3

1640 N. Damen Ave., at Concord • 773 227 2277
>> www.cansbar.com
Open to 2am Mon–Fri, 10am–2am Sat & Sun

This tongue-in-cheek tribute to the 80s has rock pouring out of the stereo and vintage video games to play on. The beer selection features plenty of canned varieties, including cheap standbys like Pabst Blue Ribbon, served more for their ironic value than for their taste.

Quenchers *an alternative alehouse*

2401 N. Western Ave., at Fullerton • 773 276 9730 • Bus No. 74
>> www.quenchers.com Open 11am–2am daily (to 3am Sat)

This Logan Square hangout has all the amenities of chilling at a friend's apartment, and then some. The interior is worn-in and welcoming and Quenchers' bonus features, such as a selection of beers from around the globe and free popcorn, catapult it into that rare list of exceptional neighborhood bars.

Sublime DJ Bars

Chicago has plenty of places to groove on the dance floor, but some spots favor the more stationary music fan. Multimedia effects meet eclectic music at **Rodan** (Map 2 A4, 1530 N. Milwaukee Ave., www.rodan.ws), a hipster hotspot that often features performances by local DJs and video artists. When you're looking for an alternative to dance beats, rock out at the semi-polished but punk **Cobra Lounge** (Map 4 A3, 235 N. Ashland Ave., 312 226 6300), where the DJs spin guitar-driven grooves. For a more chilled night, check out **Danny's Tavern** (Map 2 A2, 1951 W. Dickens Ave., 773 489 6457), a converted house in Bucktown that hosts everything from rare soul and funk nights to live jazz and experimental electronic music nights.

streetlife

To see the true Chicago, you must explore beyond the Sears Tower and deep-dish pizza. Veer off the beaten track to discover neighborhoods with a small-town feel. Join the joggers and dog-walkers making the most of the gorgeous lakefront on a sunny morning. Dip into ethnic enclaves for a taste of the immigrant experience. Every corner provides a new perspective on a city in constant motion.

Devon Avenue *South Asian flavor*

Devon Ave., bet. California & Damen
Ⓜ Loyola (Red Line) then bus No. 155
>> www.devonavenue.com

This main artery of the local Indian and Pakistani population is completely lacking in architectural charm. However, it makes up for its cheap-looking signage and battered storefronts with plenty of South Asian atmosphere. Close your eyes and you could be in Mumbai or Delhi: women chatter animatedly as they sift through bolts of gold-threaded sari silks, older men in white *kurtas* congregate on benches, and shopkeepers sing the praises of cheap phone cards.

If it's food you want, the choices are endless. Just off Devon Avenue, **Hema's Kitchen** (6406 N. Oakley Ave.), run by a very friendly woman who will urge you to fatten up, offers delicious home cooking, while **Indian Garden** (2548 W. Devon Ave.) is a more formal dining space. For treats on the go, check out the containers at the **Patel Brothers** grocery store (2610 W. Devon Ave.).

Boystown *Chicago's gay main street*

1 C3

There's no mistaking this longtime hub of gay life and commerce: if shop names such as Gay Mart and Bad Boys don't clue you in, just look at the rainbow spires jutting skyward on the end of every block.

While a few storefronts do display mannequins in leather and chains, the mood is relatively tame during the week: Boystown really comes alive in the evenings and on weekends, especially along North Halsted, where friendly crowds spill out of its many bars and clubs. **Roscoe's** (No. 3356, www.roscoes.com), which hosts events such as "wet boxer nights," pulls in a young see-and-be-seen crowd, while an older clientele loves **Sidetrack** *(see p111)* for its loungey atmosphere and roof deck. **Circuit** (No. 3641, www.circuitclub.com) is the strip's dance mecca, and **Spin** *(see p110)* draws clubbers with theme nights, as well as its infamous "shower contests." For late-night munchies, everyone heads east to the 24-hour **Melrose Restaurant** (3233 N. Broadway).

Lakeview & Wrigleyville *punk haven* 1 B3

The heart of Lakeview, around the Clark Street/Belmont Avenue intersection, hit a high (or low, depending on who's talking) in the 1980s when clubs, tattoo parlors, and goth stores moved in to cater to the punk kids who regularly assembled here. The kids still hang out, but the seediness has largely gone. Meanwhile, nearby Wrigley Field lures in jocks and sports nuts, and the gay community has a presence here thanks to the proximity of Boystown. This mish-mash of subcultures makes for a unique area that resists easy classification.

One constant is music: both the live and the recorded varieties have always been a big part of the scene here. Touring rock and pop acts play at **Metro** *(see p94)*, and the popular club **Berlin** (954 W. Belmont Ave., www.berlinchicago.com) has been going strong for over 20 years. The rock-oriented **Record Emporium** (3346 N. Paulina St.), which bills itself as the "last of the Old Time Record Stores," asserts its independence with strong opinions, frequent in-store performances, and annual cookouts.

There is also a focus on vintage clothes and clubwear, especially on Belmont Avenue. **Ragstock** (No. 812, www.ragstock.com) has everything from denims to kimonos, and **Belmont Army Navy Surplus** (No. 945, www.belmontarmy.com) stocks skateboards, new shoes, and used clothing in addition to military gear. Over on Clark Street, **Medusa's Circle** (No. 3268, www.medusacircle.com) offers bizarre garb linked to any number of musical subcategories.

For fans of ethnic food, the area is a smorgasbord of inexpensive restaurants. There's a Thai place on almost every block, with sushi coming in a close second. More unusual flavors are served up at **Mama Desta's Red Sea** Ethiopian Restaurant (3216 N. Clark St.), where you mop up spicy mixes of meat and vegetables with bread-like *injera*. And **Ann Sather** *(see p28)* is a weekend must for its pancakes and cinnamon rolls.

Lincoln Square *old and new worlds meet*

Ⓜ Western (Brown Line)
>> www.lincolnsquare.org

The center of Chicago's German community for many years, this slowly gentrifying, village-like neighborhood still retains its European flavor, complete with small shops and a tiny square. More recent stores and cafés have added some flair and a bit more energy to the diagonal main drag, Lincoln Avenue, especially between Lawrence and Montrose avenues.

You can still hear the native tongue spoken across the counter of the charmingly old-fashioned **Meyer Delicatessen** (No. 4750, www.delimeyer.com), while at the faux-gingerbread **Chicago Brauhaus** (No. 4732, www.chicagobrauhaus.com), robust diners knock back steins of pilsner as they sing and sway along to traditional oom-pah music. Across the street in the square, there are usually a few couples and kids in strollers munching on the scrumptious pastries and desserts from **Café Selmarie** (No. 4729).

The local shops tend more toward the friendly than the über-fashionable. Browse the vinyl at **Laurie's Planet of Sound** (No. 4639) and check out **Traipse**'s (No. 4724, www.traipseshoes.com) selection of cool shoes. Not a museum but a shop, the **Museum of Decorative Arts** (No. 4611) is located in a landmark building designed by Louis Sullivan, and is a great spot for buying anything from stationery to hats.

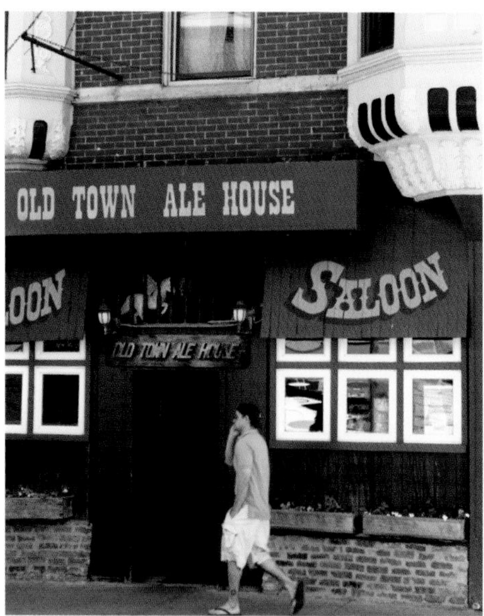

Old Town *cobblestone charm* 3 F4

Though the 19th-century character of the area has been compromised by gentrification, it's not hard to find glimpses of the original Old Town – for example in the (private but visible) cobblestone Gaslight Courtyard on the east side of the 1400 block of Wells Street, and in the faded ads for long-gone stores painted onto the sides of buildings. Old Town had its heyday in the 1960s and 70s, which was when the famed comedy improv troupe **The Second City** started up. It's still here *(see p90)*, and over the years performers and students alike have frequented the nearby traditional saloon, the **Old Town Ale House** (219 W. North Ave.). Don't confuse it with the **Old Town Pub** (1339 N. Wells St.), which draws a more yuppie crowd. There are more than a handful of good restaurants on Wells Street too: try **Kamehachi** *(see p40)* for sushi and **Salpicon** (No. 1252, www.salpicon.com) for upscale Mexican. For more on what the neighborhood has to offer see www.oldtownchicago.org.

Oak Street Beach *sun, sand, & skyscrapers* 3 H5

The combination of sun, sand, water, and spectacular backdrop draws the crowds to this beach, which is nestled in the bay created by Lake Shore Drive as it curves around the downtown area. In summer, this is an unbeatable people-watching spot. And watch many do, either perched next to the bike path *(see p132)* to check out the skaters and cyclists as they race by or sitting on the steps to ogle the sun worshippers from a respectable distance. Concrete platforms at each end also mean you can take in the scene without getting sand between your toes. Office workers, shoppers, dog walkers, and sightseers all take advantage of the beach's convenient location to dip their toes in the water or just get some fresh air. On weekends, when the beach is a dense patchwork of umbrellas, towels, and deck chairs, the pick-up scene kicks in, as men and women with toned bodies, miniscule swimwear, and determinedly casual airs wander through the maze looking for the most advantageous spot for flirting.

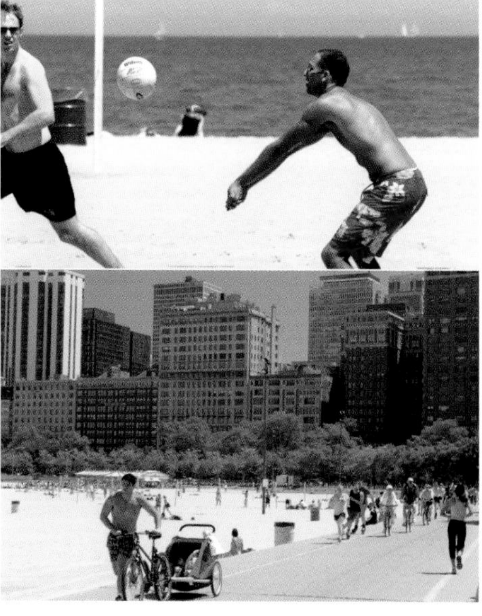

Lakefront Bike Path *miles of shoreline*

Stretching from Hollywood Avenue on the far north side all the way to 71st Street in the south, this continuous lakefront bike and walking path is the city's best-loved outdoor space, taking in five different parks, a handful of harbors, and numerous sights and cultural treasures along the way. Chicago invests generously in its most obvious asset, and it shows: the parks are well-tended and trash-free, the paths and trails are in good shape, and a discreet police presence ensures the safety of all. The downtown section can become clogged with bicyclists, joggers, and inline skaters on warm-weather weekends so, if you want some space, get up early or head for the north or south extremes, where the traffic is lighter. There are several bike rental opportunities *(see p21)* if the mood to pedal overtakes you – just remember to pay attention to the lane designations.

You'll usually see a few fishermen trying their luck off the rocks and piers, though whether their catches are fit to be eaten is a matter of some debate. Much more highly recommended are the refreshments sold at the various concession stands and ice-cream carts dotted along the path, especially near the harbors. Alcohol is not allowed in the city's parks, but cocktails are served at **Castaways Bar & Grill**, on the rooftop of the steamship-shaped North Avenue Beach House (1603 N. Lake Shore Drive, on the beach).

Up near Belmont Avenue, the rocks on the lakeshore are a popular gay meeting point, while **North Avenue Beach**'s (Map 3 H3) outdoor gym offers ogling opportunities for all persuasions. **Navy Pier** *(see p14)* is derided by city-dwellers as a tourist trap, but it does offer fine views of the skyline, frequent fireworks displays in summer, boat trips, and plenty of activities for children – most noticeably the landmark Ferris wheel. Also popular for family outings is the green expanse of the **Museum Campus** (Map 7 F1), while Hyde Park's **Promontory Point** (Map 9 G3), a beautifully landscaped area with circular stone benches, has fantastic views.

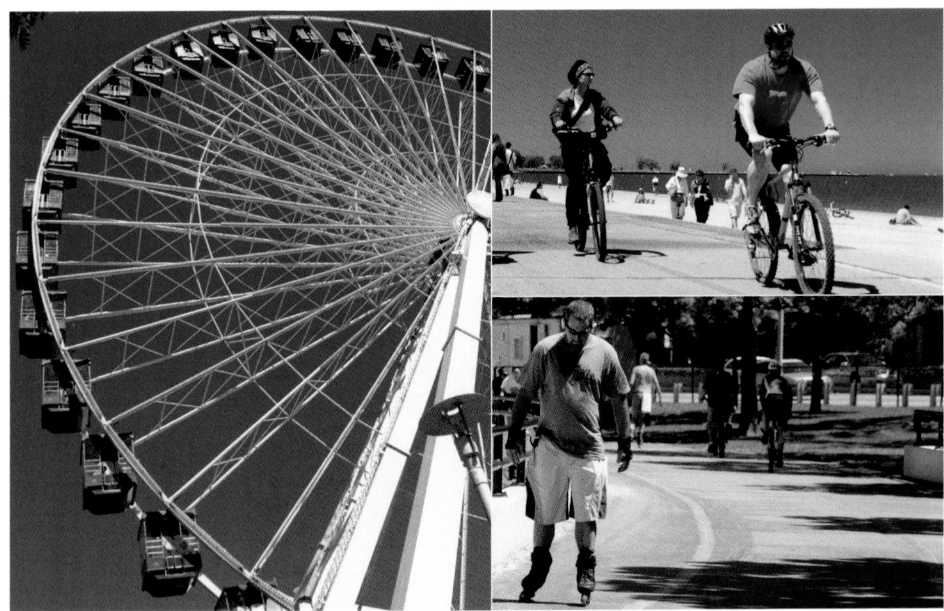

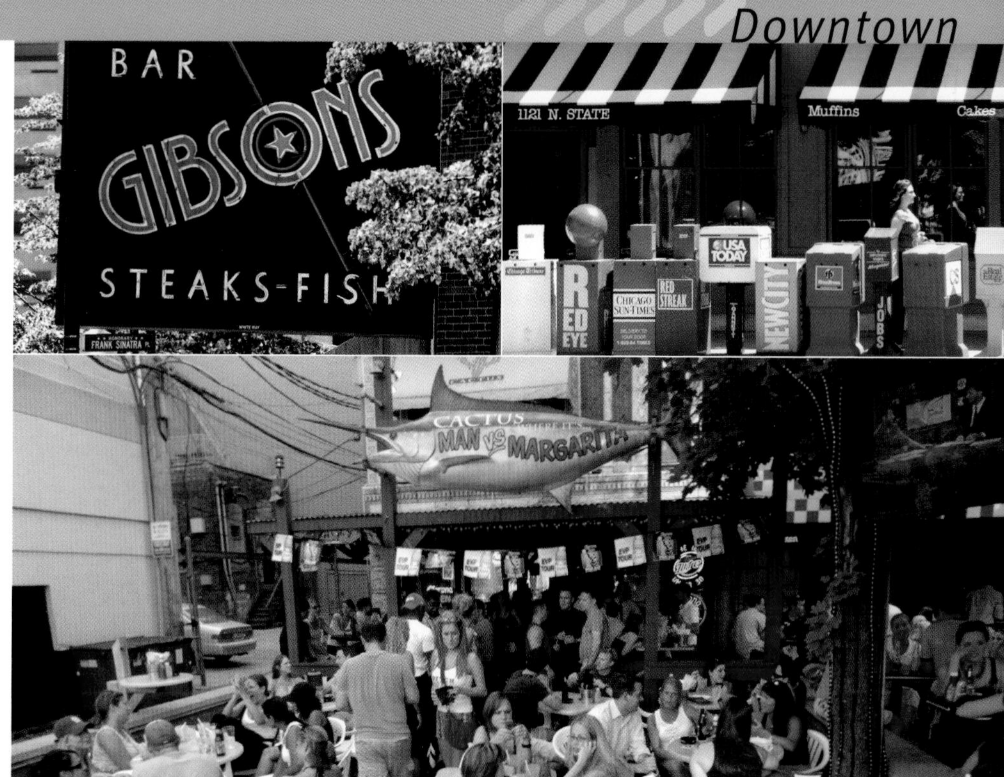

Gold Coast *flash and flesh*

3 G4

In the late 19th and early 20th centuries, prominent Chicago families built their mansions on pretty Astor Street; today it's a designated historic district known for its architecturally significant homes. The aura of wealth survives, and the whole area north of Chicago Avenue between State Street and Lake Shore Drive now attracts a mix of the rich, the famous, and the ostentatious, who come for the cool bars, well-established eateries, and chic shops. Shiny luxury cars pull up to the valet station at **Gibson's Steakhouse** (1028 N. Rush St.), while beautiful people in their best designer gear line up for entry to posh subterranean hangout **Le Passage** *(see p120)* or sip wine on one of the many restaurant terraces. A more relaxed but no less sophisticated crowd unwinds in the bar at the modern **Sofitel Chicago Water Tower** hotel *(see p159)*, with its cozy fireplace, plump chairs, and martini table service. Predictably, the prices in this part of town reflect the high income of the clientele.

No description of the Gold Coast is complete without a mention of the neon-lit bars around Rush and Division streets. A buzzing focal point during the 1970s, this intersection is now dubbed the "Viagra Triangle," and is more renowned for its cheesy pick-up lines and balding would-be Casanovas than its nightlife. Still, tanned jock types and the nubile young women who love them pack onto the shared patio of **Cactus** and **Melvin B's** (1114 N. State St.) to enjoy the pitchers of beer and the prime location, while **Elm Street Liquors** *(see p115)* winks at both sportsters and rich kids by offering super-cheap beer alongside expensive cocktails with names like "Label Whore."

» North Avenue beach is popular with singles, who often hang out to watch the frequent volleyball games

Wicker Park *boho groove*

2 A4

Originally an enclave for successful brewery owners and other wealthy citizens of German descent, the Wicker Park neighborhood grew up around a grassy triangle of the same name surrounded by ornate Victorian homes. Waves of Polish and Latino immigrants moved here in the early- and mid-1900s, then the area declined but was rediscovered toward the end of the 20th century by artists and musicians who loved the style of buildings, cheap rents, and bohemian vibe. It even gained national prominence for a burgeoning indie-rock scene during the 1990s. Since then, Wicker Park has exploded in popularity – to the dismay of many long-time residents, who decry the skyrocketing housing costs, soulless condo developments, and increasing corporatization of the area. But while parts of the area are undeniably heading back upmarket, there are enough scruffy cafés and grungy storefronts left to give a taste of the pre-gentrification era. And the **Flat Iron Arts Building** (1579 N. Milwaukee Ave.) still hosts artists' studios and galleries (many of which are open to the public), plus offices for all kinds of alternative projects.

Wicker Park's pulsing heart is the busy intersection of North, Damen, and Milwaukee avenues, where the El periodically rumbles overhead and all the different elements of the neighborhood come together in a noisy confluence: commuters, panhandlers, customized cars with stereos blasting, even the occasional enterprising designer selling stenciled T-shirts on the street. The strip of Milwaukee north of Division Street – a motley block of shabby furniture stores, luxury boutiques, dive bars, and trendy eateries – provides a comprehensive snapshot of the neighborhood, while Damen Avenue tends to be a little more refined. Division Street, which was nicknamed "Polish Broadway" in the early 1900s, still boasts a fair number of taverns, though they tend to play rock rather than the polka these days. One of the oldest is the **Rainbo Club** (1150 N. Damen Ave.), rumored to have been a hangout for local writer Nelson Algren in the 1940s and 50s. Today, many of the bar staff are respected figures in the local music scene and the red leather booths are filled with hipsters.

Other places where the cool kids like to hang out include the **Earwax Café** (1561 N. Milwaukee Ave., www.earwaxcafe.com), known for its healthy food, bizarre newspapers and magazines, and weird circus-poster decor, and **Danny's Tavern** *(see p125)*, a house turned loungey bar – look for the neon Schlitz sign. A more clean-cut crowd congregates at the **Pontiac Café** *(see p125)*, a former gas station with a patio that's bursting at the seams in summer. The huge burritos and other Costa Rican treats at little **Irazu** (1865 N. Milwaukee Ave.) are popular with just about everyone.

For sheer unadulterated consumerism, Wicker Park – a fashionista's paradise – can't be beat. Mixed in with the high-end clothing stores on N. Milwaukee Avenue are inexpensive consignment shops such as **Recycle It** (No. 1474) and one-off stores like **Una Mae's Freak Boutique** (No. 1433). You might even stumble on a tiny shop run by some recent graduates from one of the local fashion-design schools.

But one of this neighborhood's main attractions is free: the stunning architecture. While the landscape is marred here and there by newer buildings designed with absolutely no consideration for the surroundings, a ramble around the tree-lined side streets reveals a mixture of gingerbread Victorian mansions, imposing graystones, and the attractive red-brick three-flats that are typical of this part of Chicago. The most magnificent homes are found around and just to the west of Wicker Park itself, but even the more humble structures are adorned with gorgeous details. In the warmer months, you will often see residents hanging out on stoops or in gardens gossiping and chatting – perhaps about their good fortune in living here.

Taylor Street *remnants of Little Italy*

6 A1

Sad to say, much of the original character of this former "Little Italy" fell victim to urban renewal in the 1960s, and the continuing expansion of the nearby University of Illinois is also taking its toll. Now, you're as likely to find French or Asian fare as chianti and veal marsala along this leafy avenue, but a few holdouts from the old days do remain. One of them is **Al's #1 Italian Beef** (No. 1079), a Chicagoan favorite that is justly celebrated for its juicy, pepper-laden sandwiches. And just across the street, **Mario's Italian Lemonade** (No. 1068), a stand painted in the colors of the Italian flag, offers slushy and icy treats in melon, banana, and other flavors in addition to the traditional lemon. The family-owned **RoSal's Cucina** (No. 1154) is a throwback to old-style trattorias, offering Italian-American standbys to the tunes of Frank Sinatra, while longtime residents tend to meet up at the grocery-cum-delicatessen **Conte di Savoia** (No. 1438), which has a great selection of delicious olive oils, marinated anchovies and other *antipasti*, plus Italian liqueurs and cheeses.

Market Medley

The granddaddy of all Chicago's markets, **Maxwell Street Market** (Map 6 C1, Canal St. and Roosevelt Rd., 7am–3pm Sun) functioned for more than a century as a flea market, live-music venue, and grocery store combined. Sadly, its unique character was lost in the move to Canal Street, but there are still bargains to be found, plus cool junk, new T-shirts, and delicious Latino food. Most of Chicago's other markets are seasonal. At the **Chicago Antique Market** (Map 4 A3, Randolph St., between Ogden and Ada, 8am–4pm Sun May–Sep, www.chicagoantiquemarket.com) there's an entry cost to view the wares, which include everything from affordable clothing by local designers to ornate chandeliers.

Farmers' markets run roughly from June through October. The best one is the **Green City Market** (Map 3 F3, in the park between 1750 N. Clark St. and Stockton Dr., 7am–1:30pm Wed & Sat, www.chicagogreencitymarket.org), which is devoted to local organic produce and is the favorite of many Chicagoan chefs. Other markets are simpler affairs, selling seasonal produce from Midwestern farms plus the odd bakery or meat vendor. Try the **Daley Plaza Market** (Map 5 G3, Washington St. and Dearborn St., 7am–3pm Thu), right under the huge Picasso sculpture, which draws office workers selecting juicy fruit for now, or fresh herbs for later, while the **Streeterville Market** (Map 5 G1, 10am–6pm Tue), right in front of the Museum of Contemporary Art *(see p77)*, attracts a few curious shoppers from Michigan Avenue as well as museum visitors (and is occasionally shunted to the sidewalk when there's an outdoor installation going on).

Pilsen *little Mexico*

18th St., between Cermak & 16th, Canal & Damen
Ⓜ 18th (Blue Line)

Originally settled by Czechoslovakians, Pilsen is now home to a large Mexican community that has turned it into one of the most vibrant areas in the city. Though cultural hotspots like the impressive **Mexican Fine Arts Center & Museum** *(see p81)* are rare, the residents' pride in their roots is evident at every turn, from the colorful murals sweeping across buildings to the manhole covers painted with Aztec motifs. Many artists have moved into the area in recent years, and while long-time residents worry that this will bring unwelcome changes, Pilsen's identity has remained strong.

There are stretches of 18th Street that can look a bit run-down, but that's just part of the charm, as are the *curanderos* hawking herbs and other occult essentials and the stores selling communion dresses and religious statuettes. The psychedelic colored facades of two adjoining buildings mark the location of **Nuevo Leon** *(see p42)*, a busy restaurant renowned for its authentic, no-frills fare, while the cheerful **Café Jumping Bean** (No. 1439) is a real neighborhood hangout. All over Pilsen, pushcart vendors sound their horns or ring their bicycle bells to advertise corn on the cob covered in mayonnaise, cayenne pepper, and cheese – creating a constant background noise that mingles with the Latino hits spilling out of record stores.

A bit further to the east, Halsted Street between 18th and 19th streets can seem deserted by day. But on Friday evenings it comes alive with young artists and various hangers-on hopping from gallery to gallery, checking out new shows or just cadging free food and drinks. It's a very informal vibe – some of the galleries double as the artists' homes, and it shows. The same friendly atmosphere reigns at the dimly lit **Skylark** (2149 S. Halsted St.), the watering hole of choice for younger locals.

havens

With its long, freezing winters and massive urban sprawl, Chicago is about as gritty and metropolitan as it gets. Thankfully, there are lots of ways to get away from it all without even necessarily getting on a train or bus. The vast Lincoln Park is never too far away, and the city's spas, tea rooms, spiritual retreats, and high-rise hideaways offer all kinds of urban escape.

Chicago Botanic Garden *nature nurtured*

1000 Lake Cook Rd. • 847 835 5440 • Metra stop Glencoe
>> www.chicago-botanic.org Open 8am–sunset daily

The Chicago Botanic Garden is the nation's second most visited garden – the U.S. Gardens in Washington D.C. being the first – and are well worth the half-hour train ride from downtown to visit them. Once inside, you'll lose all sense of the fact that this natural paradise is surrounded by the city – albeit some of Chicago's wealthiest suburbs.

There are 23 gardens and three native areas in total covering some 383 acres (155 ha). It's easy to spend an entire day getting lost in it all, but there are some highlights that should not be missed. The English Walled Garden consists of six "rooms," including Cottage and Courtyard gardens, which typify key traditions in English garden design. Then, during the summer months, the brilliant hues of the Rose Garden are particularly spectacular. This garden is designed to highlight varietals that bloom best in the Upper Midwest and its color-coordinated planting creates an amazing effect. Equally arresting is the Prairie area. Here, however, what impresses is no vivid show, but a wild habitat – including a sea of undulating grass and lots of wildlife – of the kind that once covered much of Illinois, but which has now all but disappeared.

The garden's star attraction is thought by many to be Evening Island, designed in the New American Garden style of landscaping, which is defined by the use of swathes of grasses and perennials and the planting of relatively few species. Features on the island include the Carillion, the setting for concerts during summer, and The Arch bridge, which offers gorgeous views.

Walking and tram tours are available for different parts of the gardens throughout the year, as are special events. These tail off in the winter months, but at other times of the year include plant shows, recitals, and demonstrations by chefs using local produce.

Unique So Chique *insiders' tea room*

4600 N. Magnolia Ave., at Wilson • 773 561 0324
>> www.uniquesochique.com • Ⓜ Wilson (Red Line)
Open 11:30–7:30 Tue–Fri, 10–6 Sat, 10–5 Sun

The fact that this stylish boutique calls Uptown home just underlines how poised this neighborhood is for gentrification. The emphasis is on men and women's clothing and accessories, plus cutesy wares for the yuppie set, such as bath and beauty products, cards, stationery, and other gift items.

However, the real treasure – and a reason in itself to come – is the 22-seat tea and chocolate room buried at the back of the store. Here, a variety of sweets, savories, and a serious selection of green, red, black, and herbal teas are offered at lunch, afternoon tea (served 3–5pm), and weekend brunch. The heavenly selection of truffles come with quirky names like Black Cat and Cocorazzy: go easy otherwise you'll never fit into the Evil Kitty T-shirt and underwear collection you're bound to purchase on the way out.

Urban Tea Lounge *cozy and romantic*

838 W. Montrose, at Dayton • 773 907 8726 • Ⓜ Wilson (Red Line) Open 10–10 daily

This out-of-the-way spot is more friendly corner café than typical tea room, and its location several steps down from street level lends it an air of clandestine romance. There are almost 70 teas available and a light menu for breakfast, lunch, tea, and dinner that will satisfy meat-lovers, vegetarians, and even vegans.

Space Time Tanks *drift off*

1 B5

2526 N. Lincoln Ave., at Lill • 773 472 2700
>> www.spacetimetanks.com Open noon–9 Mon–Fri, 10:30–9 Sat, 10:30–6 Sun

For a relaxing experience, disrobe and enter a chamber filled with shallow, warm water. Epson salts keep the body afloat. To enhance a sense of inner calm, all sound and light are shut out and if you fall asleep, a knock on the door tells you when your hour is up.

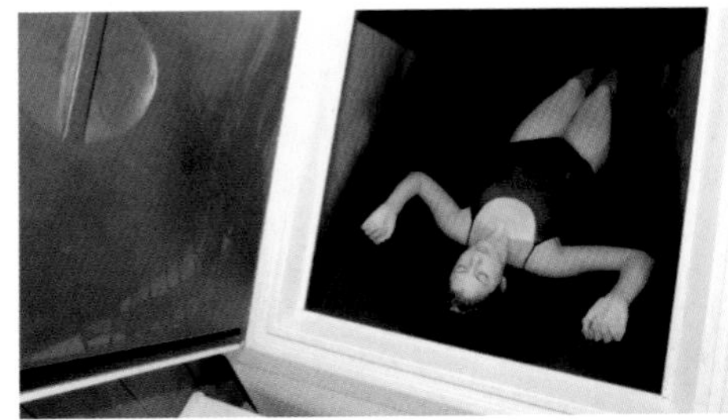

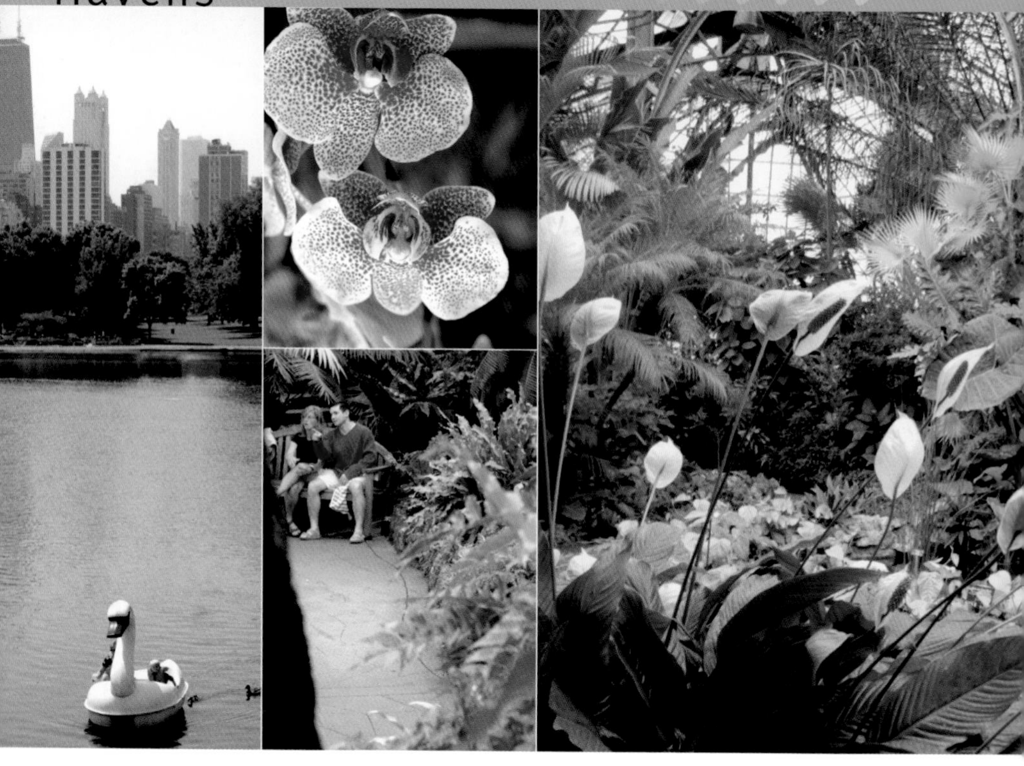

Lincoln Park *Chicago's backyard*

3 F1

600–5800 N. Lake Shore Dr. • 312 742 7529
>> www.chicagoparkdistrict.com Open 7am–11pm daily

While Chicago is blessed with over 500 parks, Lincoln Park is by the far its most impressive, giving this vast city a great swathe of much-needed and well-used greenery. Originally a cemetery in the 19th century, it was designated a park in the 1860s, due to the health concerns of local residents. Its original plan was designed by nurseryman Swain Nelson, but many prominent figures have added to the landscaping over the years, including sculptor Augustus-Saint Gaudens and landscape designer Ossian Cole.

Today, Lincoln Park offers a combination of trails, bike paths, recreational and sporting facilities, and beaches. It occupies over 1,200 acres (485 ha) of lakefront land, beginning at the touristy Navy Pier and continuing all the way to Edgewater on the far North Side, which makes it the largest urban park in the United States. Most visitors tend to head to the section between the North and South ponds, where many of the park's cultural attractions are located.

The architecturally striking **Peggy Notebaert Nature Museum** (Map 3 F1, 2430 N. Cannon Dr., 773 755 5100, www.naturemuseum.org) is full of excellent hands-on, child-oriented exhibits designed to increase an understanding of nature and the environment. However, even adults will be entranced by the hundreds of vibrant butterflies that flit about in the tranquil Butterfly Haven here. Outside, the museum's grounds are planted with beautiful native wildflowers and prairie grasses that once characterized the Midwestern landscape.

Chicago has a few excellent free greenhouses, but **Lincoln Park Conservatory** (Map 3 F1, 2391 N. Stockton Dr., 312 742 7736) is the most accessible. As you pass through its four distinct areas – the Palm House, the Fernery, the Orchid House, and the Show House – the climate rapidly switches from humid and tropical to arid, which makes for a welcome change from the snowbound city in winter. In warmer months, don't overlook the lovely, formal gardens across the street. These extend alongside the **Lincoln Park Zoo** (Map 3 F2, 2200 N. Cannon Dr., www.lpzoo.com), one of the country's last free zoos, and one of Chicago's biggest attractions. Exhibits range from American species to a center devoted to apes. The Alfred Caldwell Lily Pool, just north of the polar bear enclosure, is a quiet spot to escape from the mayhem of school groups.

While bringing a picnic is the best option, other opportunities for meals within the park range from the refined **North Pond** restaurant *(see p31)* to overpriced concession fare in the zoo. Also located within the zoo is the Prairie-style **Café Brauer** (Map 3 F2), which has a beer garden and is the only place you can officially drink within the park boundaries.

Lincoln Park's beaches are another big draw. **Oak Street Beach**, with plenty of toned bodies and diehard tourists *(see p131)*, and **North Avenue Beach**, with its swinging singles scene *(see p132)*, are very popular. **Hollywood Beach**, officially Osterman Beach (5800 N. Lake Shore Dr.) is a wide open area with a lovely pier that has become a lively hangout for Chicago's gay community. **Ohio Street Beach** (Map 5 H2) is smaller but no less crowded when the sun shines.

>> The Peggy Notebaert Nature Museum charges admission

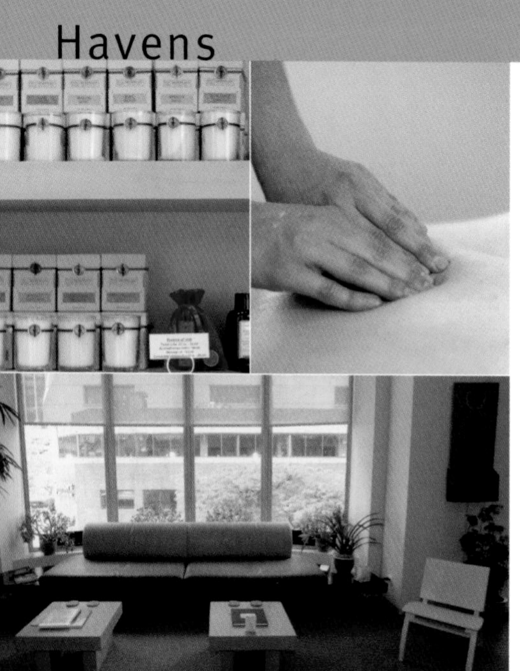

Urban Oasis *stresses melt away*

12 W. Maple St., at State • 312 587 3500
>> www.urbanoasis.biz
Open noon–8 Mon, 10–8 Tue–Thu, 9–7 Fri, 9–5 Sat, 11–5 Sun

While most Gold Coast spas cater to the area's rich residents, Urban Oasis offers everyone plenty of chic and pampering at reasonable prices. Great care is taken to make sure your visit is memorable. The spa is filled with light wood, soft music, and minimal decor, which gives it a Zen-like ambiance. In the changing rooms, guests are provided with kimonos, sandals, and towels and are offered a choice of pre-treatment showers: steam to soften the skin and relax the muscles, "European-style" using multiple spray jets, or "rain" to wash away tension.

The specialty here is massage, and therapies range from standards such as Swedish to alternatives like Reiki Light Touch and Hot Stone massage. The invigorating Salt Glow exfoliation treatment involves a sea-salt and massage-oil rub under warm infrared lamps.

Signature Room and Lounge

5 F1

875 N. Michigan Ave., at Delaware • 312 787 7230
>> www.signaturelounge.com
Lounge open 11am–12:30am daily (to 1:30am Fri & Sat); restaurant open lunch & dinner Mon–Sat, dinner Sun

Visitors and locals mix at this classic Chicago restaurant and bar perched high above the city on the 95th floor of the iconic John Hancock Center. Sadly, the prices are proportional to the elevation, but the 360-degree views are sensational – especially at night when Chicago glitters for miles in all directions.

The dining room is open for lunch, dinner and weekend brunch, serving classic American standards, but a better option is to skip this high-priced fare and head to the 96th floor where soft jazz and smooth cocktails await. The views are just as good and the atmosphere is more casual – and one expensive cocktail is at least a little easier on the wallet. If you arrive early enough to get a window seat, there's no better place in the city to watch the sun set.

Fourth Presbyterian Church

5 F1

126 E. Chestnut St., at Michigan • 312 787 4570
>> www.fourthchurch.org Open 7:30am–9pm

Step out of the bustle of Michigan Avenue and find some tranquility in this Gothic revival haven. It's a peaceful spot year round, but those in the know come on Fridays at noon, when regular recitals are held. These concerts are very popular in summer when they're held outside in the pretty courtyard.

Harold Washington Library Center

5 F5

400 S. State St., at Van Buren • 773 542 7279
>> www.chicagopubliclibrary.org
Open 9–7 Mon–Thu, 9–5 Fri & Sat, 1–5 Sun

Named for former Chicago mayor Harold Washington, the city's first African-American mayor, this building contains the U.S.'s largest public library. Apart from the enormous collection of books, the library also houses the substantial Chicago Blues Archives, well worth investigating if you're a fan, as these archives contains some rare, original concert recordings.

While you can duck out of the fast lane on any of the nine floors that are open to the public, the top floor's Winter Gardens are not to be missed. These are not actually gardens at all, but a single giant space for reading, with a glazed atrium that lets natural light pour in, even in the grey gloom of winter. The views are pretty spectacular too. The small number of tables and chairs means that the room never feels crowded, and even at full capacity you can hear a pin drop.

Kopi – A Traveler's Cafe *Andersonville hangout*

5317 N. Clark St. • 773 989 5674 • Bus No. 22
Open breakfast, lunch, & dinner daily

This quaint vegetarian café – which offers light meals, sandwiches, plenty of teas, and smoothies – is a great people-watching spot, with outdoor seating for when the weather is fine. In the back of the café is a shop and bookstore offering maps, journals, travel literature, and global gifts.

Ruby Room *spa for the spirit*

2 A5

1743 W. Division St., at Hermitage • 773 635 5000

>> www.rubyroom.com Open 11–8 Mon–Fri, 9–7 Sat, 11–6 Sun

Both a boutique and a day spa, the Ruby Room is located within an elegant building with large windows overlooking the hip Division Street scene. Its philosophy is based on the belief that energy is a force for healing, and this is translated into the provision of light-touch and non-touch treatments. While it offers traditional services such as facials, peels, and make-up sessions, what makes it different from other city spas is that most of its "menu" consists of more alternative offerings.

Curious but cautious visitors may want to try something simple such as an energy healing – designed to clear your *chakras* of stored chi – a guided meditation, or tailored astrological analysis. The more adventurous, however, can go for intuitive numero-therapy (to understand your soul's purpose), energy healing for couples, or a workshop on tantric sex.

The spa area itself is chic and urban and designed using the principles of feng shui. A giant rug softens the hardwood floors and guests are led down a hallway where semi-private rooms offer a soothing environment for the various treatment options. While it is immensely popular with women, men (and children) are equally welcome – and energy healing is even available for pets.

The inviting boutique at the front of the spa offers a selection of beauty gifts and products, such as the aromatic Ruby Room Candle Collection or luxury organic Arcana™ skin products.

Sole Nail Lounge and Beauty Emporium *fingers and toes rejoice*

2 A4

1468 N. Milwaukee Ave., at Honore • 773 486 7653
Open 11–8 Tue–Fri, 10–8 Sat, 10–5 Sun

Hands and feet are given the star treatment at this trendy mani/pedi bar set in the heart of Wicker Park's increasingly trendy main shopping strip. The spa area is nice and roomy, painted a soothing burnt sienna and serviced by a friendly and attentive staff. It's not cheap, but even men are joining the line here. The build-your-own pedicure bar, including choice of foot scrub or soak and wine or champagne to drink, is the star attraction, along with weekend DJs spinning R&B, hip-hop, and house music. Reservations are not necessary but expect to wait a while on weekends if you don't reserve ahead. And if your feet need even more pampering, note that Sole shares its space with trendy Le Fetiche shoe store, which offers high-end footwear for men and women from brands like Ugg, Dry Shod, and United Nude.

Jackson Park *historic green space*

9 F5

S. Stoney Island Ave., bet. 56th & 67th streets • 773 256 0903
>> www.chicagoparkdistrict.com Open 7am–10pm

Forming part of the greensward that occupies much of Chicago's south side lakefront, Jackson Park was the site of the great fair, the World's Columbian Exposition in 1893. The only building to survive was the Museum of Science and Industry (the original Palace of Fine Arts) – a big draw today, especially for kids. However, just south of the museum, another cherished and lesser-known attraction also owes its existence to the fair.

Occupying the north part of Wooded Island, the **Osaka Garden** is located near the site of the 1893 Japanese Pavilion. It's full of gorgeous foliage (most of the plants are native to Japan) and an abundance of water. It is said that passing through the garden's gate refreshes the spirit. The garden is designed to lead visitors around the walkways and to offer a succession of beautifully framed vistas. You might also catch a glimpse of the wild parrots that nest on the island.

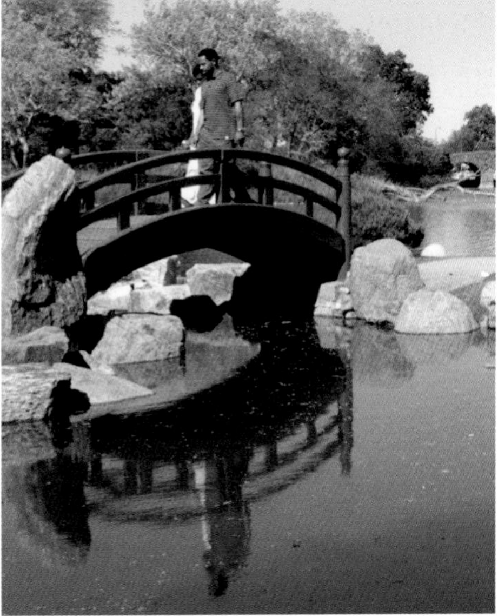

hotels

In a city that's big on conventions, it's not surprising that the major hotel chains have congregated downtown to serve the needs of the business traveler. But as more of Chicago's hoteliers embrace the lifestyle concept and more B&Bs break onto the scene, all travelers are increasingly well catered for. Most central rooms come with a high price tag, but there are still good deals to be found on the city's trendy North Side.

HOTELS

Chicago's accommodation scene is constantly improving. Boutique hotels are increasingly common and minimalist chic is "in," even though the trend peaked in other U.S. cities a few years ago. The city's B&Bs are far more varied and stylish than you might expect, and even the national chain hotels have sharpened up their interiors and added a head-turning bar or restaurant. Ask for a room with a view; in such a vertical city, you can almost always find one.

Jason Heidemann

Urban Retreats

There are lots of neighborhood gems where you can get away from the bustle of downtown. **China Doll** *(see p152)* is a stylish yet cozy short-term rental place in Lincoln Park; the literary-themed **Windy City Urban Inn** *(see p152)* occupies a rambling Victorian mansion; and the **House of Two Urns** *(see p161)* is as off-beat and eclectic as its Wicker Park location.

Individual Style

Some Chicago hotels really stand out from the crowd – like **Hotel Allegro** *(see p156)* with its morning trumpet call and vibrant rooms, or the whimsical **Hotel Monaco** *(see p157)*, which provides in-room goldfish. At the **Hard Rock Hotel** *(see p154)* and **House of Blues Hotel** *(see p158)* you'll feel like a rock star – and perhaps even get to drink with one, too.

Budget Beds

You don't have to stay in the suburbs or chase the bedbugs away to sleep cheap in Chicago. The **Cass Hotel** *(see p157)* offers great value for money just steps from Michigan Avenue, and **City Suites** *(see p153)* attracts an urbane, cost-conscious clientele to hip Lakeview. **Willows Hotel** *(see p153)* is an affordable retreat in leafy Lincoln Park.

choice stays

Great Location

With so many hotels concentrated downtown, it's not hard to find one that has a good location and/or views. The **W Chicago Lakeshore** *(see p157)* enjoys a glorious waterside setting, while **The Hotel InterContinental** *(see p157)* and the **Peninsula Chicago** *(see p156)* are both located on the Magnificent Mile, at the heart of the city.

Business Traveler Oriented

Chicago is such a big convention city that all kinds of accommodation cater to the business traveler, from the B&B experience of **Wheeler Mansion** *(see p161)* to the huge **Park Hyatt** *(see p156)*, with every business amenity you could ask for. Boutique-like **The James Chicago** *(see p156)* is a good bet for those who like to mix business with pleasure.

Living History

Several hotels are as rich in history and legend as Chicago itself. The **Hotel Burnham** *(see p155)* is considered to be the original "skyscraper," **The Drake** *(see p156)* is synonymous with old-world splendor and tradition, and **The Palmer House Hilton** *(see p154)* is a city institution that rose out of the ashes of the Great Chicago Fire in 1871.

Windy City Urban Inn *literary lodgings* 1 C5

607 W. Deming Place, at Clark • 773 248 7091
>> www.chicago-inn.com

The owners of this Lincoln Park B&B love Chicago, and their enthusiasm positively shines through. A Victorian mansion on a tranquil, tree-lined street, the Urban Inn is filled with artifacts and books that pay tribute to the Windy City and the state of Illinois – even the buffet-style breakfast is packed with locally grown produce.

Room names salute Chicago's literary giants: the cozy Carl Sandburg room features William Morris wallpaper and folk art, while the charming Gwendolyn Brooks room has an early 1900s iron bed and a mix of vintage and new fabrics. The Algren and de Beauvoir suite features a large Jacuzzi set beneath a skylight and a private sitting area. Guests can also relax in the two shared sitting rooms (one of which has a kitchen) or in the garden. A coach house contains three apartments for families and groups of friends. Reservations for a single night are sometimes not accepted. **Moderate**

China Doll *do-it-yourself luxury* 1 C5

738 W. Schubert Ave., at Burling • 773 525 4967
>> www.chinadollchicago.com

Each of the three units in this stunning ivy-clad Lincoln Park house is a home-away-from-home, with cozy fireplace, modern kitchen, oversized Jacuzzi, flat-screen TV, and business area complete with PC, printer, fax, and scanner. Laundry facilities are available, plus a DVD library to keep you entertained. **Moderate**

Days Inn Lincoln Park-North *top spot* 1 C5

644 W. Diversey Pkwy., at Clark • 773 525 7010
>> www.lpndaysinn.com

✓

With Lincoln Park and Lakeview both on the doorstep, you couldn't ask for a more energized location in all of Chicago's fashionable North Side. Rooms are clean and comfortable if a bit nondescript; some cater specifically to business needs. Generous complimentary breakfasts and passes for a nearby gym are added draws. **Cheap**

Willows Hotel *French country appeal*

1 D4

555 W. Surf St., at Pine • 773 528 8400

>> www.cityinns.com/willows

Elegant, romantic, and tucked away on a residential street, the Willows is a North-Side pearl. Its interior is decorated in a French country style and while the rooms are a little on the plain side, they're homey enough. The back of the house offers bigger guestrooms, but there are pretty views of the street from the front. **Cheap**

Best Western Hawthorne Terrace

1 C3

3434 N. Broadway Ave., at Hawthorne • 773 244 3434

>> www.hawthorneterrace.com

It may be a Best Western, but this link in the chain stands out thanks to its impressive Colonial façade and hip mix of gay and straight travelers. The rooms are big and clean if a bit staid for the youthful clientele; some offer whirlpool tubs and views over the terrace. The Boystown-Wrigleyville location is a bonus. **Cheap**

City Suites *urbane and elegant*

1 B3

933 W. Belmont Ave., at Clark • 773 404 3400

>> www.cityinns.com/citysuites

With earthy tones and a restrained interior, City Suites contrasts with its bustling and cosmopolitan Lakeview location. It's still a big hit with trendy travelers, though, and does get full in summer. Evening cookies, continental breakfasts, and an endless supply of tea and coffee are all included in the price. **Cheap**

Reservation Agencies

The cost of a hotel room in Chicago fluctuates wildly depending on the season, the day of the week, and whether there's a convention on in town, but you should be able to find a price well below the rack rate. Agencies often offer good deals: **www.expedia.com**, **www.hotels.com**, and Chicago-based **Hot Rooms** (1 800 468 3500) are good starting points.

If you're staying more than a couple of days, it may be worth reserving an apartment *(see p161)*; perks include kitchen facilities and added privacy. **At Home Inn Chicago** (312 640 1050, www.athomeinn.chicago.com) caters for both long and short stays, while the **Habitat Corporate Suites Network** (312 902 2090, www.habitatcsn.com) offers long-term (over 30 days) business accommodation.

Hard Rock Hotel *a landmark with attitude* 5 F3

230 N. Michigan Ave., at South Water • 312 345 1000
» www.hardrockhotelchicago.com

Behind the beautifully preserved Art Deco facade of the landmark Carbide and Carbon building, the interior of the Hard Rock is slick and contemporary. The brash rock 'n' roll theme prevalent in the touristy restaurants of the same name has mercifully been toned down, but a musical bent is still visible in the embroidered guitar logo on the pillows. All 381 guestrooms feature fashionably minimal furnishings in stylish zebrawood and leather, plus flat-screen TVs, 5-disc DVD/CD players, and complimentary high-speed Internet access; most also benefit from stunning views of the city. If you tire of the in-room entertainment, head downstairs to the moody Base Bar, where regular DJ slots and occasional gigs by up-and-coming local artistes will keep you rocking. The China Grill serves up larger-than-life portions of modern Asian fusion food and is a big hit with local gourmands. **Moderate**

The Palmer House Hilton *Loop legend* 5 F4

17 E. Monroe St., at State • 312 726 7500
» www.hilton.com

This Loop behemoth was a grand and lavish spectacle when it opened in 1871, but less than two weeks later it burned to the ground in the Great Chicago Fire. Not to be defeated, owner Potter Palmer started over: the new Palmer House was launched four years later and has been a Chicago institution ever since.

The building's signature wide archways and ornate ceilings hark back to its glory days. Naturally, though, all 1,639 guestrooms come complete with digital-age comforts like high-speed Internet access, cable TV, and iPod or CD listening stations alongside the good old-fashioned luxury furnishings and linens. Amenities include a fitness center, a swimming pool, a basement mall (with barber shop, beauty salon, and boutique), and four restaurants. Although Palmer House no longer attracts as many leisure travelers as it once did, it is still a huge draw for conventioneers. **Moderate**

Hotel Burnham *the original skyscraper*

5 F3

1 W. Washington St., at State • 312 782 1111
>> www.burnhamhotel.com

Staying at the Burnham, you don't just get a room in an unbeatable Loop location, you also get to experience a little bit of architectural history. Designed by Daniel Burnham and John Root in 1890 and completed by Charles Atwood in 1895, the (then) Reliance Building was built around a hidden steel skeleton – with only a delicate facade of cream-colored terra-cotta – to allow for the floor-to-ceiling windows. Although its design is perfectly in keeping with the modern cityscape, this "tower of glass" was years ahead of its time, and is considered the blueprint for the modern skyscraper.

The one-time office building was lovingly restored and converted to a hotel in 1999, retaining plenty of original features – from the old-fashioned metal room keys to the frosted glass door panels with hand-painted gold numbering. The signature quatrefoil emblem is still apparent in hallways, and the elevator lobby has been reconstructed with cast-iron grilles and imported Italian marble for the walls and ceilings.

Modern additions help to make the conversion from office block to luxury living space convincing. Rooms are furnished with mahogany writing desks, oversized gentlemen's chests, and plush chaise longues, while beds are layered in fine beige and gold fabrics and harlequin prints, and accented with rich, blue velvet pillows. Downstairs, the Beaux-Arts-inspired Atwood Café serves modern American cuisine and is at its best at lunch time, when the space is bathed in light and the inviting clatter of silverware fills the air. **Expensive**

Hotel Allegro *high-energy hotel*

171 W. Randolph St., at LaSalle • 312 236 0123
>> www.allegrochicago.com

In line with its upbeat name and lively Theater District location, the Allegro puts fun first: whimsical touches include the doorman's daily 9:01am trumpet call, all-you-can-eat Tootsie Rolls at the front desk, and a free wine reception each evening. Rooms are comfortable and vibrant, and theater deals are available. **Expensive**

The Drake Hotel *lakefront luxury*

5 F1

140 E. Walton Pl., at Michigan • 312 787 2200
>> www.thedrakehotel.com

A Gold Coast landmark since 1920, the Drake still oozes Prohibition-era opulence. It has long been a haunt of the rich and famous, and retains upscale touches such as live harp music during afternoon tea. With luxury rooms and a range of restaurants and designer boutiques on-site, you need never leave. **Expensive**

The James Chicago *downtown dream*

5 F2

55 E. Ontario St., at Rush • 877 526 3755
>> www.jameshotels.com

Part of a new hotel chain that occupies a category somewhere between boutique and luxe, The James offers gorgeous rooms with in-room dining niches, large plasma-screen TVs, and free Wi-Fi connection. Popular with business travelers looking for good facilities and a more personal, stylish stay. **Expensive**

Chicago's Elite

Chicago has a handful of top-notch hotels that are on everyone's wish list – even if it's only for a cocktail or once-in-a-lifetime meal. The **Four Seasons** (Map 5 F1, 120 E. Delaware Pl., www.fourseasons.com), with its award-winning Seasons restaurant, is a classic decorated in European style, while the trendier **Park Hyatt** (Map 5 F1, 800 N. Michigan Ave., www.parkchicago.hyatt.com) is festooned with art worth millions – from Dale Chihuly's glass sculptures in the restaurant, NoMI *(see p33)*, to the Gerhard Richter hanging in the lobby. But the *it* hotel of the moment is the starry **Peninsula Chicago** (Map 5 F1, 108 E. Superior St., chicago.peninsula.com), with its vaulted lobby where afternoon tea and Friday chocolate tastings take place.

The Hotel InterContinental *twin peaks* 5 F2

505 N. Michigan Ave., at Grand • 312 944 4100
>> www.chicago.intercontinental.com

Occupying two skyscrapers linked by a sweeping four-story lobby, this hotel is so full of historical detail that it even has its own audio tour to rent. The south tower was built for the Medinah Athletic Club in 1929 and has many original features – including the gorgeous tiled swimming pool featured in the movie *Cocoon*. **Moderate**

Cass Hotel *cheap sleep* 5 F2

640 N. Wabash Ave., at Ontario • 312 787 4030
>> www.casshotel.com

A no-frills favorite in the heart of the gallery-thronged River North district, the Cass has 150 rooms that tend toward the standard motel variety, but all have basics like cable TV and air conditioning. There is free Wi-Fi in the lobby and the Cass Café is open daily. For location and price, it may be the best deal in the city. **Cheap**

Four Points by Sheraton *stylish gem* 5 F2

630 N. Rush St., at Ontario • 312 981 6600
>> www.fourpointschicago.com

This boutique-style hotel has only 226 rooms (small for the city), each with a "four comfort" bed, Nintendo video games, refrigerator, and microwave. Suites also have whirlpools and city-view balconies. The swimming pool and landscaped patio are real pluses in this downtown location. **Moderate**

Hotel Monaco *quirky lifestyle* 5 F3

225 N. Wabash Ave., at Wacker • 312 960 8500
>> www.monaco-chicago.com

Fans of the Hotel Monaco chain's lovable lifestyle lodgings won't be disappointed by the Chicago version. The "French Deco"-style rooms offer lots of fun features like goldfish companions (upon request) and "meditation stations" overlooking the river. There are even rooms with extra-long beds for taller guests. **Moderate**

W Chicago Lakeshore *lakeside appeal* 5 H2

644 N. Lake Shore Dr., at Ontario • 312 943 9200
>> www.whotels.com

The look here is all about open-plan living: the lobby's mahogany-lined grotto and Zen fountain blend easily into a wide-open dining area. In the guestrooms, the vibe is similar, with oak shutters opening the bathroom out onto the bedroom, allowing you to enjoy stunning city and lake views even from the tub. **Expensive**

>> *Many hotel websites regularly post special deals*

House of Blues Hotel *rock 'n' roll hotel* 5 E2

333 N. Dearborn St., at Kinzie • 312 245 0333
>> www.houseofblueshotel.com

Located at the iconic Marina City complex *(see p80)*, which also houses a 36-lane bowling alley, Crunch fitness center, state-of-the-art concert hall, and the BIN 36 wine bar and restaurant *(see p33)*, the House of Blues is certainly one hotel where you could stay a weekend without ever leaving the building. The public areas are filled with a vibrant mixture of Neo-Gothic and Asian decor, while the 367 guestrooms have bold candy-striped wallpaper and exuberant color schemes that give each space a playful energy. The design rationale is visually to convey a variety of musical genres. Famous local designer Cheryl Rowley contributed the New Orleans-style furnishings, and details include folk art and black-and-white photographs. Soirées are held regularly in the large and colorful bar, where you might glimpse a rocker enjoying a drink before the show. **Moderate**

Amalfi Hotel Chicago *an alternative take* 5 F2

20 W. Kinzie St., at State • 312 395 9000
>> www.amalfihotelchicago.com

So what if there's no restaurant or bar. This boutique hotel is superb in so many other ways. The "Experience Designers" (concierges) offer exemplary service, while rooms feature multi-head showers and CD libraries. Breakfast is served in the lobby of each floor so that guests can head back for breakfast in bed. **Moderate**

Ohio House Motel *budget classic* 5 E2 ✓

600 N. LaSalle St., at Ohio • 312 943 6000
>> www.ohiohousemotel.com

With its 1950s-era aesthetic, plain but very affordable rooms, and delightful diner where servers might still call you "honey," this fabulous old-school motel offers plenty of cachet as well as value for money. Its close proximity to the many bars and clubs of the River North neighborhood will thrill some, but not all. **Cheap**

Omni Chicago Hotel *magnificent location* 5 F1

676 N. Michigan Ave., at Huron • 312 944 6664
» www.omnihotels.com

All 347 rooms here are suites comprising bedroom and parlor separated by French doors. With features such as plasma screen TVs and complimentary high speed Internet access, the hotel caters to a mix of business and leisure travelers, as well as every guest on the hugely popular Oprah Winfrey Show. **Moderate**

Gold Coast Guest House *garden haven* 3 G5

113 W. Elm St., at Clark • 312 337 0361
» www.bbchicago.com

Owner Sally Baker has largely eschewed the antiquated charms of the traditional B&B in favor of a more modern vibe. Her 1873 town house offers four cozy en-suite rooms. Guests can admire the romantic garden from the communal living/breakfast room through a ceiling-height window – or enjoy it in fine weather. **Moderate**

Sofitel Chicago Water Tower 5 F1

20 E. Chestnut St., at Rush • 312 324 4000
» www.sofitel.com

French architect Jean-Paul Viguier designed this striking Gold Coast glass skyscraper, which opened in 2002, satisfying Mayor Daley's then mandate of "no more ugly buildings" in Chicago. Part of the French Accor Group's upscale chain, the hotel is popular with both business and leisure travelers who appreciate Gallic flair.

With its dramatic high ceiling and sweeping staircase, the lobby is seriously imposing. Yet the comfy seating area is inviting and there is plenty of room to stretch out and relax. In one corner is the Café des Architectes, a casual, modern French restaurant with a terrace for alfresco dining, while at the other end of the lobby is Le Bar, a chic martini lounge with floor-to-ceiling glass walls and a library. The rooms are bright and airy, with artworks above the beds and modern conveniences such as separate shower and bathtub in bathrooms stocked with Roger & Gallet products. **Expensive**

Sutton Place Hotel *Gold Coast beauty*

3 G5

21 E. Bellevue Pl., at State • 312 266 2100
>> www.suttonplace.com

The lively location is one of many pluses at this hotel, which is adorned with original Mapplethorpe flower prints. Rooms are contemporary, with DVD players, deep tubs, and lots of bath products. Off the lobby, Rande Gerber's Whiskey Bar has plenty of sidewalk tables for people watching during summer. **Moderate**

Flemish House *lakefront getaway*

3 H5

68 E. Cedar St., at Michigan • 312 664 9981
>> www.innchicago.com

This attractive B&B contains seven well-equipped studios and small apartments, so guests enjoy plenty of independence and privacy. The owners deliver a self-serve breakfast to your kitchen the night before and are usually on hand to answer any queries. Oak Street beach is just a short stroll away. **Moderate**

Hotel Indigo *emphasis on relaxation*

3 G5

1244 N. Dearborn St., at Division • 312 787 4980
>> www.hotelindigo.com

The nautilus-shell logo encourages guests to "curl up" at this new lifestyle hotel, which also offers oversized chairs, oversized beds, and extra pillows to the same end. But Indigo isn't just about comfort and relaxation. The hotel has a fashion-conscious attitude, and seasonally changes its decor – details such as rugs, duvets, and cushion covers – in much the same way that shops update their window displays.

Like the logo, the guestrooms are designed around patterns found in nature, and use natural materials such as hardwood floors and whitewashed wood furniture to create a modern-yet-homey feel. A permanent collection of artwork by Chicago native Bill Olendorf is displayed around the hotel.

To complete the sense of wellbeing, try the Golden Bean restaurant's quick-service health food or pay a visit to the on-site spa and nail salon. **Moderate**

House of Two Urns *bohemian charm*

2 B5

1239 N. Greenview Ave., at Division • 773 235 1408

>> www.twourns.com

The House of Two Urns is among Chicago's most unique properties and offers a choice of four guestrooms, each following a different theme. Alice's Room is a colorful bolt-hole inspired by *The Princess and the Pea* and *Alice in Wonderland*; La Chambre des Chats (the cat room) is decorated with antique furniture and, of course, a mini-gallery of cat pictures; Das Porzellanzimmer (the porcelain room) is a calming blue space that takes its name from the collection of French and German plates hanging on the walls; and the Studio Suite is an open-plan attic with its own fireplace that can sleep a family of five. The common areas are cozy and inviting, with antique-style furnishings and lots of personal touches such as home-cooked snacks served throughout the day. And the owner's breakfasts are a real draw, with daily specials such as pancakes or waffles plus home-made jam from berries grown in the garden. **Moderate**

Wheeler Mansion *historic retreat*

7 F3

2020 S. Calumet Ave., at Cullerton • 312 945 2020

>> www.wheelermansion.com

One of the few remaining mansions on historic Prairie Avenue *(see p82)* to survive the Great Chicago Fire, this is an upscale South Loop retreat. Antique armoires and queen-sized canopied beds, plus modern amenities like cable and Egyptian cotton sheets, robes, and towels make this a real haven. **Moderate**

Short-Term Rental Apartments

Families and groups who just want to do their own thing are increasingly opting to stay in vacation apartments rather than hotels – and Chicago offers a number of places fit the bill. In quiet Lincoln Park, **City Scene Bed and Breakfast** (Map 2 C2, 2101 N. Clifton Ave., 773 549 1743, www.cityscenebb.com) is just one private suite with a sitting room, kitchen, and bath. Nearby **China Doll** *(see p152)* is another winner, with full business amenities and a beautiful garden. If you can handle the less convenient South Side location, **Benedictine Bed & Breakfast** (3111 S. Aberdeen St., 773 927 7424 ex.203, www.chicagomonk.org) is a private two-bedroom loft apartment set within a real, functioning, urban monastery.

CONDOS FOR SALE
31228.9904

Chicago Street Finder

The sprawling conurbation known as Chicagoland hugs the shores of Lake Michigan. Central Chicago is made up of downtown plus the northern, western, and southern suburbs. The main map below shows the division of the Street Finder, while the map to the right shows a greater area of Chicagoland. Almost every listing in this guide features a page and grid reference to the maps in this section. The few entries that fall outside the area covered by the Street Finder maps give transport details instead.

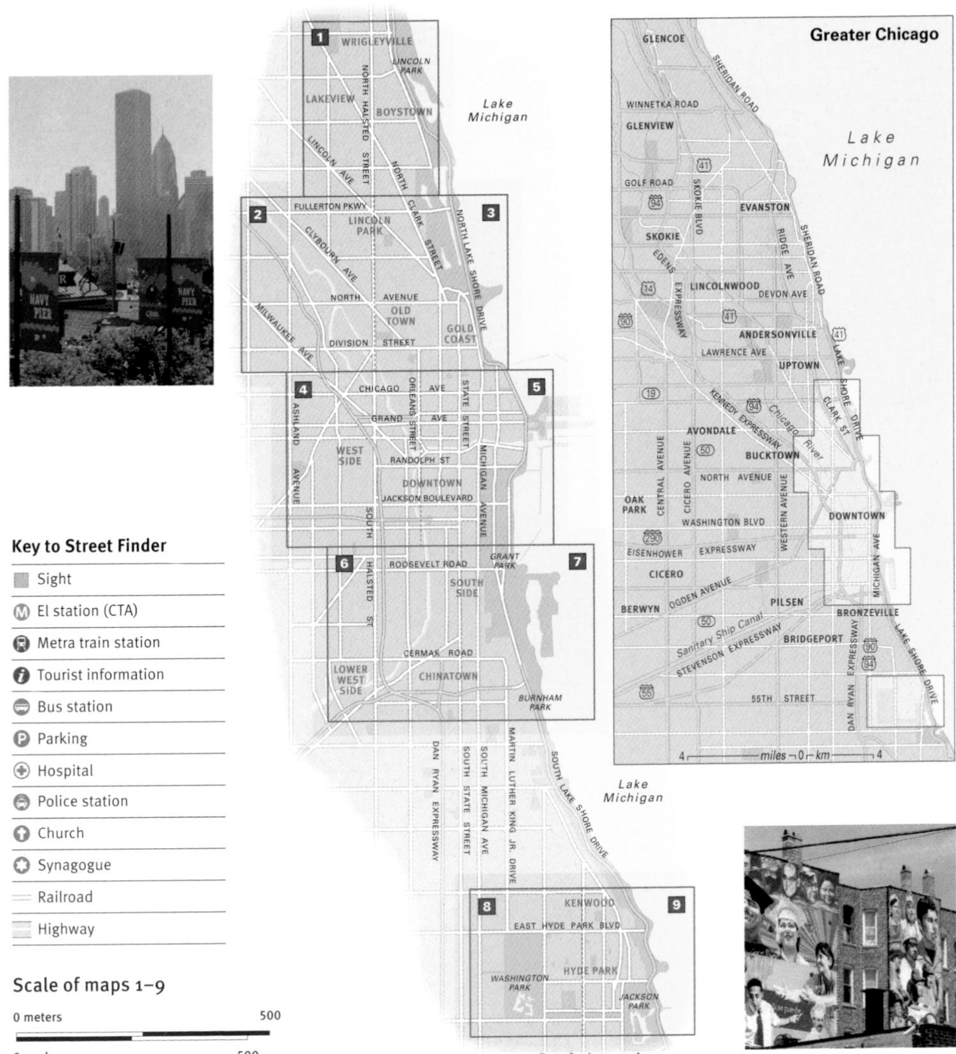

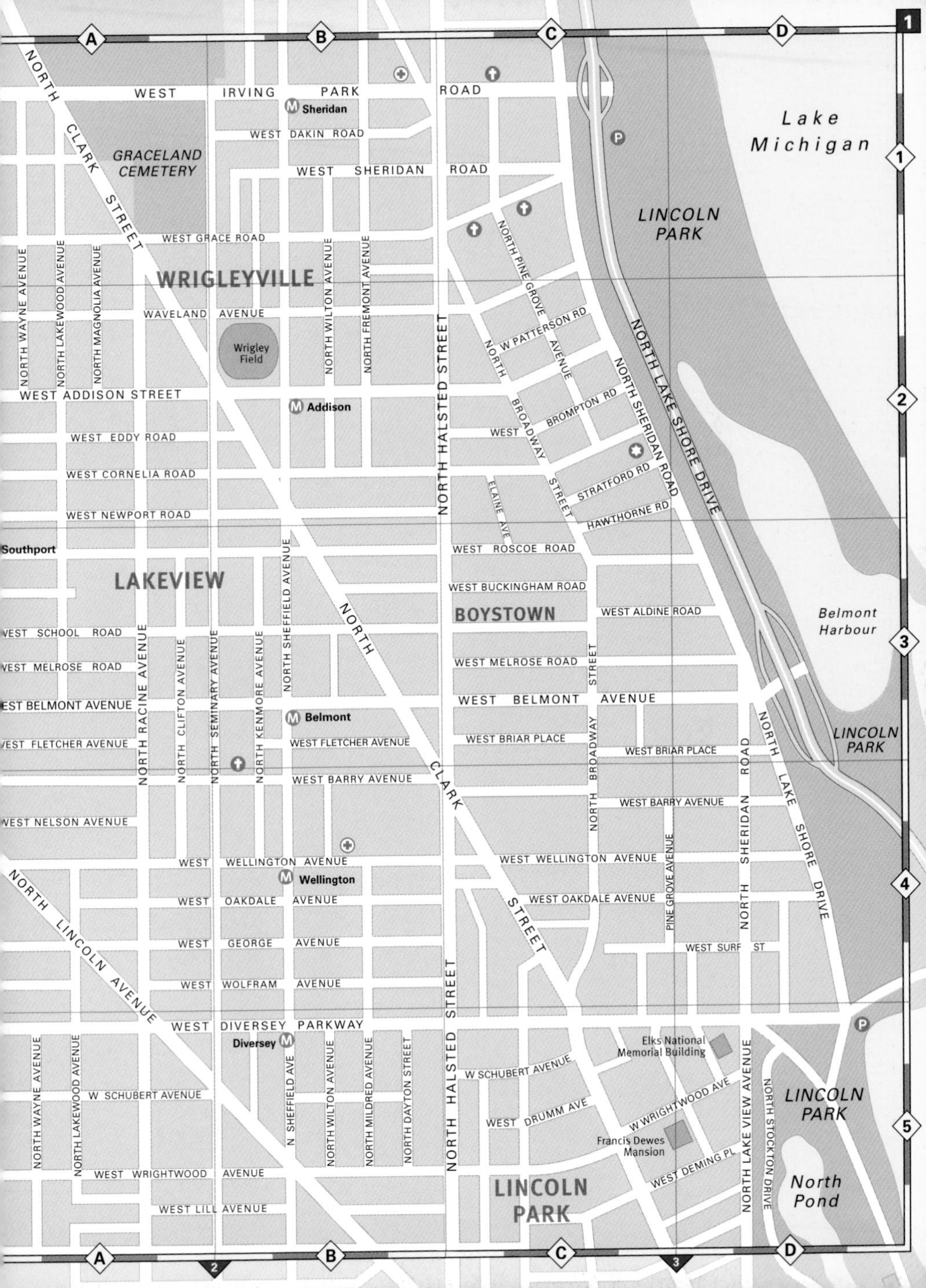

1
A
B
C
D
Lake Michigan
WEST IRVING PARK ROAD
Sheridan
WEST DAKIN ROAD
WEST SHERIDAN ROAD
GRACELAND CEMETERY
NORTH CLARK STREET
LINCOLN PARK
WEST GRACE ROAD
WRIGLEYVILLE
NORTH WAYNE AVENUE
NORTH LAKEWOOD AVENUE
NORTH MAGNOLIA AVENUE
NORTH WILTON AVENUE
NORTH FREMONT AVENUE
NORTH PINE GROVE AVENUE
WAVELAND AVENUE
Wrigley Field
W PATTERSON RD
NORTH HALSTED STREET
NORTH LAKE SHORE DRIVE
NORTH SHERIDAN ROAD
WEST ADDISON STREET
Addison
NORTH BROADWAY
WEST BROMPTON RD
WEST EDDY ROAD
WEST CORNELIA ROAD
STRATFORD RD
ELAINE AVE
STREET
HAWTHORNE RD
WEST NEWPORT ROAD
Southport
WEST ROSCOE ROAD
LAKEVIEW
NORTH SHEFFIELD AVENUE
WEST BUCKINGHAM ROAD
NORTH
BOYSTOWN
WEST ALDINE ROAD
Belmont Harbour
WEST SCHOOL ROAD
NORTH RACINE AVENUE
NORTH CLIFTON AVENUE
NORTH SEMINARY AVENUE
NORTH KENMORE AVENUE
WEST MELROSE ROAD
STREET
WEST MELROSE ROAD
WEST BELMONT AVENUE
WEST BELMONT AVENUE
Belmont
WEST FLETCHER AVENUE
WEST FLETCHER AVENUE
WEST BRIAR PLACE
WEST BRIAR PLACE
NORTH BROADWAY
LINCOLN PARK
WEST BARRY AVENUE
CLARK
WEST BARRY AVENUE
NORTH LAKE SHORE DRIVE
WEST NELSON AVENUE
PINE GROVE AVENUE
NORTH SHERIDAN ROAD
WEST WELLINGTON AVENUE
WEST WELLINGTON AVENUE
Wellington
NORTH LINCOLN AVENUE
WEST OAKDALE AVENUE
STREET
WEST OAKDALE AVENUE
WEST GEORGE AVENUE
WEST SURF ST
WEST WOLFRAM AVENUE
WEST DIVERSEY PARKWAY
Diversey
Elks National Memorial Building
NORTH WAYNE AVENUE
NORTH LAKEWOOD AVENUE
N SHEFFIELD AVE
NORTH WILTON AVENUE
NORTH MILDRED AVENUE
NORTH DAYTON STREET
NORTH HALSTED STREET
W SCHUBERT AVENUE
W SCHUBERT AVENUE
WEST DRUMM AVE
W WRIGHTWOOD AVE
NORTH LAKE VIEW AVENUE
NORTH STOCKTON DRIVE
LINCOLN PARK
Francis Dewes Mansion
WEST DEMING PL
WEST WRIGHTWOOD AVENUE
LINCOLN PARK
North Pond
WEST LILL AVENUE
2
3
4
5

2
A
B
C
D
1
2
3
4
5
4
WEST ALTGELD STREET
WEST MONTANA STREET
WEST FULLERTON AVENUE
Fullerton
De Paul University
WEST BELDEN AVENUE
N JANSSEN AVE
SOUTHPORT AVENUE
NORTH WAYNE AVENUE
N LAKEWOOD AVENUE
NORTH MAGNOLIA AVE
NORTH RACINE AVENUE
NORTH CLIFTON AVENUE
NORTH SEMINARY AVENUE
NORTH KENMORE AVENUE
WEST WEBSTER AVENUE
NORTH CLYBOURN AVENUE
NORTH DOMINICK STREET
NORTH ASHLAND AVENUE
NORTH ELSTON AVENUE
AVONDALE AVENUE
JOHN F. KENNEDY EXPRESSWAY
W DICKENS AVE
WEST DICKENS AVENUE
NORTH DAMEN AVENUE
WEST ARMITAGE AVENUE
Armitage
WEST
Chicago River North Branch
WEST CORTLAND STREET
W CORTLAND ST
NORTH WINCHESTER AVENUE
NORTH WOLCOTT AVENUE
NORTH HONORE AVENUE
NORTH WOOD STREET
MAUD AVENUE
NORTH KINGSBURY STREET
NORTH MARCEY STREET
NORTH SHEFFIELD AVENUE
NORTH BISSELL STREET
NORTH FREMONT STREET
NORTH DAYTON STREET
W BLOOMINGDALE AVE
NORTH HERMITAGE AVENUE
NORTH PAULINA STREET
NORTH MARSHFIELD AVENUE
WEST WILLOW ST
WEST WILLOW
NORTH BISSELL ST
WEST WABANSIA AVENUE
NORTH ADA ST
NTHROOP STREET
WEST CONCORD PL
Steppenwolf Theatre
WEST NORTH AVENUE
Damen
North/Clybourn
WEST PIERCE AVENUE
W WEED ST
WEST LEMOYNE STREET
WICKER PARK
WEST JULIAN STREET
W BLACKHAWK ST
WEST BEACH AVENUE
NORTH MILWAUKEE AVENUE
NORTH ASHLAND
NORTH ELSTON AVENUE
NORTH CHERRY AVENUE
NORTH KINGSBURY STREET
UKRAINIAN VILLAGE
NORTH WABANSIA AVENUE
NORTH GREENVIEW AVENUE
NORTH CLAVER STREET
N WOLCOTT AVENUE
NORTH WOOD STREET
N PAULINA ST
Division
WEST DIVISION STREET
NORTH NOBLE STREET
NORTH BRANCH STREET
NORTH HICKORY AVENUE
NORTH HOOKER STREET
WEST HADDON AVENUE
WEST THOMAS STREET
WEST THOMAS ST
WEST CORTEZ STREET

3
E
F
G
H
1
2
3
4
5
LINCOLN PARK
Peggy Notebaert Nature Museum
N ORCHARD AVE
WEST ARLINGTON PL
WEST FULLERTON PARKWAY
Lincoln Park Conservatory
NORTH LINCOLN PARK WEST
NORTH CLARK STREET
NORTH LAKE SHORE DRIVE
WEST BELDEN AVENUE
WEST GRANT PLACE
NORTH LINCOLN AVENUE
Lake Michigan
OZ PARK
Lincoln Park Zoo
NORTH CANNON DRIVE
NORTH STOCKTON DRIVE
NORTH SEDGWICK STREET
WEST DICKENS AVENUE
Café Brauer
ARMITAGE AVENUE
NORTH BURLING STREET
NORTH ORCHARD STREET
NORTH HOWE AVENUE
NORTH LARRABEE STREET
NORTH MOHAWK ST
NORTH CLEVELAND AVENUE
NORTH HUDSON AVENUE
South Pond
WEST WISCONSIN STREET
North Avenue Beach
LINCOLN PARK
WEST MENOMONEE STREET
STREET
WEST EUGENIE STREET
Chicago Historical Society
Second City
LA SALLE DR
International Museum of Surgical Science
WEST NORTH AVENUE
Sedgwick
NORTH ORLEANS STREET
NORTH PARK AVENUE
NORTH WIELAND STREET
NORTH WELLS STREET
NORTH ASTOR STREET
BURTON PL
WEST BLACKHAWK STREET
NORTH CLYBOURN AVENUE
OLD TOWN
NORTH LASALLE STREET
NORTH STATE PARKWAY
GOLD COAST
NORTH MICHIGAN AVENUE
WEST SCHILLER STREET
EVERGREEN STREET
NORTH CLARK STREET
NORTH DEARBORN STREET
EAST BANKS STREET
WEST
W SULLIVAN ST
STANTON PARK
WEST GOETHE STREET
EAST GOETHE ST
GOUDY SQUARE
N STONE ST
WEST SCOTT STREET
EAST SCOTT STREET
NORTH LARRABEE STREET
Pedestrian Tunnel
WEST DIVISION STREET
E DIVISION ST
N SEDGWICK ST
FELTON CT
Clark/Division
N ORLEANS ST
WEST ELM ST
WEST ELM STREET
EAST ELM STREET
Oak Street Beach
NORTH CROSBY STREET
W ELM ST
SEWARD PARK
EAST CEDAR STREET
WEST HILL STREET
WEST MAPLE STREET
N RUSH ST
EAST BELLEVUE PL
Pedestrian Tunnel
KINGSBURY ST
WEST WENDELL ST
EAST LAKE SHORE DR
WEST OAK ST
WEST OAK STREET
EAST OAK ST

RIVER WEST
WEST LOOP
WAREHOUSE DISTRICT
RIVER NORTH
UNION PARK
WEST CHICAGO AVENUE
WEST GRAND AVENUE
WEST KINZIE STREET
JOHN F. KENNEDY EXPRESSWAY
DWIGHT D. EISENHOWER EXPRESSWAY
DAN RYAN EXPRESSWAY
NORTH MILWAUKEE AVENUE
NORTH OGDEN AVENUE
NORTH HALSTED STREET
SOUTH HALSTED STREET
NORTH ASHLAND AVENUE
SOUTH ASHLAND AVENUE
WEST WASHINGTON BOULEVARD
WEST JACKSON BOULEVARD
WEST MADISON STREET
WEST RANDOLPH STREET
WEST HARRISON STREET
WEST CONGRESS STREET
WEST VAN BUREN STREET
Chicago River
Grand
Clinton
Ashland
UIC-Halsted
Racine
Union
Ogilvie Transportation Center
Greyhound Bus Terminal
Museum of Holography
Civic Opera House
Jane Addams' Hull-House
University of Illinois at Chicago
MERCHANDISE MART PLAZA
HUDSON PLEDGE

5
E
F
G
H
3
7
1
2
3
4
5
WALTON ST
WEST WALTON ST
EAST WALTON PL
CONNORS PARK
WASHINGTON SQUARE
LOCUST ST
E DELAWARE PL
Fourth Presbyterian Church
John Hancock Center
CHESTNUT ST
EAST CHESTNUT STREET
WEST CHESTNUT ST
NORTH LASALLE STREET
MIES V. DER ROHE WAY
N DE WITT PL
Historic Water Tower and Pumping Station
INSTITUTE PL
EAST PEARSON ST
LAKE SHORE PARK
Pedestrian Tunnel
Chicago
Hershey's Chicago
SENECA PARK
Museum of Contemporary Art
WEST CHICAGO AVENUE
EAST CHICAGO AVENUE
Chicago
NORTH FRANKLIN ST
NORTH WELLS ST
WEST SUPERIOR ST
EAST SUPERIOR STREET
STREETERVILLE
NORTH STATE STREET
NORTH WABASH AVENUE
NORTH RUSH STREET
NORTH MICHIGAN AVENUE
NORTH ST. CLAIR STREET
WEST HURON ST
EAST HURON ST
WEST ERIE ST
N FAIRBANKS COURT
EAST ERIE STREET
NORTH LAKE SHORE DRIVE
OHIO STREET BEACH
MILTON LEE OLIVE PARK
WEST ONTARIO STREET
EAST ONTARIO STREET
N MCCLURG COURT
WEST OHIO STREET
EAST OHIO STREET
NAVY PIER PARK
WEST GRAND AVENUE
EAST GRAND AVENUE
Grand
N PESHTIGO CT
Navy Pier
NORTH CLARK STREET
NORTH DEARBORN STREET
EST ILLINOIS STREET
EAST ILLINOIS STREET
GATEWAY PARK
Chicago Children's Museum
Tribune Tower
EST HUBBARD STREET
Museum of Broadcast Communication
WEST KINZIE STREET
Wrigley Building
EAST NORTH WATER STREET
Merchandise Mart
W CARROLL ST
Marina City Twin Towers
Chicago River
Merchandise Mart
EAST WACKER DRIVE
WEST WACKER DRIVE
CHESTNEY CT
E SOUTH WATER STREET
NORTH STETSON AVE
N COLUMBUS DRIVE
N FIELD BOULEVARD
N HARBOR DRIVE
West Wacker
POST PL
N WELLS ST
Clark
State
Goodman Theatre
E LAKE ST
E STREET
James R. Thompson Center
Lake
Chicago Theatre
Siskel Film Center
NORTH GARLAND CT
BEAUBIEN COURT
Randolph Street
WEST RANDOLPH STREET
E RANDOLPH STREET
Randolph
City Hall
Washington
Chicago Cultural Center
Jay Pritzker Pavilion
Washington
WEST WASHINGTON BLVD
E WASHINGTON BLVD
Reliance Building
Chase Bank
Madison
MILLENNIUM PARK
Monroe Harbor
WEST MADISON ST
E MADISON STREET
Inland Steel Building
S CLARK ST
Carson Pirie Scott
The Crown Fountain
DOWNTOWN
S WABASH AVE
SOUTH MICHIGAN AVENUE
ST MONROE STREET
E MONROE STREET
EAST MONROE DRIVE
SOUTH LAKE SHORE DRIVE
Monroe
Marquette Building
Adams
Art Institute of Chicago
WEST ADAMS STREET
E ADAMS STREET
The Rookery
Chicago Board of Trade
Quincy
Symphony Center
Federal Reserve Bank
Federal Center
Jackson
E JACKSON DRIVE
S FRANKLIN ST
Monadnock Building
SOUTH COLUMBUS DRIVE
LaSalle
W VAN BUREN ST
E VAN BUREN STREET
Library
Fine Arts Building
Van Buren Street
Harold Washington Library Center
CONGRESS PLAZA
CONGRESS PARKWAY
EAST CONGRESS DRIVE
SOUTH STATE STREET
Auditorium Theater
LaSalle
LaSalle Street
Buckingham Fountain
Chicago Harbor
EST HARRISON STREET
E HARRISON ST
Museum of Contemporary Photography
Harrison
S WELLS ST
S SHERMAN ST
S LASALLE ST
Printing House Row Historic District
S DEARBORN ST
S PLYMOUTH ST
Spertus Museum
EAST BALBO AVENUE
WEST POLK STREET
EAST 8TH STREET

6
LITTLE ITALY
University of Illinois at Chicago
LOWER WEST SIDE
CHINATOWN
WEST ROOSEVELT ROAD
WEST ROOSEVELT RD
WEST CERMAK ROAD
DAN RYAN EXPRESSWAY
STEVENSON EXPRESSWAY
ADLAI E.
SOUTH ARCHER AVENUE
SOUTH BLUE ISLAND AVENUE
SOUTH CANALPORT AVENUE
SOUTH HALSTED STREET
SOUTH RACINE AVENUE
SOUTH CANAL STREET
SOUTH CLARK STREET
SOUTH THROOP STREET
South Branch of Chicago River
Chicago River
Maxwell Street Market
Roosevelt
Cermak-Chinatown
Halsted
WILLIAMS PARK
WEST TAYLOR STREET
WEST 16TH STREET
WEST 18TH STREET
WEST 26TH STREET
SOUTH UNION AVENUE
SOUTH WENTWORTH AVENUE
SOUTH DEARBORN ST
SOUTH PLYMOUTH STREET
SOUTH FEDERAL STREET
W 27TH ST
A
B
C
D
1
2
3
4
5

7
5
E
F
G
H
1
2
3
4
5
GRANT PARK
Roosevelt Road
EAST ROOSEVELT RD
MUSEUM CAMPUS
John G. Shedd Aquarium
EAST SOLIDARITY DRIVE
Adler Planetarium
Field Museum
MCFETRIDGE DRIVE
NORTHERLY ISLAND PARK
SOUTH SIDE
Soldier Field
OLD LAKE SHORE DRIVE
Burnham Park Harbor
NORTHERLY ISLAND
EAST WALDRON DRIVE
SOUTH LAKE SHORE DRIVE
9TH STREET
11TH STREET
13TH STREET
14TH STREET
EAST 16TH STREET
EAST 18TH STREET
18TH DRIVE
18th
National Vietnam Veterans Art Museum
Glessner House
CHICAGO WOMEN'S PARK
Henry B. Clarke House
EAST CULLERTON STREET
Prairie Avenue Historic District
MEIGS FIELD
SOUTH WABASH AVENUE
SOUTH MICHIGAN AVENUE
SOUTH INDIANA AVENUE
S PRAIRIE AVENUE
McCormick Place North Building
EAST 21ST STREET
EAST CERMAK ROAD
Lakeside Center
E 23RD ST VIADUCT
Lake Michigan
E 23RD ST
23rd
SOUTH COTTAGE GROVE AVENUE
S PRAIRE AVENUE
SOUTH CALUMET AVENUE
McCormick Place South Building
BURNHAM PARK
E 24TH ST
EAST 24TH PLACE
ADLAI E. STEVENSON EXPRESSWAY
EAST 25TH STREET
MARTIN LUTHER KING JR. DR
EAST 26TH STREET
EAST 26TH ST
27th
28TH STREET
MICHIGAN AVE
SOUTH INDIANA AVE
SOUTH PRAIRIE AVE
SOUTH CALUMET AVE

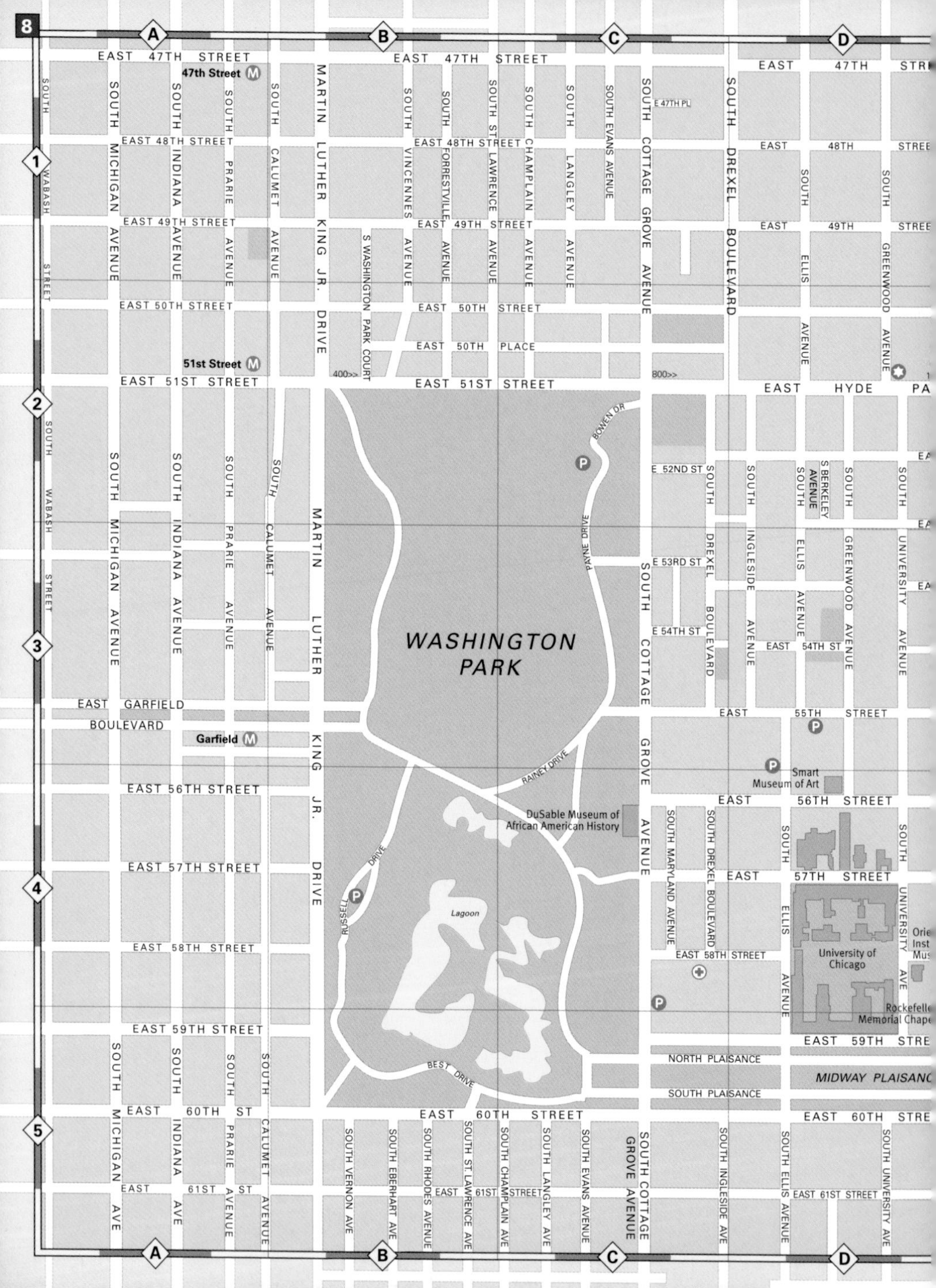

WASHINGTON PARK
47th Street
51st Street
Garfield
EAST 47TH STREET
EAST 48TH STREET
EAST 49TH STREET
EAST 50TH STREET
EAST 50TH PLACE
EAST 51ST STREET
EAST HYDE PARK
EAST GARFIELD BOULEVARD
EAST 55TH STREET
EAST 56TH STREET
EAST 57TH STREET
EAST 58TH STREET
EAST 59TH STREET
EAST 60TH STREET
EAST 61ST STREET
SOUTH WABASH STREET
SOUTH MICHIGAN AVENUE
SOUTH INDIANA AVENUE
SOUTH PRARIE AVENUE
SOUTH CALUMET AVENUE
MARTIN LUTHER KING JR. DRIVE
S WASHINGTON PARK COURT
SOUTH VINCENNES AVENUE
SOUTH FORRESTVILLE AVENUE
SOUTH ST LAWRENCE AVENUE
SOUTH CHAMPLAIN AVENUE
SOUTH LANGLEY AVENUE
SOUTH EVANS AVENUE
SOUTH COTTAGE GROVE AVENUE
SOUTH DREXEL BOULEVARD
E 47TH PL
E 52ND ST
E 53RD ST
E 54TH ST
EAST 54TH ST
SOUTH INGLESIDE AVENUE
SOUTH ELLIS AVENUE
S BERKELEY AVENUE
SOUTH GREENWOOD AVENUE
SOUTH UNIVERSITY AVENUE
SOUTH MARYLAND AVENUE
BOWEN DR
PAYNE DRIVE
RAINEY DRIVE
RUSSELL DRIVE
BEST DRIVE
Lagoon
DuSable Museum of African American History
Smart Museum of Art
University of Chicago
Rockefeller Memorial Chapel
NORTH PLAISANCE
MIDWAY PLAISANCE
SOUTH PLAISANCE
SOUTH VERNON AVE
SOUTH EBERHART AVE
SOUTH RHODES AVENUE
SOUTH ST.LAWRENCE AVE
SOUTH CHAMPLAIN AVE
SOUTH LANGLEY AVE
SOUTH EVANS AVENUE
SOUTH INGLESIDE AVE
SOUTH ELLIS AVENUE
SOUTH UNIVERSITY AVE
400>>
800>>
A B C D
1 2 3 4 5

E
F
G
H
1
2
3
4
5
47th
KENWOOD
E 47TH PL
SOUTH LAKE SHORE DRIVE
SOUTH LAKE PARK AVENUE
SOUTH CORNELL AVENUE
CHICAGO BEACH DRIVE
S KIMBARK AVENUE
S KENWOOD AVENUE
SOUTH DORCHESTER AVENUE
SOUTH BLACKSTONE AVENUE
KENWOOD PARK
CORNELL AVE
EAST 50TH STREET
EAST 50TH ST
E 50TH PL
EAST END AVE
EAST MADISON PARK AVENUE
1400>>
Lake Michigan
BOULEVARD
SOUTH KENWOOD AVE
BURNHAM PARK
52ND STREET
ELM LAYLOT PARK
53RD STREET
EAST 53RD STREET
53rd
HYDE PARK BOULEVARD
SOUTH HARPER AVENUE
SOUTH SHORE DRIVE
54TH STREET
NICHOLS PARK
SOUTH EVERETT AVENUE
PROMONTORY POINT
EAST 55TH ST
E 55TH PL
HYDE PARK
P
EAST 56TH STREET
55th-56th-57th
EAST 57TH DRIVE
EAST 57TH STREET
SOUTH KIMBARK AVENUE
SOUTH STONY ISLAND AVENUE
Museum of Science and Industry
EAST 58TH ST
SOUTH DORCHESTER AVE
EAST 59TH ST
59th
EAST 60TH STREET
Osaka Japanese Gardens
JACKSON PARK
West Lagoon
East Lagoon
S DORCHESTER AVE
SOUTH HARPER AVE
S STONY ISLAND AVE
SOUTH CORNELL DRIVE
EAST 61ST STREET
Wooded Island

8th Street, East 5 F5
9th Street, East 7 E1
11th Street, East 7 E1
13th Street, East 7 E1
13th Street, West 6 A1
14th Place, West 6 B2
14th Street, East 7 E2
14th Street, West 6 D2
15th Street, West 6 A2
16th Street, East 7 E2
16th Street, West 6 D2
17th Street, West 6 C3
18th Drive 7 F3
18th Street, East 7 E3
18th Street, West 6 C3
19th Street, West 6 A3
21st Street, East 7 E4
21st Street, West 6 D4
22nd Place, West 6 C4
23rd Place, West 6 C4
23rd Street, East 7 E4
23rd Street, West 6 C4
24th Place, East 7 E5
24th Place, West 6 C5
24th Street, East 7 E4
24th Street, West 6 C4
25th Place, West 6 C5
25th Street, East 7 E5
25th Street, West 6 D5
26th Street, East 7 E5
26th Street, West 6 B5
27th Street, West 6 D5
28th Place, West 6 C5
28th Street, East 7 E5
28th Street, West 6 C5
47th Place, East 9 E1
47th Street, East 8 D1
48th Street, East 8 D1
49th Street, East 8 D1
50th Place, East 8 B2
50th Street, East 9 E2
51st Street, East 8 A2
52nd Street, East 9 E2
53rd Street, East 9 F3
54th Street, East 8 D3
55th Place, East 9 E3
55th Street, East 8 D3
56th Street, East 8 A4
57th Drive, East 9 F4
57th Street, East 8 D4
58th Street, East 9 E4
59th Street, East 8 D4
60th Street, East 8 D5
61st Street, East 8 D5

A

Aberdeen Street, North 4 B3
Ada Maud Avenue 3 C2
Ada Street, North 4 A3
Adams Street, East 5 F4
Adams Street, West 5 E4
Addison Street, West 1 A2
Adlai E. Stevenson Expressway 7 E5
Aldine Road, West 1 C3
Alexander Street, West 6 D4
Allport Street, South 6 A3
Altgeld Street, West 2 C1
Arbour Place, West 4 A3
Archer Avenue, South 6 C4
Arlington Place, West 3 E1
Armitage Avenue, West 2 A2
Armour Street, North 1 A2
Ashland Avenue, North 2 B4
Ashland Avenue, South 4 A4
Astor Street, North 3 G4
Avondale Avenue 2 A2

B

Balbo Avenue, East 5 F5
Banks Street, East 3 G4
Barry Avenue, West 1 B4
Beach Avenue, West 2 A4
Beaubien Courts 5 F3
Belden Avenue, West 3 E1
Bellevue Place, East 3 G5
Belmont Avenue, West 1 C3
Berkeley Avenue, South 8 D2
Best Drive 8 B5
Bishop Street, North 1 A2
Bissell Street, North 2 D3
Blackhawk Street, West 2 D4
Blackstone Avenue, South 9 E3
Bloomingdale Avenue, West 2 A3
Blue Island Avenue, South 6 A1
Bowen Drive 8 C2
Branch Street, North 2 D5
Briar Place, West 1 C3
Broadway Street 1 C2
Brompton Road, West 1 C2
Buckingham Road, West 1 C3
Burling Avenue, North 3 E1
Burling Street, North 3 E3
Burton Place 3 G4

C

Cabrini Street, West 4 A5
Calumet Avenue, South 8 B1
Cambridge Avenue, North 4 D1
Canal Street, North 4 D3
Canal Street, South 6 C1
Canalport Avenue, South 6 B3
Cannon Drive, North 3 G2
Carpenter Street, North 4 B3
Carpenter Street, South 4 C5
Carroll Avenue, West 4 A3
Carroll Street, West 5 E3
Cedar Street, East 3 G5
Cermak Road, East 7 E4
Cermak Road, West 6 B4
Champlain Avenue, South 8 C1
Cherry Avenue, North 2 C4
Chestney Court 5 F3
Chestnut Street, East 5 F1
Chestnut Street, West 5 E1
Chicago Avenue, East 5 F1
Chicago Avenue, West 5 E1
Chicago Beach Drive 9 F1
Clark Street, North 1 A1
Clark Street, South 5 E4
Claver Street, North 2 B5
Cleveland Avenue, North 3 E3
Clifton Avenue, North 1 A3
Clinton Street, North 4 D3
Clinton Street, South 4 D4
Clybourn Avenue, North 3 E4
Columbus Drive, North 5 G3
Columbus Drive, South 5 G4
Concord Place, West 2 D3
Congress Drive, East 5 F5
Congress Parkway, West 4 D5
Congress Plaza 5 F5
Congress Street, West 4 A5
Cornelia Road 1 A2
Cornell Avenue, South 9 F3
Cornell Drive, South 9 F5
Cortez Street, West 2 B5
Cortland Street, West 2 B2
Cottage Grove Avenue, South 8 C3
Crosby Street, North 3 E5
Cullerton Street, East 7 E3
Cullerton Street, West 6 A3

D

Dakin Road, West 1 B1
Damen Avenue, North 2 A3
Dan Ryan Expressway 6 C5
Dayton Street, North 1 B5
De Witt Place, North 5 G1
Dearborn Street, North 5 E2
Dearborn Street, South 6 D2
Dekoven Street, West 6 C1
Delaware Place, East 5 F1
Deming Place, West 1 C5
Des Plaines Street, North 4 D3
Des Plaines Street, South 4 D4
Dickens Avenue, West 2 A2
Diversey Parkway, West 1 A5
Division Street, East 3 G5
Division Street, West 2 A5
Dominick Street, North 2 B2
Dorchester Avenue, South 9 E4
Drexel Boulevard, South 8 C4
Drumm Avenue, West 1 C5
Dwight D. Eisenhower Expressway 4 A5

E

East End Avenue 9 F2
Eberhart Avenue, South 8 B5
Eddy Road, West 1 A2
Elaine Avenue 1 C2
Elizabeth Avenue, North 4 B3
Elizabeth Street, North 4 B1
Ellis Avenue, South 8 D4
Elm Street, East 3 G5
Elm Street, West 3 E5
Elston Avenue, North 2 B3
Emerald Avenue, South 6 B5
Erie Street, East 5 G2
Erie Street, West 4 D2
Eugenie Street, West 3 F3
Evans Avenue, South 8 C1
Everett Avenue, South 9 G3
Evergreen Street, West 3 F4

F

Fairbanks Court, North 5 G2
Federal Park Terrace, South 6 D1
Federal Street, South 6 D4
Felton Court 3 F5
Field Boulevard, North 5 G3
Fletcher Avenue, West 1 B3
Flournoy Street, West 4 A5
Forrestville Avenue, South 8 B1
Franklin Street, North 5 E1
Franklin Street, South 5 E4
Fremont Avenue, North 1 B2
Fremont Street, North 2 D3
Fullerton Avenue, West 2 B1
Fullerton Parkway, West 3 E1
Fulton Market, West 4 B3
Fulton Street, West 4 A3

G

Garfield Boulevard, East 8 A3
Garland Court, North 5 F3
George Avenue, West 1 A4
Goethe Street, East 3 G5
Goethe Street, West 3 F5
Goudy Square 3 G5
Grace Road, West 1 A1
Grand Avenue, East 5 G2
Grand Avenue, West 5 E2
Grant Place, West 3 E1
Green Street, North 4 C3
Green Street, South 4 C4
Greenview Avenue, North 4 A1
Greenwood Avenue, South 8 D2
Grove Street, South 8 D1

H

Haddon Avenue, West 2 A5
Halsted Street, North 4 C3
Halsted Street, South 4 C5
Harbor Drive, North 5 G3
Harper Avenue, South 9 F3
Harrison Street, East 5 F5
Harrison Street, West 5 E5
Hastings Street, West 6 C2
Hawthorne Road 1 C2
Hermitage Avenue, North 2 A3
Hickory Avenue, North 2 D5
Hill Street, West 3 F5
Honore Avenue, North 2 A3
Hooker Street, North 2 D5
Howe Avenue, North 3 E3
Hubbard Street, West 5 E2
Hudson Avenue, North 3 F3
Huron Street, East 5 G1
Huron Street, West 4 D1
Hyde Park Boulevard, East 8 D2
Hyde Park Boulevard, South 9 F2

I
Illinois Street, East 5 F2
Illinois Street, West 5 E2
Indiana Avenue, South 7 E4
Ingleside Avenue, South 8 D2
Institute Place, West 5 E1
Irving Park Road, West 1 A1

J
Jackson Boulevard, West 4 D4
Jackson Drive, East 5 F4
Janssen Avenue, North 2 B1
Jefferson Street, North 4 D3
Jefferson Street, South 6 B1
John F. Kennedy Expressway 2 A2
Julian Street, West 2 A4
Just Street, North 4 A3

K
Kenmore Avenue, North 1 B3
Kenwood Avenue, South 9 E4
Kimbark Avenue, South 9 E4
Kingsbury Street, North 2 C3
Kinzie Street, West 5 E2

L
Laflin Street, North 4 A3
Laflin Street, South 4 A4
Lake Park Avenue, South 9 F4
Lake Shore Drive, East 3 H5
Lake Shore Drive, North 3 G1
Lake Shore Drive, South 9 G4
Lake Street, East 5 F3
Lake Street, West 4 A3
Lake View Avenue, North 1 D5
Lakewood Avenue, North 1 A2
Langley Avenue, South 8 C1
Larrabee Street, North 3 E5
LaSalle Street, North 5 E1
LaSalle Street, South 5 E5
Lemoyne Street, West 2 A4
Lill Avenue, West 1 A5
Lincoln Avenue, North 3 E1
Lincoln Park, North 3 F2
Locust Street, West 5 E1
Loomis Street, South 4 A4
Lowe Avenue, South 6 B5
Lumber Street, South 6 C4
Lytle Street, South 6 A1

M
Madison Park Avenue, East 9 E2
Madison Street, East 5 F4
Madison Street, West 5 E4
Magnolia Avenue, North 1 A2
Maple Street, West 3 G5
Marcey Street, North 2 C3
Marshfield Avenue 2 B3
Martin Luther King Jr. Drive 8 B1
Maryland Avenue, South 8 C4
Maxwell Street, West 6 C1
May Street, North 4 B3
May Street, South 6 A3
McClurg Court, North 5 G2
Mcfetridge Drive 7 F2
Melrose Road, West 1 C3
Menomonee Street, West 3 F3
Merchandise Mart Plaza 4 D3
Michigan Avenue, North 5 F2
Michigan Avenue, South 5 F4
Mies van der Rohe Way 5 G1
Mildred Avenue, North 1 B5
Miller Street, South 6 A2
Milwaukee Avenue, North 4 B1
Mohawk Street, North 3 E3
Monroe Drive, East 5 F4
Monroe Street, East 5 F4
Monroe Street, West 5 E4
Montana Street, West 2 C1
Morgan Street, North 4 C3
Morgan Street, South 4 C4

N
Nelson Avenue, West 1 A4
Newberry Avenue, South 6 B2
Newport Road, West 1 A2
Noble Street, North 3 C5
Normal Avenue, South 6 C3
Normal Street, South 6 c3
North Avenue, West 3 E4
North Water Street, East 5 G2

O
Oak Street, East 3 G5
Oak Street, West 3 E5
Oakdale Avenue, West 1 C4
Ogden Avenue, North 4 B2
Ohio Street, East 5 G2
Ohio Street, West 5 E2
Old Lake Shore Drive 7 F2
Ontario Street, East 5 G2
Ontario Street, West 5 E2
Orchard Avenue, North 3 E1
Orchard Street, North 3 E3
Orleans Street, North 4 D2

P
Park Avenue, North 3 F4
Patterson Road, West 1 C2
Paulina Street, North 2 B3
Payne Drive 8 C3
Pearson Street, East 5 G1
Peoria Street, North 4 C3
Peoria Street, South 4 C4
Peshtigo Court, North 5 H2
Pierce Avenue, West 2 A4
Pine Grove Avenue, North 1 C1
Plaisance, North 8 C5
Plaisance, South 8 C5
Plymouth Street, South 5 F5
Polk Street, West 5 E5
Poplar Avenue, South 6 A5
Post Place 5 E3
Prarie Avenue, South 7 E3
Princeton Avenue, South 6 C4

R
Racine Avenue, North 1 A3
Racine Avenue, South 6 A2
Rainey Drive 8 C4
Randolph Street, East 5 G3
Randolph Street, West 5 E3
Rhodes Avenue, South 8 B5
Roosevelt Road, East 7 E1
Roosevelt Road, West 6 C1
Roscoe Road, West 1 C3
Rube Street, South 6 B3
Rush Street, North 5 F1
Russell Drive 8 B4

S
St. Clair Street, North 5 G1
St. Lawrence Avenue, South 8 B1
Sangamon Street, North 4 C3
Sangamon Street, South 4 C4
Schiller Street, West 3 F4
School Road, West 1 A3
Schubert Avenue, West 1 C5
Scott Street, East 3 G5
Scott Street, West 3 F5
Sedgwick Street, North 3 F2
Seminary Avenue, North 1 B3
Sheffield Avenue, North 1 B3
Sheridan Road, North 1 D4
Sheridan Road, West 1 B1
Sherman Street 5 E5
Shore Drive, South 9 G3
Solidarity Drive, East 7 F2
South Water Street, East 5 F3
Southport Avenue, North 1 A2
State Parkway, North 3 G5
State Street, North 5 F1
State Street, South 5 F5
Stetson Avenue, North 5 G3
Stewart Street, South 6 C3
Stockton Drive, North 3 F2
Stone Street, North 3 H5
Stony Island Avenue, South 9 F4
Stratford Road 1 C2
Sullivan Street, West 3 E4
Superior Street, West 4 A1
Surf Street, West 1 D4

T
Taylor Street, West 6 A1
Thomas Street, West 2 A5
Throop Street, North 2 C3
Throop Street, South 6 A3

U
Union Avenue, South 6 B2
University Avenue, South 8 D4

V
Van Buren Street, East 5 F5
Van Buren Street, West 5 E5
Vernon Avenue, South 8 B5
Vernon Park Place 4 B5
Vincennes Avenue, South 8 B1

W
Wabansia Avenue, North 2 B4
Wabansia Avenue, West 2 A3
Wabash Avenue, North 5 F2
Wabash Avenue, South 7 E1
Wacker Drive, East 5 G3
Wacker Drive, North 4 D3
Wacker Drive, South 4 D4
Wacker Drive, West 5 E3
Waldron Drive, East 7 F2
Wallace Avenue, South 6 C5
Walton Place, East 5 F1
Walton Street, West 4 A1
Washburn Avenue, West 6 A1
Washington Boulevard, East 5 F3
Washington Boulevard, West 5 E3
Washington Park Court, South 8 B1
Waveland Avenue, West 1 A2
Wayman Street, West 4 C3
Wayne Avenue, North 1 A2
Webster Avenue, West 2 D2
Weed Street, West 2 D4
Wellington Avenue, West 1 C4
Wells Street, North 3 F4
Wells Street, South 5 E5
Wendell Street, West 3 F5
Wentworth Avenue, South 6 D4
Wieland Street, North 3 F4
Willow Street, West 2 D3
Wilton Avenue, North 1 B2
Winchester Avenue, North 2 A3
Wisconsin Street, West 3 F3
Wolcott Avenue, North 2 A3
Wolfram Avenue, West 1 A4
Wood Street, North 2 A3
Woodlawn Avenue, South 9 E1
Wrightwood Avenue, West 1 A5

North

Restaurants

For further restaurants, cafés, and tea rooms, see also Streetlife and Havens p177

Andersonville

Jin Ju (p33) $$
Korean

Boystown

Kit Kat Lounge & Supper Club (p28) $$
New American

pingpong (p30) $
Asian

Edgewater

Moody's Pub (p33) $
American

Far North Side

Arun's (p40) $$$
Thai

Café 28 (p32) $$
Cuban

Tiffin (p32) $$
Indian

Lakeview

Ann Sather (p28) $
Swedish

Mia Francesca (p29) $$
Italian

Orange (p29) $
American

Pepper Lounge (p29) $$
New American

Lincoln Park

Alinea (p30) $$$
New American

Bourgeois Pig (p31) $
Café

Charlie Trotter's (p40) $$$
New American

Half Shell, Inc. (p30) $$
Seafood

Karyn's Fresh Corner (p32) $$
Vegetarian

North Pond (p31) $$$
New American

Penny's Noodles (p28) $
Asian

The Wiener's Circle (p32) $
American

Shopping

Andersonville

His Stuff (p52)
Menswear

Women & Children First (p65)
Books & Records

Boystown

Unabridged Bookstore (p65)
Books & Records

Edgewater

Broadway Antique Market (p53)
Vintage & Retro

Lakeview

Chicago Comics (p56)
Books & Records

Mint (p55)
Accessories

Lincoln Park

Art Effect (p55)
Homewares

Calvin Tran (p54)
Womenswear

CB2 (p55)
Homewares

Dave's Records (p57)
Books & Records

Endo-Exo Apothecary (p53)
Health & Beauty

Eskell (p56)
Womenswear

Lori's Shoes (p54)
Shoes & Accessories

Reckless Records (p57)
Books & Records

Lincoln Square

The Chopping Block (p52)
Homewares

Merz Apothecary (p52)
Health & Beauty

Uptown

Unique So Chique (p141)
Womenswear

Wrigleyville

Jake (p56)
Mens- & Womenswear

Trousseau (p56)
Lingerie

Art & Architecture

Lincoln Park

International Museum of Surgical Science (p72)
Museum

Rogers Park

Leather Archives & Museum (p72)
Museum

Performance

Lakeview

Athenaeum Theater (p91)
Dance & Theater

Link's Hall (p91)
Dance, Live Music & Theater

Lincoln Park

B.L.U.E.S. (p94)
Jazz & Blues

Facets Cinémathèque (p90)
Movie Theater

Kingston Mines (p94)
Jazz & Blues

Lincoln Square

Old Town School of Folk Music (p102)
Live Music

Uptown

Annoyance Theatre (p91)
Comedy

Aragon Ballroom (p94)
Live Music & Spectator Sports

Green Mill Jazz Club (p92)
Jazz & Blues

Wrigleyville

I.O. (p91)
Comedy

Live Bait Theatre (p91)
Theater

Metro (p94)
Live Music

Music Box Theatre (p90)
Movie Theater

Bars & Clubs

For further bars & clubs, see also Streetlife p177

Andersonville

Big Chicks (p114)
Bar

Hopleaf (p114)
Bar

Boystown

Hydrate (p111)
Bar

Sidetrack (p111)
Bar

Spin (p110)
Club

Lincoln Park

Aliveone (p110)
Bar

The Apartment (p109)
Bar

John Barleycorn's (p110)
Bar

Kincade's (p122)
Sports Bar

Lilly's (p108)
Bar

Lion's Head Pub (p109)
Bar

Webster's Wine Bar (p108)
Wine Bar

Wrightwood Tap (p108)
Bar

Uptown

Carol's (p114)
Bar

Crew (p113)
Sports Bar

Holiday Club (p113)
Bar

Wrigleyville

Cubby Bear Lounge (p122)
Sports Bar

Delilah's (p111)
Bar

Sluggers (p122)
Sports Bar

Smartbar (p113)
Club

Wild Hare (p112)
Bar

Streetlife

Boystown

Boystown (p128)

Circuit (p128)
Bar

Melrose Restaurant (p128)
Restaurant

Roscoe's (p128)
Bar

Sidetrack (p128)
Bar

Spin (p110)
Club

Far North

Devon Avenue (p128)

Hema's Kitchen (p128)
Restaurant

Indian Garden (p128)
Restaurant

Patel Brothers (p128)
Store

Lincoln Park

Green City Market (p136)
Shopping

Lakeview & Wrigleyville

Anne Sather (p28)
Restaurant

Army Navy Surplus (p129)
Store

Berlin (p129)
Club

Lakeview & Wrigleyville (p129)

Mama Desta's Red Sea (p129)
Restaurant

Medusa's Circle (p129)
Store

Metro (p94)
Live Music Venue

Ragstock (p129)
Store

Record Emporium (p129)
Store

Wrigley Field (p101)
Spectator Sports

Lincoln Square

Café Selmarie (p130)
Café

Chicago Brauhaus (p130)
Restaurant

Laurie's Planet of Sound (p130)
Store

Lincoln Square (p130)

Meyer Delicatessen (p130)
Store

Museum of Decorative Arts (p130)
Store

Traipse's (p130)
Store

Havens

Andersonville

Kopi – A Traveler's Café (p141)
Café

Glencoe

Chicago Botanic Garden (p12, p140)
Green Space

Lincoln Park

Café Brauer (p143)
Café

Lincoln Park (pp142–3)
Green Space

Lincoln Park Conservatory (p143)
Conservatory

Lincoln Park Zoo (p13, p143)
Zoo

North Pond (p31)
Restaurant

Peggy Notabaert Nature Museum (p142)
Museum

Space Time Tanks (p141)
Health & Beauty

Uptown

Unique So Chique (p141)
Tea Room

Urban Tea Lounge (p141)
Tea Room

Hotels

Lakeview

Best Westerm Hawthorne Terrace (p153)
Cheap

City Suites (p153)
Cheap

Lincoln Park

China Doll (p152)
Moderate

City Scene Bed and Breakfast (p161)
Moderate

Days Inn Lincoln Park-North (p152)
Cheap

Willows Hotel (p153)
Cheap

Windy City Urban Inn (p152)
Moderate

Downtown

Restaurants

For further restaurants, cafés, and tea rooms, see also Streetlife p179

Gold Coast

Morton's (p31) $$$
American

The Loop

Everest (p40) $$$
French

Lou Mitchell's (p39) $
American

Perry's (p39) $
Sandwich Bar

Old Town

Kamehachi (p40) $$$
Japanese

Twin Anchors (p38) $
American

River North

BIN 36 (p33) $$
New American

Café Iberico (p34) $$
Spanish

David Burke's Primehouse (p31) $$$
American

Japonais (p35) $$$
Japanese

Lou Malnati's (p34) $$
Pizza

Mr. Beef (p34) $
Sandwiches

Downtown

Restaurants *continued*

Pizzeria Uno (p34) $$
Pizza

Spiaggia (p40) $$$
Italian

Tru (p40) $$$
New American

Streeterville

NoMI (p33) $$$
French

Osteria Via Stato (p38) $$$
Italian

Shopping

Gold Coast

G'bani (p58)
Mens- & Womenswear

Ikram (p58)
Womenswear

Oak Street (p62)

The Loop

Rock Records (p57)
Books & Records

Old Town

Sara Jane (p59)
Womenswear

River North

Carson, Pirie, Scott (p58)
Department Store

Europa Books (p65)
Books & Records

Jazz Record Mart (p57)
Books & Records

Macy's (p58)
Department Store

Material Possessions (p59)
Homewares

Paper Source (p59)
Specialist

Streeterville

Bloomingdales (p58)
Department Store

Fox & Obel (p59)
Food & Drink

H&M (p63)
Chain Stores

Lord & Taylor (p58)
Department Store

Marshall's (p63)
Chain Stores

Neiman Marcus (p58)
Department Store

Nordstrom (p58)
Department Store

Sak's (p58)
Department Store

Streeterville Market (p136)
Market

TJ Maxx (p63)
Chain Stores

Vosges Haut Chocolat (p57)
Food & Drink

Art & Architecture

The Loop

Art Institute of Chicago (p14, p73)
Museum

"Batcolumn" (p83)
Public Art

Chicago Architecture Foundation (p76)
Museum

Chicago Cultural Center (p76)
Mixed Media

"Flamingo" (p83)
Public Art

"Four Seasons" (p83)
Public Art

Gallery 37 Center for the Arts (p76)
Art Gallery

James R. Thompson Center (p77)
Modern Building

The Monadnock (p80)
Historic Building

"Monument With Standing Beast" (p83)
Public Art

"the Picasso" (p83)
Public Art

The Reliance Building (p80)
Historic Building

The Rookery (p76)
Historic Building

Sears Tower (p80)
Modern Building

West Wacker Drive Riverwalk (p72)
Modern Buildings

Millennium Park

Millennium Park (p13, p74)
Green Space

River North

Carl Hammer (p84)
Art Gallery

Marina City (p80)
Modern Building

Streeterville

John Hancock Building (p80)
Modern Building

Museum of Broadcast Communications (p77)
Museum

Museum of Contemporary Art (p14, p77)
Museum

Tribune Tower (p80)
Historic Building

Wrigley Building (p80)
Historic Building

Performance

The Loop

Chicago Theatre (p95)
Live Music & Theater

Civic Opera House (p98)
Opera

Gene Siskel Film Center (p98)
Movie Theater

Goodman Theatre (p98)
Theater

Symphony Center (p98)
Classical Music & Live Music

River North

Jazz Showcase (p99)
Jazz & Blues

Millenium Park

Joan W. & Irving B. Harris Theatre for Music & Dance (p99)
Classical Music, Dance, Live Music & Theater

Old Town

The Second City (p90)
Comedy

Steppenwolf Theatre Company (p95)
Theater

Zanies (p91)
Comedy

Streeterville

Lookingglass Theatre Company (p95)
Theater

Bars & Clubs

For further bars & clubs, see also Streetlife and Havens p179

Gold Coast

Bella Lounge (p120)
Cocktail Lounge

Cactus (p120)
Bar

Elm Street Liquors (p115)
Cocktail Lounge

Hunt Club (p122)
Sports Bar

Le Passage (p120)
Cocktail Lounge

Old Town

Jet Vodka Lounge (p115)
Cocktail Lounge

Spoon (p108)
Cocktail Lounge

River North

Howl at the Moon (p115)
Bar

Jet Vodka Lounge (p115)
Cocktail Lounge

Rock Bottom Brewery (p120)
Bar

Rockit Bar and Grill (p119)
Sports Bar

Sound-bar (p118)
Club

Whiskey Sky (p120)
Bar

Streeterville

Signature Room & Lounge (p120)
Cocktail Lounge

Weed Street

Zentra (p108)
Club

Streetlife

Gold Coast

Cactus (p120)
Bar

Elm Street Liquors (p133)
Cocktail Lounge

Gold Coast (p133)

Melvin B's (p133)
Bar

Oak Street Beach (p136)

Le Passage (p120)
Cocktail Lounge

Sofitel Chicago Water Tower (p159)
Bar

The Loop

Daley Plaza Market (p136)
Shopping

Old Town

Old Town (p131)

Old Town Ale House (p131)
Bar

Old Town Pub (p131)
Bar

Salpicon (p131)
Restaurant

The Second City (p90)
Comedy

Streeterville

Castaways Bar & Grill (p132)
Restaurant

Lakefront Bike Path (p132)

Museum Campus (p132)
Green Space

Navy Pier (p132)
Attraction

North Avenue Beach (p132)
Beach

Promontory Point (p132)
Green Space

Streeterville Market (p136)
Shopping

Havens

Gold Coast

Fourth Presbyterian Church (p145)
Religious Building

Urban Oasis (p144)
Spa

The Loop

Harold Washington Library Center (p145)
Library

Streeterville

Signature Room and Lounge (p144)
Cocktail Lounge

Hotels

Gold Coast

Flemish House (p160)
Moderate

Gold Coast Guest House (p159)
Moderate

Hotel Indigo (p160)
Moderate

Sutton Place Hotel (p160)
Moderate

The Loop

Hard Rock Hotel (p154)
Moderate

Hotel Allegro (p156)
Expensive

Hotel Burnham (p155)
Expensive

Hotel Monaco (p157)
Moderate

The James Hotel (p156)
Expensive

The Palmer House Hilton (p154)
Moderate

River North

Amalfi Hotel Chicago (p158)
Moderate

Cass Hotel (p156)
Cheap

Four Points by Sheraton (p157)
Moderate

House of Blues Hotel (p158)
Moderate

Ohio House Motel (p158)
Cheap

Streeterville

The Drake (p156)
Expensive

The Four Seasons (p156)
Expensive

The Hotel InterContinental (p157)
Moderate

The James Hotel (p156)
Expensive

Omni Chicago Hotel (p159)
Moderate

The Park Hyatt (p156)
Expensive

The Peninsula (p156)
Expensive

Sofitel Chicago Water Tower (p159)
Expensive

W Chicago Lakeshore (p157)
Expensive

West

Restaurants

For further restaurants, cafés, and tea rooms, see also Streetlife and Havens pp180–1

Bucktown

Le Bouchon (p44) $$
French

Cafe Bolero (p44) $$
Cuban

Coast (p44) $$
Japanese

Spring (p43) $$$
New American

Greektown

Greek Islands (p42) $$
Greek

Little Italy

Tufanos (p42) $$
Italian

Pilsen

Nuevo Leon (p42) $
Mexican

River West

Green Zebra (p46) $$
Vegetarian

Moto (p47) $$$
New American

Twisted Spoke (p46) $
American

West Loop

avec (p45) $$
Mediterranean

Blackbird (p45) $$$
New American

West

Restaurants *continued*

Nine Steakhouse (p31) $$$
American

Sushi Wabi (p45) $$$
Japanese

Wicker Park

Bongo Room (p42) $
American

Hot Chocolate (p43) $$
New American

Piece (p34) $$
Pizza

Pizza Metro (p34) $
Pizza

Shopping

Bucktown

Apartment No. 9 (p67)
Menswear

Robin Richman (p67)
Womenswear

Stitch (p67)
Lifestyle

Ukrainian Village

Dusty Groove (P57)
Books & Records

Wicker Park

City Soles (p64)
Shoes & Accessories

Le Fetiche (p147)
Shoes & Accessories

Hefjina (p63)
Lifestyle

Jolie Joli (p64)
Mens- & Womenswear

Myopic Books (p65)
Books & Records

Niche (p64)
Shoes & Accessories

p45 (p66)
Womenswear

Penelope's (p63)
Mens- & Womenswear

Quimby's (p64)
Books & Records

Silver Moon (p65)
Vintage & Retro

Silver Room (p63)
Shoes & Accessories

Art & Architecture

Oak Park

Oak Park (p80)
Modern Buildings

Pilsen

Dubhe Carreño Gallery (p84)
Art Gallery

Mexican Fine Arts Center & Museum (p81)
Museum

Ukrainian Village

Intuit (p81)
Art Gallery

West Loop

Douglas Dawson Gallery (p77)
Art Gallery

Linda Warren Gallery (p84)
Art Gallery

Museum of Holography (p77)
Museum

Performance

Avondale

Abbey Pub (p102)
Live Music

Logan Square

Rosa's Lounge (p99)
Jazz & Blues

Roscoe Village

Viaduct Theatre (p99)
Live Music, Movie Theater & Theater

Ukranian Village

Chopin Theatre (p100)
Dance, Live Music, Movie Theater & Theater

Empty Bottle (p102)
Live Music

Hideout (p102)
Live Music

Bars & Clubs

For further bars & clubs, see also Streetlife p180

Bucktown

Cans Bar and Canteen (p125)
Bar

Danny's Tavern (p134)
DJ Bar

darkroom (p124)
bar

Logan Square

Quenchers (p125)
Bar

Roscoe Village

Hungry Brain (p113)
Bar

Ukrainian Village

Rodan
DJ Bar

Sonotheque (p123)
Club

West Loop

Cobra Lounge (p125)
DJ Bar

Fulton Lounge (p123)
Bar

Funky Buddha Lounge (p122)
Club

reserve (p122)
Club

Union Park (p121)
Bar

Wicker Park

Pontiac Café (p125)
Bar

Salud Tequila Lounge (p124)
Bar

Vintage Wine Bar (p124)
Wine Bar

Streetlife

Near West Side

United Center (p101)
Spectator Sports

Pilsen

Café Jumping Bean (p137)
Restaurant

Mexican Fine Arts Center & Museum (p81)
Museum

Pilsen (p137)

Skylark (p137)
Bar

Rosemont

Allstate Arena (p101)
Spectator Sports

Taylor Street

Al's #1 Italian Beef (p136)
Restaurant

Conte de Savoia (p136)
Store

Mario's Italian Lemonade (p136)
Kiosk

RoSal's Cucina (p136)
Restaurant

Taylor Street (p136)

West Loop

Chicago Antique Market (p136)
Shopping

Wicker Park

Danny's Tavern (p134)
Bar

Earwax Café (p134)
Café

Flat Iron Arts Building (p134)
Art Gallery

Irazu (p134)
Restaurant

Pontian Café (p125)
Bar

Rainbo Club (p134)
Bar

Recycle It (p135)
Store

Una Mae's Freak Boutique (p135)
Store

Wicker Park (pp134–5)

Havens

Wicker Park

Ruby Room (p146)
Health & Beauty

Sole Nail Lounge and Beauty Emporium (p147)
Health & Beauty

Hotels

Wicker Park

House of Two Urns (p161)
Cheap

South

Restaurants

Bronzeville

Spoken Word Café (p101) $
Café

Chinatown

The Phoenix (p41) $$
Chinese

Hyde Park

Dixie Kitchen (p41) $$
American

Near South Side

Manny's Coffee Shop (p40) $
American

South Side

Eleven City Diner (p39) $$
South/South Side

Gioco (p40) $$
Italian

Opera (p41) $$$
Chinese

Shopping

Hyde Park

57th St. Books (p65)
Books & Records

O'Gara & Wilson (p65)
Books & Records

Seminary Co-op (p65)
Books & Records

Near South Side

Maxwell Street Market (p136)
Markets

Millennium Park

The Savvy Traveller (p65)
Books & Records

Art & Architecture

Bridgeport

Illinois Institute of Technology (p85)
Modern Buildings

Hyde Park

DuSable Museum (p83)
Museum

Frederic C. Robie House (p83)
Modern Building

Museum of Science & Industry (p15)
Museum

Oriental Institute (p83)
Museum

Smart Museum (p83)
Museum

University of Chicago Campus (p83)
Historic Buildings

Museum Campus

Adler Planetarium & Astronomy Museum (p15)
Museum

The Field Museum (p13)
Museum

Shedd Aquarium (p15, p82)
Aquarium

South Loop

Museum of Contemporary Photography (p81)
Museum

Spertus Museum (p82)
Museum

South Side

Historic Pullman District (p84)
Historic Buildings

Prairie Avenue Historic District (p82)
Historic Buildings

Performance

Bronzeville

Spoken Word Cafe (p101)
Jazz & Blues, Comedy & Live Music

Chinatown

Velvet Lounge (p101)
Jazz & Blues

Far South

eta Creative Arts Foundation (p102)
Theater

New Apartment Lounge (p102)
Jazz & Blues

Hyde Park

Court Theatre (p102)
Theater

South Loop

Buddy Guy's Legends (p94)
Jazz & Blues

HotHouse (p103)
Live Music, Movie Theater & Theater

South Side

Cotton Club (p94)
Jazz & Blues

Bars & Clubs

Bronzeville

Chicago Legends (p121)
Bar

Near South Side

Junior's Sports Lounge (p121)
Sports Bar

South Loop

Wabash Tap (p121)
Bar

South Side

Tantrum (p121)
Cocktail Lounge

Streetlife

Bridgeview

Bridgeview Stadium (p101)
Spectator Sports

Far South Side

Doyle Stadium (p101)
Spectator Sports

Museum Campus

Soldier Field (p101)
Spectator Sports

Near South Side

Maxwell Street Market (p136)
Shopping

South Side

U.S. Cellular Field (p101)
Spectator Sports

Havens

Jackson Park

Jackson Park (p147)
Green Space

Osaka Gardens (p147)
Green Space

Hotels

Bridgeport

Benedictine Bed & Breakfast (p161)
Moderate

South Loop

Wheeler Mansion (p161)
Moderate

Restaurants

American

Al's #1 Italian Beef (p136) $
West/Taylor Street

Bongo Room (p42) $
West/Wicker Park

Castaways Bar & Grill (p132) $$
North/Lincoln Park

David Burke's Primehouse (p31) $$$
Downtown/River North

Dixie Kitchen (p41) $$
South/Hyde Park

Eleven City Diner (p39) $$
South/South Side

Gibson's Steak House (p133) $$$
Downtown/Gold Coast

Lou Mitchell's (p39) $
Downtown/The Loop

Manny's Coffee Shop (p40) $
South/Near South Side

Melrose (p128) $
North/Boystown

Moody's Pub (p33) $
North/Edgewater

Morton's (p31) $$$
Dowtown/Gold Coast

Nine Steakhouse (p31) $$$
West/West Loop

Orange (p29) $
North/Lakeview

Twin Anchors (p38) $
Downtown/Old Town

Twisted Spoke (p46) $
West/River West

The Wiener's Circle (p32) $
North/Lincoln Park

Asian

Penny's Noodles (p28) $
North/Lincoln Park

pingpong (p30) $
North/Boystown

Cafés

Bourgeois Pig (p31) $
North/Lincoln Park

Café Brauer (p143) $
North/Lincoln Park

Café Jumping Bean (p137) $
West/Pilsen

Café Selmarie (p130) $
North/Lincoln Square

Earwax Café (p125) $
West/Wicker Park

Spoken Word Café (p101) $
South/Bronzeville

Chinese

Opera (p41) $$$
South/South Side

The Phoenix (p41) $$
South/Chinatown

Cuban

Café 28 (p32) $$
North/Far North Side

Café Bolero (p44) $$
West/Bucktown

Ethiopian

Mama Desta's Red Sea (p129) $$
North/Lakeview

French

Le Bouchon (p44) $$
West/Bucktown

Everest (p40) $$$
Downtown/The Loop

NoMI (p33) $$$
Downtown/Streeterville

Greek

Greek Islands (p42) $$
West/Greektown

Indian

Hema's Kitchen (p128) $
North/Far North

Indian Garden (p128) $$
North/Far North

Tiffin (p32) $$
North/Far North Side

Italian

Gioco (p40) $$
South/South Side

Mia Francesca (p29) $$
North/Lakeview

Osteria Via Stato (p38) $$$
Downtown/Streeterville

RoSal's Cucina (p136) $
West/Taylor Street

Spiaggia (p40) $$$
Downtown/River North

Tufanos (p42) $$
West/Little Italy

Japanese

Coast (p44) $$
West/Bucktown

Japonais (p35) $$$
Downtown/River North

Kamehachi (p40) $$$
Downtown/Old Town

Sushi Wabi (p45) $$$
West/West Loop

Korean

Jin Ju (p33) $$
North/Andersonville

Mediterranean

avec (p45) $$
West/West Loop

Mexican

Irazu (p134) $
West/Wicker Park

Nuevo Leon (p42) $
West/Pilsen

Salpicon (p131) $$
Downtown/Old Town

New American

Alinea (p30) $$$
North/Lincoln Park

BIN 36 (p33) $$
Downtown/River North

Blackbird (p45) $$$
West/West Loop

Charlie Trotter's (p40) $$$
North/Lincoln Park

Hot Chocolate (p43) $$
West/Wicker Park

Kit Kat Lounge & Supper Club (p28) $$
North/Boystown

Moto (p47) $$$
West/River West

North Pond (p31) $$$
North/Lincoln Park

Pepper Lounge (p29) $$
North/Lakeview

Spring (p43) $$$
West/Bucktown

Tru (p40) $$$
Downtown/River North

Pizza

Lou Malnati's (p34) $$
Downtown/River North

Piece (p34) $$
West/Wicker Park

Pizza Metro (p34) $
West/Wicker Park

Pizzeria Uno (p34) $$
Downtown/River North

Sandwich Bars

Mr. Beef (p34) $
Downtown/River North

Perry's (p39) $
Downtown/The Loop

Seafood

Half Shell, Inc. (p30) $$
North/Lincoln Park

Spanish

Café Iberico (p34) $$
Downtown/River North

Swedish

Ann Sather (p28) $
North/Lakeview

Thai

Arun's (p40) $$$
North/Far North Side

Vegetarian

Green Zebra (p46) $$
West/River West

Karyn's Fresh Corner (p32) $$
North/Lincoln Park

Shopping

Books & Records

57th St. Books (p65)
South/Hyde Park

Chicago Comics (p56)
North/Lakeview

Dave's Records (p57)
North/Lincoln Park

Dusty Groove (p57)
West/Ukrainian Village

Europa Books (p65)
Downtown/River North

Jazz Record Mart (p57)
Downtown/River North

Laurie's Planet of Sound (p130)
North/Lincoln Square

Myopic Books (p65)
West/Wicker Park

O'Gara & Wilson (p64)
South/Hyde Park

Quimby's (p64)
West/Wicker Park

Reckless Records (p57)
North/Lincoln Park

Record Emporium (p129)
North/Lakeview

Rock Records (p57)
Downtown/The Loop

The Savvy Traveller (p65)
South/Millennium Park

Seminary Co-op (p65)
South/Hyde Park

Unabridged Bookstore (p65)
North/Boystown

Women & Children First (p65)
North/Andersonville

Chain Stores

H&M (p63)
Downtown/Streeterville

Marshall's (p63)
Downtown/Streeterville

TJ Maxx (p63)
Downtown/Streeterville

Department Stores

Bloomingdales (p58)
Downtown/Streeterville

Carson, Pirie, Scott (p58)
Downtown/River North

Lord & Taylor (p58)
Downtown/Streeterville

Macy's (p58)
Downtown/River North

Neiman Marcus (p58)
Downtown/Streeterville

Nordstrom (p58)
Downtown/Streeterville

Sak's (p58)
Downtown/Streeterville

Food & Drink

Fox & Obel (p59)
Downtown/Streeterville

Conte de Savoia (p136)
West/Taylor Street

Meyer Delicatessen (p130)
North/Lincoln Square

Patel Brothers (p128)
North/Far North

Vosges Haut Chocolat (p57)
Downtown/Streeterville

Health & Beauty

Endo-Exo Apothecary (p53)
North/Lincoln Park

Merz Apothecary (p52)
North/Lincoln Square

Homewares

Art Effect (p55)
North/Lincoln Park

CB2 (p55)
North/Lincoln Park

The Chopping Block (p52)
North/Lincoln Square

Material Possessions (p59)
Downtown/River North

Lifestyle

Hefjina (p63)
West/Wicker Park

Stitch (p67)
West/Bucktown

Lingerie

Trousseau (p56)
North/Wrigleyville

Markets

Chicago Antique Market (p136)
West/West Loop

Daley Plaza Market (p136)
Downtown/The Loop

Green City Market (p136)
North/Lincoln Park

Maxwell Street Market (p136)
South/Near South Side

Streeterville Market (p136)
Downtown/Streeterville

Mens- & Womenswear

Belmont Army Navy Surplus (p129)
North/Lakeview

G'bani (p58)
Downtown/Gold Coast

Jake (p56)
North/Wrigleyville

Jolie Joli (p64)
West/Wicker Park

Medusa's Circle (p129)
North/Wrigleyville

Oak Street (p62)

Penelope's (p63)
West/Wicker Park

Menswear

Apartment No. 9 (p67)
West/Bucktown

His Stuff (p52)
North/Andersonville

Shoes & Accessories

City Soles (p64)
West/Wicker Park

Lori's Shoes (p54)
North/Lincoln Park

Mint (p55)
North/Lakeview

Niche (p64)
West/Wicker Park

Silver Room (p63)
West/Wicker Park

Traipse's (p130)
North/Lincoln Square

Specialist

Museum of Decorative Arts (p130)
North/Lincoln Square

Paper Source (p59)
Downtown/River North

Vintage & Retro

Broadway Antique Market (p53)
North/Edgewater

Ragstock (p129)
North/Lakeview

Silver Moon (p65)
West/Wicker Park

Index by Type

Shopping

Womenswear

Calvin Tran (p54)
North/Lincoln Park

Eskell (p56)
North/Lincoln Park

Ikram (p58)
Downtown/Gold Coast

p45 (p66)
West/Wicker Park

Recycle It (p135)
West/Wicker Park

Robin Richman (p67)
West/Bucktown

Sara Jane (p59)
Downtown/Old Town

Una Mae's Freak Boutique (p135)
West/Wicker Park

Unique So Chique (p141)
North/Uptown

Art & Architecture

Aquarium

Shedd Aquarium (p15, p82)
South/Museum Campus

Art Galleries

Carl Hammer (p84)
Downtown/River North

Douglas Dawson Gallery (p77)
West/West Loop

Dubhe Carreño Gallery (p84)
West/Pilsen

Flat Iron Arts Building (p134)
West/Wicker Park

Gallery 37 Center for the Arts (p76)
Downtown/The Loop

Intuit (p81)
West/Ukrainian Village

Linda Warren Gallery (p84)
West/West Loop

Green Spaces

Millennium Park (p13, p74)
Downtown/Millennium Park

Historic Buildings

Historic Pullman District (p84)
South/South Side

The Monadnock (p80)
Downtown/The Loop

Prairie Avenue Historic District (p82)
South/South Side

The Reliance Building (p80)
Downtown/The Loop

The Rookery (p76)
Downtown/The Loop

Tribune Tower (p80)
Downtown/Streeterville

University of Chicago Campus (p83)
South/Hyde Park

Wrigley Building (p80)
Downtown/Streeterville

Mixed Media

Chicago Cultural Center (p76)
Downtown/The Loop

Modern Buildings

Illinois Institute of Technology (p85)
South/Bridgeport

Frederic C. Robie House (p83)
South/Hyde Park

James R. Thompson Center (p77)
Downtown/The Loop

John Hancock Building (p80)
Downtown/Streeterville

Marina City (p80)
Downtown/River North

Oak Park (p80)
West/Oak Park

Sears Tower (p12, 80)
Downtown/The Loop

West Wacker Drive Riverwalk (p72)
Downtown/The Loop

Museums

Adler Planetarium & Astronomy Museum (p15)
South/Museum Campus

Art Institute of Chicago (p14, p73)
Downtown/The Loop

Chicago Architecture Foundation (p76)
Downtown/The Loop

DuSable Museum of African-American History (p83)
South/Hyde Park

The Field Museum (p13)
South/Museum Campus

International Museum of Surgical Science (p72)
North/Lincoln Park

Leather Archives & Museum (p72)
North/Rogers Park

Mexican Fine Arts Center & Museum (p81)
West/Pilsen

Museum of Broadcast Communications (p77)
Downtown/Streeterville

Museum of Contemporary Art (p14, p77)
Downtown/Streeterville

Museum of Contemporary Photography (p81)
South/South Loop

Museum of Holography (p77)
West/West Loop

Museum of Science & Industry (p15)
South/Hyde Park

Oriental Institute (p83)
South/Hyde Park

Smart Museum (p83)
South/Hyde Park

Spertus Museum (p82)
South/South Loop

Public Art

"Batcolumn" (p83)
Downtown/The Loop

"Flamingo" (p83)
Downtown/The Loop

"Four Seasons" (p83)
Downtown/The Loop

"Monument With Standing Beast" (p83)
Downtown/The Loop

"the Picasso" (p83)
Downtown/The Loop

Performance

Classical Music

Joan W. & Irving B. Harris Theatre for Music & Dance (p99)
Downtown/Millennium Park

Symphony Center (p98)
Downtown/The Loop

Dance

Athenaeum Theater (p91)
North/Lakeview

Chopin Theatre (p100)
West/Ukrainian Village

Joan W. & Irving B. Harris Theatre for Music & Dance (p99)
Downtown/Millennium Park

Link's Hall (p91)
North/Lakeview

Comedy

Annoyance Theatre (p91)
North/Uptown

I.O. (p91)
North/Wrigleyville

The Second City (p90)
Downtown/Old Town

Spoken Word Café (p101)
South/Bronzeville

Zanies (p91)
Downtown/Old Town

Jazz & Blues

B.L.U.E.S. (p94)
North/Lincoln Park

Buddy Guy's Legends (p94)
South/South Loop

Cotton Club (p94)
South/South Side

Green Mill Jazz Club (p92)
North/Uptown

Jazz Showcase (p99)
Downtown/River North

Kingston Mines (p94)
North/Lincoln Park

New Apartment Lounge (p102)
South/Far South

Rosa's Lounge (p99)
West/Logan Square

Spoken Word Café (p101)
South/Bronzeville

Velvet Lounge (p101)
South/Chinatown

Live Music

Abbey Pub (p102)
West/Avondale

Aragon Ballroom (p94)
North/Uptown

Chicago Theatre (p95)
Downtown/The Loop

Chopin Theatre (p100)
West/Ukrainian Village

Empty Bottle (p102)
West/Ukrainian Village

Hideout (p102)
West/Ukrainian Village

HotHouse (p103)
South/South Loop

Joan W. & Irving B. Harris Theatre for Music & Dance (p99)
Downtown/Millennium Park

Link's Hall (p91)
North/Lakeview

Metro (p94)
North/Wrigleyville

Old Town School of Folk Music (p102)
North/Lincoln Square

Spoken Word Café (p101)
South/Bronzeville

Symphony Center (p98)
Downtown/The Loop

Viaduct Theatre (p99)
West/Roscoe Village

Movie Theaters

Chopin Theatre (p100)
West/Ukrainian Village

Facets Cinémathèque (p90)
North/Lincoln Park

Gene Siskel Film Center (p98)
Downtown/The Loop

HotHouse (p103)
South/South Loop

Music Box Theatre (p90)
North/Wrigleyville

Viaduct Theatre (p99)
West/Roscoe Village

Opera

Civic Opera House (p98)
Downtown/The Loop

Joan W. & Irving B. Harris Theatre for Music & Dance (p99)
Downtown/Millennium Park

Spectator Sports

Allstate Arena (p101)
West/Rosemont

Aragon Ballroom (p94)
North/Uptown

Bridgeview Stadium (p101)
South/Bridgeview

Doyle Stadium (p101)
South/Far South Side

Soldier Field (p101)
South/Museum Campus

United Center (p101)
West/Near West Side

U.S. Cellular Field (p101)
South/South Side

Wrigley Field (p101)
North/Wrigleyville

Theaters

Athenaeum Theater (p91)
North/Lakeview

Chicago Theatre (p95)
Downtown/The Loop

Chopin Theatre (p100)
West/Ukrainian Village

Court Theatre (p102)
South/Hyde Park

eta Creative Arts Foundation (p102)
South/Far South

Goodman Theatre (p102)
Downtown/The Loop

HotHouse (p103)
South/South Loop

Link's Hall (p91)
North/Lakeview

Live Bait Theatre (p91)
North/Wrigleyville

Lookingglass Theatre Company (p95)
Downtown/Old Town

Steppenwolf Theatre Company (p95)
Downtownn/Old Town

Viaduct Theatre (p99)
West/Roscoe Village

Bars & Clubs

Bars

Aliveone (p110)
North/Lincoln Park

The Apartment (p109)
North/Lincoln Park

Big Chicks (p114)
North/Andersonville

Cactus (p120)
Downtown/Gold Coast

Cans Bar and Canteen (p125)
West/Bucktown

Carol's (p114)
North/Uptown

Castaways Bar & Grill (p132)
North/Lincoln Park

Chicago Brauhaus (p130)
North/Lincoln Park

Chicago Legends (p121)
South/Bronzeville

darkroom (p124)
West/Bucktown

Delilah's (p111)
North/Wrigleyville

Fulton Lounge (p123)
West/West Loop

Holiday Club (p113)
North/Uptown

Hopleaf (p114)
North/Andersonville

Howl at the Moon (p115)
Downtown/River North

Hydrate (p111)
North/Boystown

Hungry Brain (p113)
West/Roscoe Village

John Barleycorn's (p110)
North/Lincoln Park

Lilly's (p102)
North/Lincoln Park

Lion's Head Pub (p109)
North/Lincoln Park

Melvin B's (p133)
Downtown/Gold Coast

Moody's Pub (p33)
North/Edgewater

Pontiac Café (p125)
West/Wicker Park

Old Town Ale House (p131)
Downtown/Old Town

Old Town Pub (p131)
Downtown/Old Town

Bars & Clubs

Bars *continued*

Quenchers (p125)
West/Logan Square

Rainbo Club (p134)
West/Wicker Park

Roscoe's (p128)
North/Boystown

Rock Bottom Brewery (p120)
Downtown/River North

Salud Tequila Lounge (p124)
West/Wicker Park

Sidetrack (p111)
North/Boystown

Skylark (p137)
West/Pilsen

Tufanos (p42)
West/Little Italy

Twisted Spoke (p46)
West/River West

Union Park (p121)
West/West Loop

Wabash Tap (p121)
South/South Loop

Whiskey Sky (p120)
Downtown/River North

Wild Hare (p112)
North/Wrigleyville

Wrightwood Tap (p108)
North/Lincoln Park

Clubs

Berlin (p129)
North/Lakeview

Funky Buddha Lounge (p122)
West/West Loop

reserve (p122)
West/West Loop

Smartbar (p113)
North/Wrigleyville

Sonotheque (p123)
West/Ukrainian Village

Sound-bar (p118)
Downtown/River North

Spin (p110)
North/Boystown

Zentra (p110)
Downtown/Weed Street

Cocktail Lounges

Bella Lounge (p120)
Downtown/Gold Coast

Elm Street Liquors (p115)
Downtown/Gold Coast

Jet Vodka Lounge (p115)
Downtown/Old Town

Kit Kat Lounge & Supper Club (p28)
North/Boystown

Le Passage (p120)
Downtown/Gold Coast

Signature Room & Lounge (p120)
Downtown/Streeterville

Spoon (p108)
Downtown/Old Town

Tantrum (p121)
South/South Side

DJ Bars

Danny's Tavern (p125)
West/Bucktown

Cobra Lounge (p125)
West/West Loop

Rodan (p125)
West/Wicker Park

Sports Bars

Crew (p113)
North/Uptown

Cubby Bear Lounge (p122)
North/Wrigleyville

Hunt Club (p122)
Downtown/Gold Coast

Junior's Sports Lounge (p121)
South/Near South Side

Kincade's (p122)
North/Lincoln Park

Rockit Bar and Grill (p119)
Downtown/River North

Sluggers (p122)
North/Wrigleyville

Wine Bars

BIN 36 (p33)
Downtown/River North

Vintage Wine Bar (p124)
West/Wicker Park

Webster's Wine Bar (p108)
North/Lincoln Park

Havens

Cafés & Tea Rooms

Café Brauer (p143)
North/Lincoln Park

Kopi – A Traveler's Café (p141)
North/Andersonville

Unique So Chique (p141)
North/Uptown

Urban Tea Lounge (p141)
North/Uptown

Cocktail Lounge

Signature Room and Lounge (p138)
Downtown/Streeterville

Conservatory

Lincoln Park Conservatory (p143)
North/Lincoln Park

Green Spaces

Chicago Botanic Garden (p12, p140)
North/Glencoe

Jackson Park (p147)
South/Jackson Park

Lincoln Park (pp142–3)
North/Lincoln Park

Museum Campus (p132)
South/Museum Campus

Osaka Gardens (p147)
South/Jackson Park

Promontory Point (p132)
South/Hyde Park

Health & Beauty

Ruby Room (p146)
West/Wicker Park

Sole Nail Lounge and Beauty Emporium (p147)
West/Wicker Park

Space Time Tanks (p141)
North/Lincoln Park

Urban Oasis (p144)
Downtown/Gold Coast

Library

Harold Washington Library Center (p145)
Downtown/The Loop

Museum

Peggy Notabaert Nature Museum (p142)
North/Lincoln Park

Religious Building

Fourth Presbyterian Church (p145)
Downtown/Gold Coast

Zoo

Lincoln Park Zoo (p13, p143)
North/Lincoln Park

Hotels

Cheap

Best Western Hawthorne Terrace (p153)
North/Lakeview

Cass Hotel (p156)
Downtown/River North

Days Inn Lincoln Park-North (p152)
North/Lincoln Park

City Suites (p153)
North/Lakeview

Ohio House Motel (p158)
Downtown/River North

Willows Hotel (p153)
North/Lincoln Park

Moderate

Amalfi Hotel Chicago (p158)
Downtown/River North

Benedictine Bed & Breakfast (p161)
South/Bridgeport

China Doll (p152)
North/Lincoln Park

City Scene Bed and Breakfast (p161)
North/Lincoln Park

Flemish House (p160)
Downtown/Gold Coast

Four Points by Sheraton (p157)
Downtown/River North

Gold Coast Guest House (p159)
Downtown/Gold Coast

Hard Rock Hotel (p154)
Downtown/Loop

House of Blues Hotel (p158)
Downtown/River North

House of Two Urns (p161)
West/Wicker Park

Hotel Indigo (p160)
Downtown/Gold Coast

The Hotel InterContinental (p157)
Downtown/Streeterville

Hotel Monaco (p157)
Downtown/Loop

Omni Chicago Hotel (p159)
Downtown/Streeterville

The Palmer House Hilton (p154)
Downtown/Loop

Sutton Place Hotel (p160)
Downtown/Gold Coast

Wheeler Mansion (p161)
South/Bridgeport

Windy City Urban Inn (p152)
North/Lincoln Park

Expensive

The Drake Hotel (p156)
Downtown/Streeterville

The Four Seasons (p156)
Downtown/Streeterville

Hotel Allegro (p156)
Downtown/Loop

Hotel Burnham (p155)
Downtown/Loop

The James Chicago (p156)
Downtown/Streeterville

The Park Hyatt (p156)
Downtown/Streeterville

The Peninsula (p156)
Downtown/Streeterville

Sofitel Chicago Water Tower (p159)
Downtown/Streeterville

W Chicago Lakeshore (p157)
Downtown/Streeterville

57th Street Art Fair **16**
57th Street Bookstore **65**

A

A1 Limousines **21**
Abbey Pub **102**
Adler Planetarium **15**
airports **20**
Alinea **30**
Aliveone **110**
Allstate Arena **101**
Al's #1 Italian Beef **136**
Amalfi Hotel Chicago **158**
Ann Sather **28, 129**
Annoyance Theater **91**
Apartment/Lion Head Pub **108**
Apartment No. 9 **67**
apartments, efficiency **161**
Aquarium, Shedd **15, 82**
Aragon Ballroom **94**
architecture
 see art and architecture
Around the Coyote **18**
art and architecture **69–85**
 architectural icons **80**
 Downtown public art **83**
 major art hubs **84**
Art Institute of Chicago **14, 73**
Art Effect **55**
Arun's **40**
At Home Inn Chicago **153**
Athenaeum Theatre **91**
ATMs **22**
avec **45**

B

banks **22**
 opening hours **22, 23**
Barney's New York **62**
bars and clubs **105–25**
 DJ bars **125**
 drinks with a view **120**
 ID in **23**
 opening hours **22**
 sports bars **122**
 tipping **23**
baseball **101**
Bella Lounge **120**
Belmont Army Navy Surplus **129**
Benedictine Bed & Breakfast **161**
Berlin **129**
Best Western
 Hawthorne Terrace **153**
bicycles **21**
Big Chicks **114**
Bike Chicago **21**
Bin 36 **33**
Blackbird **45**
Bloomingdale's **58**
Blue Chicago **94**
B.L.U.E.S. **94**
blues clubs **94**
Blues Fest **16–17**
boats **21**
Bongo Room **42**
bookstores, independent **65**
Le Bouchon **44**
Bourgeois Pig **31**
Boystown **22, 128**
BP Bridge **74**
Bravco **62**
Bridgeview Stadium **101**
Broadway Antique Market (BAM) **53**
Buddy Guy's Legends **94**
budget shopping **63**
Burnham, Daniel **80**
buses **20**

C

Cactus **120, 133**
Café 28 **32**
Café Bolero **44**
Café Brauer **143**
Café Iberico **34**
Café Jumping Bean **137**
Café Selmarie **130**
Calder, Alexander **83**
Calvin Tran **54**
Camper **62**
Cans Bar and Canteen **125**
Carl Hammer Gallery **84**
Carol's **114**
cars **21**
Carson Pirie Scott **58**
Casimir Pulaski Day Parade **16**
Cass Hotel **157**
Castaways Bar & Grill **132**
CB2 **55**
Chagall, Marc **13, 83**
Charlie Trotter's **40**
Chasalla **62**
Chicago Antique Market **136**
Chicago Architecture Foundation
 21, 76
Chicago Blues Festival **16–17, 94**
Chicago Botanic Garden **12, 140**
Chicago Brauhaus **130**
Chicago Comics **56**
Chicago Cultural Center **76**
Chicago Dental Society **22, 23**
Chicago Dyke March **16**
Chicago Legends **121**
Chicago Office of Tourism **23**
Chicago Outdoor Film Festival **17**
Chicago River **21**
Chicago Theatre **95**
Chicago Transit Authority (CTA)
 20, 21, 22
Chicago Visitor Centers **23**
China Doll **152, 161**
Chinese New Year **19**
Chocolate Festival at Garfield Park
Conservatory **19**
Chopin Theatre **100**
The Chopping Block **52**
Christmas **18**
churches
 Fourth Presbyterian Church **145**
 Unity Temple **80**
Circuit **128**
City Scene Bed and Breakfast **161**
City Soles & Niche **64**
City Suites **153**
CityPass **77**
Civic Opera House **98**
Clarke House Museum **82**
classical music **98**
clubs *see bars and clubs*
Coast **44**
Cobra Lounge **125**
comedy clubs **91**
communications **23**
Conte de Savoia **136**
Continental Airport Express **20, 21**
Cotton Club **94**
Court Theatre **102**
credit cards **22**
Crew **113**
crime **22**
Crown Fountain **74**
CTA (Chicago Transit Authority)
 20, 21, 22
Cubby Bear Lounge **122**
currency exchanges **22**
CVS **22, 23**
cycling **21**

D

Daley Plaza Market **136**
dance **91, 94, 99**
Danny's Tavern **125, 134**
darkroom **124**
Dave's Records **57**
David Burke's Primehouse **31**
Days Inn Lincoln Park-North **152**
Delilah's **111**
dentists **22**
department stores **58**
Devon Avenue **128**
dialling codes **23**
disabled travellers **22**
Dixie Kitchen **41**
DJ bars **125**
Do-it-Yourself Messiah **19**
doctors **22**
Dominick's **22, 23**
Douglas Dawson Gallery **77, 84**
Doyle Stadium **101**
The Drake Hotel **156**
driving in Chicago **21**
drug stores **22**
Dubhe Carreño Gallery **84**
Dubuffet, Jean **83**
DuSable Museum of African-
 American History **83**
Dusty Groove **57**

E

Earwax Café **134**
efficiency apartments **161**
"The El" trains **20**
Eleven City Diner **39**
Elm Street Liquors **115, 133**
emergencies **22**
The Empty Bottle **102**
Endo-Exo Apothecary **53**
Enterprise Rent-a-Car **21**
entertainment *see performance*
Eskell **56**
eta Creative Arts Foundation **102**

Europa Books 65
events 16–19
Everest 40

F

Facets Cinémathèque 90
fall events 18–19
festivals 16–19
Field Museum 13, 82
57th Street Art Fair 16
57th Street Bookstore 65
Filene's Basement 63
film
Chicago Outdoor Film Festival 17
Gene Siskel Film Center 98
Music Box Theatre 90
fine dining favorites 40
Fire Brigade 23
Flash Cab Chicago 21
Flat Iron Arts Building 134
Flemish House 160
Folk and Roots Festival 17
football 101
Four Points by Sheraton 157
Four Seasons 156
Fourth Presbyterian Church 145
Fox & Obel 59
Frederick C. Robie House 83
Fulton Lounge 123
Funky Buddha Lounge 122

G

Gallery 37 Center for the Arts 76
gardens and parks 140, 142–3, 147
opening hours 23
gay and lesbian Chicago 22
bars and clubs 111, 113, 114
Boystown 128
Lesbian & Gay Helpine 22, 23
Pride Parade 16
G'bani 58
Gehry, Frank 74
Gene Siskel Film Center 98
German-American Fest 18
Gibson's Steakhouse 133
Gioco 40
Glessner House Museum 82
Gold Coast 133
Gold Coast Guest House 159
Goodman Theatre 98
Greek Islands 42
Green City Market 136
Green Mill Jazz Club 92–3
Green Zebra 46
Greyhound buses 20, 21
grid system 20

H

H&M 63
Habitat Corporate Suites
Network 153
hairdressers, tipping 23
Half Shell, Inc. 30
harbor taxi 21
Hard Rock Hotel 154
Harold Washington Library
Center 145
Harris Theatre for Music & Dance 99
havens 139–47
health care 22
Hejfina 63
Hema's Kitchen 128
Hermès 62
Hertz Rent-a-Car 21
Hideout 102
His Stuff 52
historic buildings 72, 76, 80, 82, 84
Historic Pullman District 84
hockey 101
Holiday Club 113
Hollywood Beach 143
Hopleaf 114
hospitals 22
Hot Chocolate 43
Hot Rooms 153
Hot Tix 98
Hotel Allegro 156
Hotel Burnham 155
Hotel Indigo 160
The Hotel InterContinental 157
Hotel Monaco 157
hotels 148–61
elite hotels 156
reservation agencies 153
taxes 23
tipping 23
HotHouse 103
House of Blues Hotel 158
House of Two Urns 161
Howl at the Moon 115
Hungry Brain 113
Hunt Club 122
Hydrate 111

I

ID 23
Ikram 58
Illinois Bureau of Tourism 23
Illinois Institute of Technology
(IIR) 85
Improv Festival 91
Indian Garden 128
indie music venues 102
inline skates 21
insurance, medical 22
International Museum of Surgical
Sciences 72
Internet cafés 23
Intuit 81
Irazu 134

J

Jackson Park 147
Jake 56
The James Hotel 156
James R. Thompson Center 77
Japonais 35
Jay Pritzker Pavilion 74
jazz
Green Mill Jazz Club 92–3
Jazz Record Mart 57
Jazz Showcase 99
Jet Vodka Lounge 115
Jewels 22, 23
Jil Sander 62
Jin Ju 33
Joan W. & Irving B. Harris Theatre
for Music & Dance 99
John Barleycorn 110
John Hancock Centre 80, 144
Jolie Joli 64
Junior's Sports Lounge 121

K

Kamehachi 40, 131
Kapoor, Anish 74
Karyn's Fresh Corner 32
Kate Spade 62
Kincaide's 122
Kingston Mines 94
Kit Kat Lounge & Supper Club 28
Kleihues, Josef Paul 14, 77
Kohn Pederson Fox Associates 72
Koolhaas, Rem 85
Kopi – A Traveler's Café 145

L

Lakefront Bike Path 132
Lakeview 129
Lanyon, Ellen 72
LaSalle Bank Chicago Marathon 18
LaSalle Bank Do-it-Yourself
Messiah 19
LaSalle Currency Exchange 23
Laurie's Planet of Sound 130
Leather Archives & Museum 72
Lesbian and Gay Helpline 22, 23
lesbians
see gay and lesbian Chicago
library 145
Lilly's 108
Lincoln Park 142–3
Lincoln Park Conservatory 143
Lincoln Park Zoo 13, 143
Lincoln Square 130
Linda Warren Gallery 84
Links Hall 91
listings 22
Live Bait Theater 91
Lookingglass Theatre Company 95
Lord & Taylor 58
Lori's Shoes 54
Lou Malnati's 34
Lou Mitchell's 39
Lurie Garden 75

M

MAC 62
Macy's 58
magazines, listings 22
Magnificent Mile 12, 56
Magnificent Mile Lights Festival 18
mail services 23
La Maison du Parfum 62
Mama Desta's Red Sea 129
Manny's Coffee Shop 40
marathon 18
Marina City 80
Mario's Italian Lemonade 136
markets 136

Marshall's **63**
Material Possessions **59**
Maxwell Street Market **94, 136**
Mayor's Office for People with Disabilities **23**
medical care **22**
Medusa's Circle **129**
Melrose Restaurant **128**
Melvin B's **133**
Merz Apothecary **52**
Messiah, LaSalle Bank Do-it-Yourself **19**
Metra trains **20**
Metro **94, 129**
Mexican Fine Arts Center & Museum **81, 137**
Meyer Delicatessen **130**
Mia Francesca **29**
Midway International Airport **20, 21**
Mies van der Rohe, Ludwig **72, 83, 85**
Millennium Monument **75**
Millennium Park **13, 74–5**
Millennium Park Bike Station **21**
Mint **53**
Mr. Beef **34**
Monadnock Building **80**
money **22**
Moody's Pub **33**
Morton's **31**
Moto **47**
movie theaters
  Gene Siskel Film Center **98**
  Music Box Theatre **90**
Museum of Broadcast Communications **77**
Museum Campus **132**
Museum of Contemporary Art **14, 77**
Museum of Contemporary Photography **81**
Museum of Decorative Arts **130**
Museum of Holography **77**
Museum of Science and Industry **15**
museums, CityPass **77**
music
  independent record stores **57**
  indie music venues **102**
  outdoor summer music festivals **16–17**
  performance **87–103**
Music Box Theatre **90**
Myopic Books **65**

N

National Vietnam Veterans Art Museum **82**
Navy Pier **14, 132**
neighbourhood festivals **17**
Neiman Marcus **58**
New Apartment Lounge **102**
Nine Steakhouse **31**
NoMI **33**
Nordstrom **58**
North Avenue Beach **132, 143**
North Pond **31, 143**
Northwestern Memorial Hospital **22, 23**
Nuevo Leon **42, 137**

O

Oak Park **80**
Oak Street **62**
Oak Street Beach **131, 143**
O'Gara & Wilson **65**
O'Hare International Airport **20, 21**
Ohio House Motel **158**
Ohio Street Beach **143**
Old Town **131**
Old Town Ale House **131**
Old Town Pub **131**
Old Town School of Folk Music **17, 102**
Oldenburg, Claes **83**
Omega Airport Shuttles **20, 21**
Omni Chicago Hotel **159**
opening hours **22–3**
opera **98**
Opera (restaurant) **41**
Orange **29**
Oriental Institute **83**
Osaka Garden **147**
Osteria Via Stato **38**
outdoor summer music festivals **16–17**

P

p45 **66**
Pace suburban buses **20**
The Palmer House Hilton **154**
Paper Source **59**
Park Hyatt **156**
parks and gardens **140, 142–3, 147**
  opening hours **23**
Le Passage **120, 133**
passes
  CityPass (museum pass) **77**
  transportation **20**
passports **23**
Patel Brothers **128**
Peggy Notebaert Nature Museum **142–3**
Penelope's **63**
Peninsula Chicago Hotel **156**
Penny's Noodles **28**
The Pepper Lounge **29**
performance arts **87–103**
  blues clubs **94**
  comedy clubs **91**
  indie music venues **102**
  spectator sports **101**
  tickets **98**
Perry's **39**
pharmacies **22**
The Phoenix **41**
phones **23**
Picasso, Pablo **83, 136**
Piece **34**
Pilsen **137**
pingpong **30**
Pizza Metro **34**
pizzas **34**
Pizzeria Uno **34**
Planetarium, Adler **15**
Plensa, Jaume **74**
police **22, 23**
Pontiac Café **125, 134**
post offices, opening hours **22, 23**
postal services **23**
Prada **62**
Prairie Avenue Historic District **82**
Pride Parade **16**
Promontory Point **132**
public art **83**
public transportation **20**

Q

Quenchers **125**
Quimby's **64**

R

Ragstock **129**
rail travel **20**
  disabled travellers **22**
Rainbo Club **134**
Ravinia Festival **17**
Reckless Records **57**
Record Emporium **129**
record stores, independent **57**
Recycle It **135**
Regional Transportation Authority (RTA) **20, 21**
Reliance Building **80, 155**
reservation agencies, hotels **153**
reserve **122**
restaurants **25–47**
  fine dining favorites **40**
  ID in **23**
  opening hours **22–3**
  pizza **34**
  steakhouses **31**
  tipping **23**
Richardson, H.H. **82**
Richman, Robin **67**
River North **84**
river taxi **21**
Robie House **83**
Robin Richman **67**
Rock Bottom Brewery **120**
Rock Records **57**
Rockit Bar and Grill **119**
Rodan **125**
The Rookery **76**
RoSal's Cucina **136**
Rosa's Lounge **94, 99**
Roscoe's **128**
RTA (Regional Transportation Authority) **20, 21**
Ruby Room **146**

S

St. Laurent, Yves **62**
St. Patrick's Day Parades **16**
Saks **58**
sales tax **23**
Salpicon **131**
Salud Tequila Lounge **124**
Sandburg, Carl **75**
Sander, Jil **62**

Sara Jane 59
The Savvy Traveller 65
Sears Tower 12, 80
seasonal lights 18
The Second City 90, 91, 131
security 23
self-catering apartments 161
Seminary Co-op 65
Shedd Aquarium 15, 82
shoe stores 54, 64
shopping 49–67
  budget shopping 63
  department stores 58
  independent bookstores 65
  independent record stores 57
  Magnificent Mile 56
  opening hours 22
Shoreline Sightseeing 21
Sidetrack 111, 128
Signature Room and Lounge 120, 144
Silver Moon 65
Silver Room 63
skates, inline 21
Skidmore, Owings and Merrill 72
Skylark 137
Slugger's 122
Smartbar 113
Smart Museum 83
Sofitel Chicago Water Tower 133, 159
Soldier Field 101
Sole Nail Lounge and Beauty Emporium 147
Sonotheque 123
Sound-bar 118
Space Time Tanks 141
Spade, Kate 62
spas 144, 146
Spertus Museum 82
Spiaggia 40
Spin 110, 128
Spoken Word Café 101
Spoon 108
sports 101
sports bars 122
Spring 43
spring events 16–17
stamps, postage 23
steakhouses 31
Steppenwolf Theatre Company 95
Stitch 67
street numbering 20
Streeterville Market 136
streetlife 127–37
  markets 136
streets, grid system 20
Sugar Magnolia 62
Sullivan, Louis 130
summer events 16–17
Sushi Wabi 45
Sutton Place Hotel 160
Symphony Center 98

T

Tantrum 121
tax, sales 23
taxis 20, 21
  tipping 23
Taylor Street 136
tea lounges 141, 145
telephones 23
theatres 87–103
Theater on the Lake 17
Ticketmaster 98
tickets
  entertainments 98
  transportation 20
Tiffin 32
tipping 23
TJ Maxx 63
Tod's 62
tourist information 23
tours 21
trains 20
  disabled travelers 22
Traipse's 130
Tran, Calvin 54
travel 20–1
  disabled travelers 22
traveler's checks 22
Tribune Tower 80
Trousseau 56
Tru 40
Tufanos 42
Twin Anchors 38
Twisted Spoke 46

U

Ultimo 62
Una Mae's Freak Boutique 135
Unabridged Bookstore 65
Union Park 121
Union Station 20, 21
Unique So Chique 141
United Center 101
United States Postal Service 23
Unity Temple 80
University of Chicago Campus 83
Urban Oasis 144
Urban Tea Lounge 141
U.S. Cellular Field 101

V

Velvet Lounge 101
Viaduct Theater 99
views, bars with 120
Viguier, Jean-Paul 159
vintage shops 53, 65
Vintage Wine Bar 124
Visitor Centers 23
Vosges Haut Chocolat 57

W

W Chicago Lakeshore 157
Wabash Tap 121
Walgreens 22, 23
walks 20
Webster's Wine Bar 108
Wells Street 84
West Loop 84
West Wacker Drive Riverwalk 72
wheelchair access 22
Wheeler Mansion 161
Whiskey Sky 120
Wicker Park 134–5
The Wieners Circle 32
Wild Hare 112
Willows Hotel 153
Windy City Urban Inn 152
Winter Delights 19
winter events 18–19
Women and Children First 65
Wright, Frank Lloyd 76, 80, 83
Wrightwood Tap 108
Wrigley Building 80
Wrigley Field 101
Wrigleyville 129
www.expedia.com 153
www.hotels.com 153

Y

Yahoo Yellow Pages 23
Yellow Cab Chicago 21
Yves St. Laurent 62

Z

Zanies 91
Zentra 108
Zoo, Lincoln Park 13, 143

Acknowledgments

Produced by Departure Lounge LLP
Editorial Director Naomi Peck
Art Director Lisa Kosky
Editor Debbie Woska
Indexer Hilary Bird
Proofreader Gary Werner
Picture Research Joaquim Carneiro and Debbie Woska
Digital Retouching Charlie Murphy

Published by DK
Publishing Managers Jane Ewart and Scarlett O'Hara
Senior Editor Christine Stroyan
Senior Designer Paul Jackson
Website Editor Gouri Banerji
Cartographic Editor Casper Morris
DTP Designers Jason Little and Natasha Lu
Production Coordinator Rita Sinha
Fact Checker Jennifer Sodini

PHOTOGRAPHY PERMISSIONS

Dorling Kindersley would like to thank all the museums, restaurants, hotels, bars, clubs, shops, and other sights for their help and kind permission to photograph at their establishments, and the companies below for permission to reproduce their photographs:

Placement Key: tc = top center; tl = top left; tr = top right; c = center; cl = centre left; cla = center left above; cr = center right; crc = center right center; bl = bottom left; br = bottom right.

ALAMY IMAGES: Jason Lindsey 1; ADLER PLANETARIUM AND ASTRONOMY MUSEUM, Chicago: 15cl; ART INSTITUTE OF CHICAGO: *At the Moulin Rouge*, Toulouse-Lautrec 71tc; CHICAGO OFFICE OF TOURISM: 19tr; CHICAGO PARK DISTRICT: Caroline O'Boyle, Cloud Gate: 74bl; CITY OF CHICAGO: Mark Montgomery 17tr, 17tc, 70cr; Peter Schultz 70crc; THE DRAKE HOTEL, Hilton Group: 156crc; THE FIELD MUSEUM: 13br, 15tl; HARRIS THEATER FOR MUSIC AND DANCE, Chicago Opera Theater performs Britten's *A Midsummer Night's Dream* 89cr; HIS STUFF: Bret Grafton: 52tl; ILLINOIS INSTITUTE OF TECHNOLOGY: 71cl; INTERNATIONAL MUSEUM OF SURGICAL SCIENCES: 72tl; JAMES HOTEL CHICAGO: 156cla; JOLIE JOLI: Jacob VanVooran photography: 64crc; LASALLE BANK CHICAGO MARATHON: Victor Sailer and staff: 19c; LASALLE BANK DO-IT-YOURSELF MESSIAH: Brian Eaves: 19tl; LOOKINGGLASS THEATRE COMPANY: Steve Hall & Hendrich Blessing 95cla; MAYORS' OFFICE OF SPECIAL EVENTS: 17tl; MUSEUM OF SCIENCE & TECHNOLOGY, Chicago: Apollo 8 Command Model, first manned spacecraft to orbit the moon on display 15crc; THE ROOKERY: 70tl; SIDETRACK: 111cla; SONOTHEQUE: Douglas Reid Fogelson: 123bl; STEPPENWOLF THEATRE COMPANY: *Intimate Apparel*, Michael Brosilow: 95tr; MUSIC BOX THEATRE: 90br; THE WRIGLEY BUILDING AND DESIGN are registered trademarks of the W. M. Wrigley Jr. Company: used by permission 12bl.

Full Page Picture Captions: Dusable Museum: 2–3; Jazz Showcase: 8–9; Alinea: 24–5; Dixie Kitchen: 36–7; Lori's Shoes: 48–9; p45: 60–61; The Rookery: 68–9; Oriental Institute, University of Chicago Campus: 78–9; eta Creative Arts Foundation: 86–7; Green Mill Jazz Club: 96–7; Jet Vodka Lounge: 104–5; Sound Bar: 116–17; Aztec motifs, Pilsen: 126–7; Lincoln Park Conservatory: 138–9; Hotel Monaco: 148–9; Chicago Skylines: 162, 164.

Jacket Images
Front and Spine: ALAMY IMAGES: Jason Lindsey.
Back: DK IMAGES: all.

Chicago Downtown Transport Map